The

Travel
Writer's
Guide

Earn Three Times Your Travel Costs by
Becoming a Published Travel Writer!

Revised 3rd Edition

Gordon Burgett

Please visit our website at http://www.sops.com for information on more resources for writers, speakers, and publishers.

Library of Congress Cataloging Data

Burgett, Gordon, 1938 -
    The travel writer's guide: how to earn at least thrice what you spend on travel by writing magazine and newspaper articles / Gordon Burgett.—Rev. 3rd ed.
      p. cm.
    Includes bibliographical references and index.
    ISBN 0-9708621-1-3
    1. Travel—Authorship. I. Title.
808´.06691—dc20

ISBN 0-9708621-1-3

Cover design by Steve Nosse

ACKNOWLEDGMENTS

I needed encouragement and help to update and revise this book that was first published by Prima about a decade back, while I continue to write, expand my publishing business, and speak hither and yon, although, in truth, I've yet to actually speak in yon.

Much of the encouragement has come from those who read the first two editions and bugged me for a new one. And I need proven, easy-to-use material in print for the many hundreds who attend my travel writing seminars each year, mostly in California. They will now have this book to help guide them on their writing journey.

I also want to particularly thank those who made it possible to bring this information well into the 21st century, to Bev Schulz for her assistance in a new land, that of digital photography; to Steve Nosse, with a sleek new cover; and to my long-time friends Suzanne and Jerry Hogsett, who kept me current about air couriers and field details of travel in general. Most of all, to Linda Lange, who not only keeps my many ventures flowing and my books balanced, but was directly involved in converting the text into modern English and churning the new pages out.

DEDICATIONS

This book is dedicated to those who love this Earth, who travel to see and enjoy it, who leave it better for their visit, and who enjoy writing about it and its very odd inhabitants.

But also to my Barbershopping golf buddies—Lu Hintz, Larry Long, Larry Los, and Ralph Guthrie—who kept me in quarters and in tune while this book was updated and rewritten.

PART FOUR
AFTER THE TRIP

PART FIVE
RELATED INFORMATION

INTRODUCTION

When I first wrote this book in 1991 I spoke tentatively of computers as great editing tools but still not ready for use in prime time manuscript submission. Today, writers pecking out prose on typewriters conjure up images of cavemen chipping flint. All that in a little over a decade!

We query as often as not by e-mail now, send final text as a download, post digital photos on our website for the editor's easy perusal, and do much of our research late at night using spiders and gigabytes.

So I've rewritten much of the first and second (1994) editions to include the new digital toys and procedures. Even the "365 Ideas for Travel Articles" got a facelift and tune-up, in an era when much of the world is less hospitable, we spend vacations waiting in airports, and domestic sightseeing marvels in the United States are being rediscovered in record numbers.

Technology has removed much of the drudgery of the copy capture—putting the sentences together, moving the text about, dropping in artwork with the touch of a key, and mailing the masterpiece almost instantly without a stamp.

But I was even more impressed, when rereading both of the earlier manuscripts, with how little the article creation aspect of travel writing has changed. It's still one-on-one, labor-intensive work plucking facts, images, and procedures from places that readers want to visit, injecting clarity, and transporting those readers there with nothing but words. Articles still require pre-trip research, foot leather on-site, a half-dozen interviews, scores (or hundreds) of photos—and getting all those niggling details right so the reader can tell the difference between Manaus and Managua!

I left out a key step: for the words to work we still have to sell what we saw to a harried editor who has another dozen writers figuratively banging on her door or literally filling her monitor's message screen, each hawking his or her own geographic wonder.

So most of the old book is still here too. That's because we sell articles today just about the same way I first sold them (1,700 sales ago) in the early 1960s—talk about flint chipping! Selling articles are still composed of facts, quotes, and anecdotes, plus a photo or two. And we still have to wrestle with the same old words to make people and places jump into published existence.

I even added another chapter that has little to do with electronics! The question that I am most frequently asked by successful users of my earlier books is "Does it get any easier the more you sell?" You bet. Details in the new Chapter 15.

The opportunities open to you as a successful travel writer include the mastery of a new skill, that of writing for publication. This in turn requires the attainment of other skills, like interviewing, marketing, and editing. And by plying your new trade you can increase your income, secure in the knowledge that the same skill used in writing about travel can be used to write about any other marvel for the reading world!

Better yet, travel writing can be great fun, take you to any part of the globe your desires and purse will reach, pay you far more than you spend, let you share with others the joy and awe of seeing new places, and even allow you to deduct from your taxes the expenses necessary to conduct this wonderful business!

So that's what this book is about: the step-by-step process of travel writing for publication in magazines and newspapers.

It is a show-and-tell book. The basic text, the how-to element, is the "tell." The "show" comes by example, usually at the end of a chapter, to illustrate the points made. More about the books mentioned in the text can also be found in the bibliography and the source section at the end.

The model example in this book is based on an actual trip I took to Santa Barbara, California. The site is arbitrary—it could have been almost any place. I picked Santa Barbara because the places mentioned from there are truly spectacular and because California in general is such a common travel direction for most North American readers. But the principles used in selling articles about any other location would be the same.

There is a final joy that I hope to impart to you through this book. That of taking raw facts and observations and crafting from them a new and totally personal element: an article at once as singular as a snowflake and as useful as a word map. For writing is also an art and an article is a creation. By helping to create new artists, this book might help elevate you and your readers to a higher creative plain. If that sounds a bit presumptuous, it is really only a modest hope that you, the reader, putting into practice what these pages share, will make a reality.

PART ONE

An Overview
of
Travel Writing

Chapter One
The Professional Way for Professional Results

Chapter One

TRAVEL WRITING: THE PROFESSIONAL WAY FOR PROFESSIONAL RESULTS

"I've got $500 and the whole summer free!" announced a young school teacher at my travel writing seminar in San Francisco when I asked if anybody was going to try their hand at some articles right away.

"I've only got $10 and a coupla hundred *days* left," retorted an old-timer loudly to the laughing back row. "What do *I* do?"

Travel and write. Let the articles pay for your trips, reap a fat profit, and deduct the travel costs from your taxes.

Choose where you go, how long you stay, what you do. And when you return (or while you're on-site), by sharing what you've seen, heard, and learned, you can develop a skill and sharpen a trade that can bring you more profits, more sights, and more new knowledge—until your days do run out or you put yourself out to pasture. With luck, an exotic pasture.

Who benefits the most? You *and* your readers. If you do your job well—if your writing is honest and balanced and embodies the full measure of life as you see it—readers learn about other people and places without taking a step. And beyond the obvious benefits of fun and profit to yourself, you perform a valuable function through good travel writing: You help bring all mankind closer together.

In a step-by-step process, this book shows you how professionals profit from travel in print, and how you too can do the same.

There *are* some basics: You must be literate. Clarity of expression is a plus. Curiosity is mandatory. And hard work is the order of the day. In addition, five points apply to the whole field of travel writing. Let's take a look at them.

1. TRAVEL WRITING SELLS

Great news: Nothing is easier to sell in the writing world than travel! It's estimated that one million articles are published each year. Somebody writes them. They get paid. They could be you.

First, think magazines. They are the travel writer's best market. They pay from several hundred to several thousand dollars per article, photos extra, and you only write for them when you know they are interested. (More on that later.)

Divide magazines into two main categories: consumer (called "slicks") and specialty/trade. Consumer magazines are sold on the racks and by subscription. Almost all of them use travel regularly.

Some of them are standard, well-known magazines, like *Travel & Leisure* and the *National Geographic Traveler*. Others are less well known: *Adventure Cyclist*, *Cruise World*, *Interline*, and *Northwest Travel*. Some are published by travel-related sponsors, like *AAA Going Places* and *Highroads Magazine* (automobile associations) and *Voyageur* (hotel chain).

Still others have a theme or purpose that involves travel. These include RV/motor home publications (*Motorhome*, *Trailer Life*, and *Western RV News*), in-flight magazines (*American West Airlines Magazine*, *Attaché Magazine*, *Hemispheres*, *Meridian*, *Washington Flyer Magazine*, and *Zoom! Magazine*); and publications about automobiles, motorcycles, aviation, camping, cruises, food and drink, nature, photography, geographic locations, and many more.

Examples of the more obvious consumer magazines are easy to find. Libraries subscribe to them, supermarkets and newsstands sell them, and dentists age them and leave them in their waiting rooms. However, a less obvious market, the specialty/trade magazines, may be hungrier, and sometimes, though rarely, may pay better.

Some of these specialty magazines are easy enough to imagine: They are for people in the travel trade, like *Leisure Group Travel*,

Specialty Travel Index, Star Service, and *Vacation Industry Review.*

But others take more creative thinking. For instance, let's imagine there's a magazine called *The Plumber's Journal,* and let's say you want to go to Guatemala. While there you research the Guatemalan plumbing trade. Upon returning you write an article called "Plumbing in Guatemala," which *The Plumber's Journal* buys because its readers are interested in all facets of plumbing—plumbing trends, plumbing history, plumbing how-to, and even plumbing in exotic places. For them yours is a plumbing piece; for you, an article that helps support your habit: traveling on a full stomach with a cooperative wallet.

If you know a field well—as a teacher, architect, gardener, plumber, or whatever—you can provide those specialty/trade publications with solid articles from new or unusual sites. You have an advantage over the rest of us: In addition to the consumer magazines open to all, you have access to those magazines that cater to your expertise. You know what readers of those magazines would enjoy reading more about, the special vocabulary they use, and how they might benefit from that knowledge.

You needn't be a specialist to write for those pages, however. I've sold to horticulture publications (I can't get weeds to grow); stamp collecting newsletters (my collection is a roll of unused 33-centers); the Lions, Rotarians, and Kiwanis publications (though I'm not a member of any of them—like Groucho, "I wouldn't join a club that would have me"); children's pages (though I'm six times their age), many academic journals (do they give doctorates in spelling?), and, yes, *Modern Bride,* repeatedly, though I'm a devoutly outdated male and, in my near-dotage, single—again!

Let me share two quick examples to sharpen your vision for seeing those harder-to-find trade and specialty markets.

A friend of mine normally covered Portuguese-speaking Africa, Diu, and Goa. She was given an assignment in Beirut (in the days when it was a glittering resort town). While in the area she decided to visit Egypt and see the pyramids. Surprising—since she was a seasoned traveler who preferred going it alone—she signed on with a tour group.

When she boarded the tour bus she found it full of architects fresh from a world conference in Athens. Whipping out her stenographer's notepad, she began interviewing. By the end of the tour she had spoken with them all, plus squeezed in three rolls of color slides. The result, some months later, was over $2,500 from sold freelance articles—almost all to architectural magazines!

Three points worth noting. One, she had never read an architectural magazine before, had trouble spelling *Egypt*, and hadn't planned to write about her Egyptian side trip. She simply took advantage of a reportable situation.

Two, she gained her architectural expertise from the experts she interviewed and from follow-up research and magazine reading after her trip.

Three, she let the architects lead the interviews. Rather than trying to imagine what the editor might want, she asked the architects at the pyramids, "Why is this particularly interesting to you?" From the answers and related comments, she built (and sold) articles based on in-depth listening.

The second example is of an agriculture major from the University of Illinois who took his wife on a belated wedding gift trip to Japan some time after he had graduated. Although he'd never been in print before (nor to my knowledge has he since), he turned one day's digging into seven articles and about $1,500 (helping to pay for his trip!).

He became interested in the intensive form of farming in Japan, in contrast to the extensive system practiced in the Midwest. He wanted to share that with his college ag cronies, now scattered around the country, so he decided to write an article.

Cleverly, he persuaded the Ministry of Agriculture in Tokyo to "lend" him an English-speaking employee. The two then spent a day visiting three model farms, where our writer toured, pinched, bowed, tasted, interviewed, and photographed. When he returned home he actually wrote two different articles and sent them to 20 regional (mostly county) agricultural magazines, all outside each other's distribution range. Seven bought, six paid, all used photos—and knowledge was spread.

Anybody can write for architectural or agricultural magazines. The articles simply must work, the information must be correct, and it must meet the readers' needs.

The hardest part for beginners is to let their minds expand to see those less obvious markets, then dare to approach them with a good idea or article.

After consumer and specialty/trade magazines, newspapers are the third market for travel articles. Usually newspapers don't buy much from freelancers. They are largely staff written, with most of the rest picked up from syndicates and wire services. Freelancers are a headache for most editors, and they have enough headaches already.

Except for travel. It costs far less to buy a travel article and photos from a freelancer than to send a staffer half way around the world. So this is a particularly receptive market that responds quickly and pays promptly, though modestly, once the words have appeared in print. More about newspapers in Chapter 12.

2. THINK AND ACT LIKE A PROFESSIONAL

More than half the battle is thinking and acting like a professional, of wearing the suit while you grow into it. In fact, it's unlikely that unless you do—you sell, then write like a pro—you'll ever become one.

Although the world is full of people who can write well, editors have trouble finding responsible, energetic, and accurate super people who can observe, listen, research—and *then* write well and deliver their product in a timely fashion. In other words, professionals who give what they promise when they promise it in a reliable, usable form.

If you're going to compete with professionals like these, you must do it right from the moment you get to the starting line. And keep doing it right from then on.

If you aren't literate you just aren't in the race. That's not fatal. Millions of Americans, most of them literate, have no desire whatsoever to be in print and they still lead exciting, positive lives. Join them and do something else very well.

But if you do want to write and are literate, just as important is the ability to sell. This is something you can learn to do: it's akin to wearing the right shoes, training the right way, and eating the right foods before you enter a race. Likewise, selling your travel writing simply has its own rules and methods.

This book will show you how to get in the race in the first place—and how to win every time. Professionals win with every article they put in print. Which takes us to our next step.

3. WRITING IS EASIER THAN SELLING

If you can make a place, an idea, or a people come alive, wrap your prose around a central theme, keep the paragraphs short, write clearly in words that readers understand, be accurate, and help readers experience *your* experience with all their senses, you won't have much problem with the writing. And the more you do it, the sharper you'll become. But that is only half the battle—selling is definitely the other half.

How do you sell your work? Begin by examining the magazine or newspaper in which you'd like to appear. What did the editor just buy? What was the topic? How was it treated? What was the ratio of fact, quote, and anecdote? What angle did the writer take? Any humor? How much? What kind of photos accompanied the piece? Who took them? How many sentences per paragraph? What made the piece "work"?

Remember, you can be the greatest writer in captivity, bursting with electric text and sparkling dialogue, but unless you sell those words you're an outsider looking in, pockets hanging. The old adage (which I made up a couple of decades ago) that "amateurs write, then try to sell; professionals sell, then write" is true. But it took me, a kid in Illinois writing up a storm, a long time to learn it. I believed that editors wanted to see what they were buying *before* they actually bought it. Wrong! (And I've got the rejection slips to prove it.)

What I didn't know was that professionals promised an exciting piece *before* they took a trip. They got the editor's interest and tentative approval, gathered the information and photos on their travels, and tailored their piece to the magazine's readers—they sent off customized prose and got back a customized check.

Then they sold that same piece again and again! And they rewrote it into other articles. And they sold other items based on the same trip to newspapers. After spending $1,500 and a few weeks in some magic spot, they ended up with $4,500, a great trip, and lots of deductions. This makes for success, and selling is as much a key to it as writing.

4. DO MOST OF THE WORK
BEFORE YOU GO!

Although this may sound odd, it makes good sense. Get most of the work done before you reach your destination, then you'll have lots more time to enjoy the place!

How do you do this? By studying the writings of others. By combing encyclopedias, geography books, maps, the Internet, press releases, and the odd item in the library's vertical file. By checking out videos or watching TV shows or travelogues. By talking with others who were there. By reviewing the *Reader's Guide to Periodical Literature* (or its computer equivalent) and the newspaper indexes, then reading the articles themselves.

In Chapter 2 I'll show you how to create a solid information base before you take the trip, so that you spend most of your time on-site adding to, correcting, and expanding that base. Plus gathering invaluable observations, taking photos, talking with locals, and blending left brain-right brain elements into a full-dimensional manuscript that includes facts, quotes, and anecdotes.

Every research hour well spent at home is another hour uncommitted once you're there.

5. DOUBLE OR TRIPLE YOUR INCOME
BY TRAVELING SMART

Occasionally you'll have time for only a short visit to one place. But if you have more time at your disposal, as a travel writer you can greatly increase the amount of articles you write (and the money you make). By planning well you can include many stops coming and going, with enough time to branch out locally from your destination. Not only is it far less expensive to do this than visit the same number of places separately, but each stop can be lucrative.

Let me explain by example. Suppose you live in or near Los Angeles and you want to write a piece about Reno, Nevada, some 470 miles north. If you have little time, you'll fly directly there, gather what you need quickly, and fly back.

But if you have more time, you can jump in the car and head to Santa Barbara, "where the Westerns were born and the stars now hide." Check out La Purísima Mission near Lompoc, the best preserved and reconstructed in the chain, and stop at Solvang, the Danish village a few miles east. Pismo Beach, San Luis Obispo, or Morro Bay are travel havens along the way. Then head up Highway 1 to Hearst Castle, the San Antonio Mission (half-hidden behind Big Sur), and the "17-Mile Drive" in Carmel.

Stories beg to be written about Monterey, once the state capital. Santa Cruz and nearby seaside villages are throwbacks to beatnik days, and San Jose, in the throes of a massive downtown rebuilding, glistens with unwritten articles.

In San Francisco find tightly focused pieces on Burmese restaurants, bed-and-breakfast inns tucked away in the city, ferry boating, the fortifications near Lake Merced.

Cross the Golden Gate Bridge for a matching article, "The Other Highway 1," from Marin to Leggett, a day or more of the wildest, snakiest, prettiest stretch of sea-hugging road imaginable. Write about it and the places along the way: Point Reyes, Fort Ross, Mendocino, and more.

From there it's either up the "Valley of the Giants" (a road lined with towering redwoods) to Arcata or Eureka, or back down to Highway 20, Marysville, and the fabled Feather River. Why not swing north to Oroville and its magnificent dam, and a few miles more to Cherokee (a shard of a town but still full of earlier mining tailings, a museum, and a full cemetery)? Some of America's only diamonds were found here.

The back roads will take you to Nevada City and Grass Valley, through Truckee (where, in 1846, the Donner Party site became stranded and turned to cannibalism), then off to Squaw Valley, Lake Tahoe, and finally, an hour later, to Reno!

On the way back head a bit north to Highway 49 (the "Road of Gold") and Camptonville, with its magnificently preserved hydraulic mining remains. South then to record and photograph the remnants of the gilded age: to Coloma, where gold was first found at

Marshall's mill; to Hangtown (Placerville), Amador City, Jackson, Angel's Camp; to Columbia, where a gold town has been completely preserved

You may want to stop in Sacramento, since the highway passes nearby, and later head east to Yosemite. Go through the park to the highlands, continue on to Mono Lake, and snake skyward to Bodie, a silver ghost town that rings with authenticity and photographic charm. Then home to Los Angeles and a much-deserved rest!

This could apply to any sector of America...or the world! I've shown you how a straight-line trip can be bent and expanded to pick up another 20 articles coming and going. What I call "pocket-trip stories," two to three hours of on-site work each (well researched in advance), most of the time there interviewing, taking sharp photos, and capturing the impressions and sense of the place in a notebook, to be molded later into compelling copy for magazines and newspapers.

You start at the end, the purpose of your trip. Determine how many days you need to do it properly, add another day or two, then pick up the other stories on both sides, determining what you can add coming and going by the time, money, and energy you have available.

By conducting your travel writing venture professionally, you'll be able to have great success and fun too. It's an ideal job. As long as you, your legs, and your curiosity hold out, you can be desk-free, poking around wherever in the world you want, and getting paid for doing what you'd otherwise gladly pay to do!

THE TRAVEL WRITER'S TASKMASTERS

Even though it *is* an ideal job, it's more than fun and games. Four taskmasters watch your every merry turn: travel editors back home, the clock, your working budget, and—the most exacting of all—the reader.

Locate "Big Ben" in Bangkok, encourage readers to tramp across Lapland in shorts and sandals, or extol the virtues of seeing "the real New York" (or almost any big city) by strolling downtown at 2:00 a.m. and that will be your last advice in any magazine or newspaper foolish enough to print it. Irate readers become red-penned writers, which puts editors on notice: Buy more from you and that red could become the pink of their dismissal slip.

Obligations of a Travel Writer

Your job is to tell the truth. Sounds good, doesn't it? Virtuous. Yet just telling the truth won't sell articles. You must dip into the vat of truths and pick out those that create an article about a place, event, or topic that editors want for their pages, that readers will eagerly read, and that, in the blending of smaller truths, still remain true in their totality.

Let's look more closely at the first two qualifications: (1) what editors want for their pages and (2) what readers will eagerly read.

What Editors Want

Magazines and newspapers exist to inform the public, either the general public or people with special interests. Some are general public magazines like the *Newsweek* or the *Smithsonian Magazine*; special interest magazines like *Skydiving* and the *Mustang Monthly*; general newspapers like the *Christian Science Monitor* and the *New York Times*; and very specific newspapers like the *Santa Barbara News-Press* and the *Des Plaines Suburban Times*.

No matter what type of publication—general or special interest—editors want articles that will attract and keep readers, that will entice them to buy the magazine or newspaper from the newsstand and later to order a subscription. Editors also want complete accuracy: places mentioned that are identical to places in reality, names correctly spelled, quotes as they left the speakers' mouths. And they usually want prose that evokes the time and place in telling detail—a smell and feel of a place, a sense of the actors and action. In short, words that come alive to paint pictures of people and places.

What Readers Want

One of the best ways to determine what readers want is to first determine who your readers are.

If you are writing an article for the general public about the beaches from Santa Barbara to San Francisco, you should ask yourself: Why would the readers of the *Chicago Sun-Times*, say, read this? What are their expectations? What do they want to know from my words and photos? What does the editor expect?

You can make educated guesses about the readers' expectations. If you have access to earlier *Sun-Times* issues, you can see what kinds of similar articles the editor bought to give you an idea of what the editor wants.

You can also put yourself in the readers' shoes. What would you want to read if you were in Chicago or were thinking of heading west to actually see those beaches? Your list might look like this:

Readers' Expectations List

1. How many beaches are there?

2. What do they look like? White sand? Rock? Dunes? Swamp mud?

3. Are they continuous? If not, what separates them? Can you hike over or around the separations? If so, how far? Or how much of the total shoreline is continuously accessible?

4. Where is it safe—or best—to swim there? Where are dangerous riptides usually found? Any problems with sharks, jellyfish, or other unpleasant critters? Where? Seasonal?

5. Is any of the beach inaccessible for other reasons? Military preserve? Nuclear generators? Private land?

6. Are the beaches accessible by car? Four-wheel truck? On foot only?

7. Is it possible to leave a vehicle at one spot, hike a long way, and get back to your vehicle by other means?

8. What are the best times of day and seasons to visit this beach? When are other people there? What are they like? Friendly? Hermits? How much of the beach is underwater or impassable during high tide? How can you find out when it will be high tide?

9. Is a particular beach reasonably flat or is it steeply sloping into the sea? Does that make it harder to hike along?

10. Can you camp at or near these beaches? Should arrangements be made in advance? What are the busy/open seasons?

11. Is food available at these beaches? Which? All year? Can one cook on or near the beaches? Any restrictions?

12. Is it dangerous to stay at these beaches at night? Or leave your vehicle unattended to hike during the day?

13. Can you surf between Santa Barbara and San Francisco? Where? Are rental boards available? Where? Cost? Security required?

14. What kind and amount of clothing and sun screen is needed on these beaches? Can you go barefoot or do you need shoes? Sandals or sand-proof running shoes?

15. If you could pick the three most interesting beaches, offering the widest variety of activity, beauty, and flora/fauna, which would they be? Why? How can one specifically get to these three sites?

16. Following up on (15), the next three? What are the three worst places—and why?

General public readers would eagerly devour a story incorporating this information, whether in Chicago or elsewhere, if the facts are accompanied by quotes, visuals, anecdotes, and other telling details that add color and spunk.

Special interest readers require more tightly targeted stories. If your goal is an article in the *Sea Kayaker* rather than the *Chicago Sun-Times*, your readers' expectations would naturally center around the sea and kayaking. To fulfill these expectations, you would first make yourself familiar with sea kayaking in general (read back issues of the magazine itself, for instance). You'd then want to find out where along this coast sea kayaking is done (which would lead you to the zone from Nipomo to Morro Bay). To complete your survey you would interview any sea kayakers you could locate. All this would allow you to devise a set of questions from which you'd later compose a query to the editor. The result would be an article of fresh interest to the readers of *Sea Kayaker*.

This chapter provided you with an overview of the travel writing profession and how travel writers go about their business. The rest of this book deals with the nitty-gritty of the profession—in hopes of providing you with the knowledge and tools to begin your own career or hobby of travel writing.

PART TWO

Before the Trip

Chapter Two

GETTING ORGANIZED

Many travel writers never take the "big trip," a major excursion undertaken for fun and profit. Instead they specialize in one region, almost always where they live, probably where they were born, and about which they know best. Sometimes they write about other regions as well, usually in conjunction with a business or family trip.

Yet because the big trip requires the fullest use of the travel writer's professional skills, this book will focus on it. For writing jaunts of a more modest scope, pluck what you need from the spread of skills described in these pages.

At this point I'd like to introduce a checklist that shows all the steps needed for a big trip: preparing for it, taking it, and writing and then selling your articles about it. We'll spend the rest of the book bringing each step to life. (Any terms not explained in the checklist—like query letters, query responses, and feasibility study—will be defined later as needed.)

Big Trip Checklist

1. Select a place you want to visit, can afford, and where there is likely to be sufficient material for many articles. If you route yourself wisely almost any site qualifies.

2. Determine whether the time you can travel is the best time to go to that particular site. If it will be under water, scorchingly hot, buried in unskiable snow, or just plain miserable, pick another season in which to visit.

3. Assuming your visit is well timed, figure out precisely how many hours or days you will need to travel, how much time you

want to spend at the ultimate site, what percentage of the time you should allot to writing-related tasks, and how much idle time you want or need.

4. Then plot a rough travel itinerary, remembering to select sites for articles en route, if possible.

5. Research everything reasonably accessible about the ultimate destination(s) and any of the locations you plan to visit en route. Research articles that have been written about these sites, in which publications they appeared, what topics and angles they chose, and so on. Then complete a feasibility study, composing as many market lists as you have subjects to sell.

6. Develop both a writing and sales plan. Leave ample time between the initial planning and the trip itself (as much as six months is advisable) because you will need to send queries and receive responses, a process as vital to your status with the IRS as it is to the direction and success of your writing.

7. Send query letters to the top magazines on your lists. If you receive a rejection, move on to the next publication on that list, querying until you get a "go-ahead."

8. When you receive those positive replies, study the last three issues of each publication and draw up a rough outline of the kind of material each seems to prefer: facts, quotes, anecdotes, types of photos (black-and-white[b/w] or color, vertical or horizontal, people or scenery, etc.). Take this outline on-site with you.

9. If the publications have someone you can contact at the site, get letters of recommendation or introduction. Get other letters of introduction if they are commonly used in the area. These letters can be from government officials, the clergy, academics, friends—anyone who has useful contacts or can open doors in the country you'll visit.

10. Before leaving double-check everything related to your trip: itinerary, tickets, layovers, shots, equipment, writing tools, clothes, glasses, immunization, medication, camera, film, and so on.

11. Go and have fun! You should be so well prepared that all you have left are the interviews, verifications, and plenty of photo taking. (a) Complete the work on your queried go-aheads first, then gather material for later newspaper articles or magazine post-trip queries. (b) Acquire any local printed material you can use, to read now and pluck from later. (c) Fill your notebook(s) with quotes and

anecdotes; verify facts. (d) Take many, many photos. It's far cheaper to toss out or delete the losers than to fly back for that "one key shot" you didn't take!

12. Back home get your photos developed, if you used film: proof sheets for b/w's, paper-mounted slides for color.

13. Write your queried go-ahead articles. Take time to compare your final rough draft with the articles in the latest issue of the magazine. Edit, write, edit, write, then send the package (text, photographs, maps, etc.) to the editor. Do this for all the go-aheads before or by the deadline(s).

14. Send post-trip query letters regarding those sites you visited or those topics you investigated but did not query beforehand. You may need to do some of the same research that you did for the queried articles, including a full feasibility study, of which the market list is a part. As you receive positive responses to these queries, write the copy, select the photographs, and sell them.

15. In the meantime, write your newspaper travel articles and other nonqueried pieces and send them out, taking care not to glut a market. For example, if most of your articles are about the Amazon, send them to the newspapers every few months, or even every month, but not three articles at once! Alternating with your Amazon pieces, submit those written about other sites.

16. Submit your published pieces for reprints or query for rewrites. Look to syndications that sell abroad for resales too. If you have scraps of facts left over, work them into fillers (items of one page or less) and get those out. Find a market for your good, unsold photographs (read the current edition of *Photographer's Market* or Rohn Engh's *Sell & Resell Your Photos* to see what can be done with them).

17. Gather and itemize your receipts for tax purposes.

Next, let's focus on four key areas from the Big Trip Checklist that are vital to planning your big trip. First, you must pick a destination and make an itinerary, determine how long you can stay, decide how much money you can afford to spend, and select the necessary writing tools you'll need. Second, see what is available in print about that area: articles, books, guides, and maps—then review them. Third, you must create a writing plan, and fourth, a sales plan (the last two areas will be covered in Chapter 3).

WHERE TO GO AND WHAT TO TAKE

Where and When

Choosing a destination is often the easiest part. Make a wish list and shoot for the top. Time and money will then determine how far up that list you actually go!

Almost anywhere in the world can yield good copy. In fact, where you go is less important than your ability to discover those topics that will appeal to editors and readers. I apply a simple rule of thumb: What grabs my attention or piques my curiosity will do the same for others.

Given the above, the time of year that you travel can influence the salability of your articles. Some sites work well all year whereas others are definitely tied to seasons. Yosemite offers copy for articles about cross country skiing in the winter, surviving inner-tube river rides in the spring, sheer outdoor magnificence in the summer, and superb riverbed hiking in the fall. But Siberia in the winter or Panama during the rainy season are hard to sell to even the most generous editor—unless you discover a secret delight that any editor would be happy to reveal to his or her readers.

As with choosing a destination, your length of stay is also determined by the uncommitted time you have and the funds you can spend.

I use two guides to measure desired trip time in advance: how many hours I like to work each day and how many on-site hours I feel each article requires. I like to work four hard hours a day, preferably in the morning, during which I observe, gather information, and take photos. In addition, I figure six hours of on-site time will be required for each major article. So if I send out a flock of query letters each suggesting an article about a different topic, and four return with positive replies, I will need six half-day periods to gather the basic requirements, six full days there.

Why do I work only four hours a day? Because I want to have fun on the trip too. But I don't necessarily spend the rest of my time gawking or carousing. What I do in the other hours will probably find its way into other articles. I might walk or cycle, camera and notepad at hand. Or enjoy a harp concert, interviewing and snapping photos as well as listening. Or visit a now-retired adventurer and tape our conversation. These activities would easily find their way into other articles.

Prudence also suggests that I add another day or two, just in case I find a super article idea that simply begs for my full attention, in addition to the other commitments I've made in advance.

So now we're up to eight days at the prime destination. How many days then, if any, can I add for writing/touring stops coming and going? Or similar stops at places within easy distance of the prime destination?

Other points: (1) Remember that you can lose or add days when you cross the international date line. (2) Jet lag is real: it reduces your ability to work and think at full capacity, so factor it in when traveling longitudinally. (3) Much of your first and last day can be spent just getting to and from the airport, with delays at each step.

Given all these considerations, when you ask yourself how long can you spend, remember: Too much time is always better than too little.

Money

How much money can you afford to spend? How much do you have and how much will the trip cost? How much will you earn from it? And later, after you've created a clientele that gives you assignments and pays in advance, how much will you need up front? Answer those questions and you will know approximately what capital you will need on hand.

At the outset assume that no editor is going to give you an advance, however eye-popping your query. At this point all the editor knows is that you have a good idea and can write a smashing query. If the article is as good, you'll be paid soon enough (by the editor's lights); if it isn't, thank God you paid for the trip yourself!

Since it's almost certain that you will pay for your first trips out of your own pocket, you must figure out what you can afford. Trim the sail to match the wind. Prepare an estimated budget, then adjust the distance and time on tour to match what you can comfortably afford to spend. You'll be nervous enough traveling afar to research and write for vaguely known editors and unknown readers without mortgaging your house and car.

What must you take into consideration when planning your budget? Suzanne Hogsett's *Bargain Travel Handbook* (the details

Figure 1 *Estimated Budget Worksheet*

FIXED COSTS

Airfare (_____ per person x _____ people) $ _____
Train pass, bus passes, etc. $ _____
Car rental $ _____
            TOTAL FIXED COSTS $ _____

VARIABLE COSTS

Transportation (tickets for train, boat, bus, subway; taxis; transport porters; others, including costs for transport porters and other personnel) $ _____
Food (restaurant meals, groceries, nonmeal drinks, snacks, other) $ _____
Lodging (hotel/motel, campsite, hostel, family, hotel porters, other, including costs for hotel porters and other personnel) $ _____
Sightseeing (admissions fees, sightseeing tours, other) $ _____
Entertainment (movies, plays, shows, other) $ _____
Rental car additional expenses (gas, tolls, parking, other) $ _____
Shopping $ _____
Other expenses (equipment rental, lessons, other) $ _____
Pre- and post-trip expenses (immunizations, passports, and visas; guidebooks and maps; clothes, luggage, and travel goods; camera, film, and development; other) $ _____
         TOTAL VARIABLE COSTS $ _____

Multiply the Variable Costs by 1.2 to allow for a margin of error of 20% $ _____

TOTAL ADJUSTED VARIABLE COSTS $ _____

Add the Total Fixed Costs and Total Adjusted Variable Costs $ _____

TOTAL ESTIMATED TRIP COST $ _____

about all books listed are found in the Sources section at the end of the book), offers an easy-to-use worksheet which I have slightly modified in Figure 1.

It used to be that whatever you calculated, it was wise to bring about a third more in traveler's checks, just in case. Now, with credit cards usable worldwide, that wisdom is a bit dated, though a few hundred dollars in twenties come in very handy in small, rural towns where the cards (or you) may be suspect. So that amount of emergency near-tender might be added to the worksheet above.

Once you know the approximate cost and the length of time of your trip, get out a map and a schedule book and block out the area you can afford to visit and the time you can afford to invest.

Personal Items

What remains of the preplanning is figuring out which personal items and writing tools you will need on your trip.

First, keep in a safe place all tickets and documentation (passport, visas, tourist cards, personal identification cards, credit cards, letters of introduction, vaccination certificate). Check these regularly during your trip to make sure they haven't been stolen. In addition, pack all necessary legal papers, plus a driver's license for a car rental and a copy of your car insurance, if valid in that area.

If you're traveling abroad, bring at least $25 in small currency, including change, to tide you over until you can get your American dollars exchanged for the local currency. I bring an additional $20 in U.S. singles, which are the best kind of tip in some countries.

Bring a watch that you know how to operate, since time changes are the bane of travel writers. A reliable, inexpensive alarm clock is also valuable and makes an appreciated tip for the maid at the last hotel.

One umbrella per person if it might be wet, proper attire for normal and inclement weather, and always a second pair of comfortable shoes are other essentials.

Remember to include prescriptions for all medicine, lest you be jailed as a junkie, and if you wear glasses, bring a second set, or at least a recent lens prescription should the first set get lost or damaged.

Pack at least one full set of proper, conservative business clothes (including a tie for men) for interviews or other similar occasions.

Business cards are very useful abroad. They can include personal information as well as professional (you can have "Professional Travel Writer" set in bold type at the top!). You might also bring evidence of your intent, that is, query go-ahead or assignment letters. Even a copy or two of recent articles in print.

Tools of the Trade

As a travel writer you will need a camera, two if possible: one for color slides and one for b/w's, 35mm or larger. Plus filters, a sturdy carrying case (or two), plenty of film, and waterproof/weatherproof coverings are essential. If using a digital camera, remember a spare battery and extra memory sticks or discs.

In addition, tape recorders, small and battery-run, are very useful for interviewing and keeping personal observations. Include an extra set of batteries and plenty of cassettes, particularly if they are an odd size.

You will also need file folders (which you may be able to buy locally). Steno pads too, and perhaps some large manila envelopes to hold receipts, booklets, and anything worth keeping that you pick up.

I like to carry an old manual typewriter, worth $25 or less, to bring up my notes every evening. I tape the purchase receipt inside its cover and, at that price, it will pass customs in any country.

You will have additional needs, idiosyncratic to you. Mine include running shoes, trunks, and sweat bands. Remember—you're not headed to boot camp or a monastery! Bring whatever you need to turn your working trip into a thoroughly enjoyable adventure!

THE RESEARCH PLAN

There are two very important reasons why you want to study what's been said about your destination before you go. The first, so you have solid information about potential articles around from which you will write your query letters. The second, so you can use your time most effectively once you're there.

Some of the sources you'll use are predominantly factual: maps, weather charts, hotel and tour lists, encyclopedias, even promotional sheets and fliers from tourism bureaus and the countries themselves (although the objectivity of the last may not be absolute!). Scour the Internet too.

The more subjective accounts should be particularly helpful. These are usually articles written by other travel writers like yourself. Go as far back as ten years, locate all accounts in print through the *Reader's Guide to Periodical Literature* (or its computerized equivalent, both located in your library's reference section), academic indexes, and the respective newspaper indexes (we'll discuss this in greater detail in the next section). Make a copy of each article.

Then draw a large grid on a sheet of paper. On the left side list all the attractions mentioned in the articles, top to bottom. Along the top, each heading a vertical column, list an article or book, its author, publication, and date, from the oldest to the most recent. In each box indicate whether that attraction was mentioned in the particular article. Put a plus or minus to show a strong positive or negative reaction. Add any key words the author used about it: "Not worth the time," "Spectacular," "See at night," and so on. This exercise will show what other travel editors thought was worth seeing, how reactions have changed over time, and may reveal lesser-known features you might also want to investigate.

Before you leave home you will know what you want to see at a particular site, the restaurants and hotels worth exploring, local cuisine you should sample, seasonal activities to consider, items to buy, and problems others have encountered. Between the objective fact sheets and the more subjective reporting, you'll be better able to prioritize your time.

At this point you'll also be able to ask two important questions: "Is the promised article feasible to write?" and "Is it feasible to sell?"

You can answer the first question now, and we'll address the second in Chapter 3. If your research has unearthed a solid article about the topic—all the better if several have seen light—you can rest assured there is something to write about.

Now you must read those accounts, add information from other sources, and based on these materials write three or four relatively short paragraphs about the topic in a query letter that promises more depth and a current review of the topic when you visit the site. Your letter says to the editor, by implication: Here is something your readers will want to know about, it exists, I will look into it more fully when there and can give a reliable, interesting, and accurate account of it when I return. Are you interested?

At this point let me share a 15-step process called "How to Prepare and Market Magazine Articles That Sell" from another of my writing books, *How to Sell More Than 75% of Your Freelance Writing*, currently out of print but soon to see light in its fourth reincarnation! You can use this checklist for any travel pieces you wish to compose.

How to Prepare and Market Magazine Articles That Sell

1. In one sentence, what is the subject of the article you want to write and sell?
2. Who would benefit from reading your article? Who would be most interested? What kinds of readers would select your specific subject from a variety of choices? Rank all those potential readers in order, placing those who would derive the most benefits first.
3. Which publications do these readers buy and read? Prepare a market list of those publications that are the most likely to buy your manuscript.
4. In addition to the publications checked in (3), it is necessary to review the broader publishing field for articles similar or identical to yours. Therefore, you must check both the *Reader's Guide to Periodical Literature* (or the computer equivalent) and specific subject indexes for at least the previous three years, then
   (a) list the articles that are closest to your subject, in order, with the most similar first: subject, author, title, publication, page reference, length, and when they appeared. Where the subjects appear to be very similar, how does yours differ?
   (b) cross-check newspaper indexes for the past three years and provide the same information.
5. Have the publications listed in (3) and (4) printed articles within the past three years that are similar to the one you propose?
6. After each publication, note the name of the person you should contact (editor, managing editor, etc.), with title and address. Then provide the following information about each publication:

(a) Does it pay on acceptance or publication?
(b) How much does it pay for articles as long as yours?
(c) Does it prefer a query or a direct submission?
(d) How often is it published?
(e) What percentage of it is written by freelancers?
(f) What is its preferred manuscript length?
(g) Is any other information provided that will affect its placement on your list?

7. Now rank your market list in priority order, based on when the buyers pay (on acceptance or on publication), how much, the frequency of publication, and the percentage of freelance material used per issue.

8. Read the latest issues of your target publication, front to back. Select the articles that are the most similar, in form if not topic, to the piece you will prepare. Outline each article. Write out the lead and conclusion of each, by hand. Attempt to identify the publication's readers by age, sex, occupation, income range, education, residence, and other pertinent factors.

9. To verify the availability of resource information
   (a) read as many of the articles in (5) as necessary or possible, then list the sources of information found in each,
   (b) consult the library computer catalogue and list books you will refer to for factual information: title, author, call number, date of publication, and library, and
   (c) list the people you should consult for additional information and quotes, working with the reference librarian for information that you do not already have: their name, position, and current affiliation (if related to the topic), academic title and degrees (if relevant), and reasons for their being consulted.

10. From the information you've gathered on the specific target publication and the research you've done on your topic, select the material needed to write a professional query letter. Verify its accuracy.

11. Write a selling query letter to an editor of your target publication. If you do not receive a positive reply, write a query letter to the editor of the next publication on your list, and so on, one editor at a time, until an editor does respond positively. Repeat as much of (9) as necessary for each new publication queried.

12. When you receive that positive response to your query, plan your article to determine what is still needed to finish it.
13. Complete the needed research.
14. Write the manuscript in final draft form.
15. Try five different leads. Select the best, edit the draft, type a final manuscript (keeping a copy), and mail it, with illustrations (if needed and available), to the editor who gave you the go-ahead.

The most profitable hours on a trip are spent at home, often months before you pack. In those hours you gather information, ideas, opinions, quotes; you look at other articles, check the web, read books, study photographs and slides. It's called research. Better before the trip, so you know what you must see and where it is and why it's crucial for your articles, than after you're back!

Libraries

There are two kinds of libraries for travel writers: your own at home, and everybody's, in town or at the university. To function as a professional writer certain resources are mandatory for your personal library. To begin, you need a dictionary, a thesaurus, and a general atlas (with many good maps also downloadable from the Internet).

The dictionary should be reasonably current and comparable to *Webster's New Collegiate* (or *New World*) *Dictionary*. Even though most computer word-processing programs include a spell checker, real writers need to get their hands on real dictionaries. A writer avoiding a dictionary is like a pianist practicing on paper keys.

You need a thesaurus for the same reason. Good writing isn't hit-and-miss when it comes to words. It's precise, the right word for a specific meaning. Winston Churchill urged "short words rather than long, old words rather than new"—so use your thesaurus to find the exact word, and when appropriate choose the short, old, comfortable word.

Don't spend hundreds of dollars on a multicolored atlas that will become obsolete the next time an island changes its name. Buy an inexpensive atlas that gives you a current overview of continents, nations, and topographical features, then add to your information before the trip with more detailed maps (from the library, a good map store, or the Internet).

You'll also need a current *Writer's Market*, which you can update monthly through the *Writer's Digest Magazine*, available at all public libraries. If you are pursuing photography with the same vigor, then *Photographer's Market* will also be needed.

You'd be surprised how often you'll turn to an almanac if you have one at hand. Buy either the most recent *Information Please Almanac* or the *World Almanac and Book of Facts*.

Those are the absolute essentials, unless your grammar is shaky. If so, add a basic English grammar handbook.

Travel writers in for the long haul tend to fall into two camps: generalists and specialists. Generalists add assorted, eclectic items to their shelf. Specialists stock up on everything available about a country, a region, or even city. Since collections like this grow over time, there's no reason to invest heavily in your home library at the outset, especially if you are lucky enough to live near a well-stocked public library or, even luckier, a good college or university library. What they don't have, they can get nationwide through interlibrary loan.

Why so much printed research? So you know what to expect and what to see before you go (and what to stress in your query letters) and so you won't have to spend hours on-site gathering this information. You'll also know what to look for and where to get more information when you return.

I always start with the encyclopedia, to get a quick, comprehensive overview of the area or subject. From the general encyclopedia—like the *Encyclopaedia Britannica* or the *Encyclopedia Americana*—I might move to a specific one. When checking into gray whales and their migration, for example, I continued with the *Encyclopedia of Science and Technology* to find out more about cetaceans.

Akin to the encyclopedia is a specific sourcebook for travelers called the *Webster's New Geographical Dictionary*, ideal for the spelling of place names, the population of cities and countries, and other such details.

While at the library you'll find its manual or computerized card catalogue a primary tool for your research. Check four things: the books in stock (and their call numbers), cross-references for your topic, any microfiche material listed, and any microfilm material noted, though most of that is not digitally available on websites. Follow up the cross-references (so you can add more books related to your topic) as well as the microfiche and microfilm items.

Then head for the stacks, browsing each call-number area to see if something else is there that wasn't catalogued or was listed under another heading but nonetheless meets your needs. Write down the key call information about each book and check out the most important ones.

You may have to use the library machinery to read the microfiches (usually found at academic libraries) and microfilm (most often used for back issues of magazines and newspapers).

Beginners tend to ignore microfiche altogether, either because they don't know about it or haven't bothered to learn how to use it. Microfiche consists of transparent plastic sheets containing miniscule photocopies of book pages, which are read on a magnified light machine. They are absolute boons to historians and as valuable for travel and history. An example shows how.

Some years back I was writing a series of articles on the year 1876, when I noticed that three things dating from that year had been preserved on microfiche in the library where I was doing research. Two were guidebooks of the 1876 Philadelphia Centennial Exposition, each many hundreds of pages long with superb line drawings of the exhibits, including the new Otis elevator, a revolutionary new floor covering called linoleum, and a novel sound machine being displayed by Alexander Graham Bell called, later, the telephone.

Of equal interest on the third microfiche was the diary of an Illinois lad, Jerry Bryan, who had gone to Deadwood in the Black Hills, drawn by a new gold rush. The diary, *An Illinois Goldhunter in the Black Hills*, was reproduced exactly as written. Where else could I have found this firsthand account of actual events occurring on August 2, 1876?

> About noon a man was found just a cross the creek Dead, cause of Death poor whiskey. An exciting day in Dead Wood. The fun commenced early this morning by a crowd of 20 armed men escorting a Murderer through Town. Just after dinner Wild Bill was Shot through the Head. Killed instantly.

While the crowd was Debating whether to hang the assassin or not. Reports came from Crook City that the Indians have Surrounded the Town and that help was wanted. All those that could get Horses went down to render assistance. Just at Sundown a Greaser came in with an Indian head. This caped the climax. [Wild] Bill and every thing else was thrown in the Shade... It is getting to dangerous here to be healthy. (Illinois State Historical Society, 1960)

"Wild Bill" was Hickok. Less than a month before he, his friend and fellow scout of earlier days "Buffalo Bill" Cody, and a prostitute named "Calamity Jane" had been camped together near Deadwood when they heard of Custer's "last stand."

I wouldn't have been able to add this colorful bit of history to my article if I hadn't been moseying through the microfiche. Another good source for authenticity and verve are old newspaper accounts, found on microfilm.

To infuse history into travel, check the *New York Times Index* for that period or date, plus some days before and after. See what was reported, then call up the microfilm copy of the actual edition. Local newspapers may also have indexes, and most have files or a morgue that they will let you use, particularly if you're a writer. Although the major newspaper indexes seldom list travel articles per se, news about specific locations in the U.S. is listed. Local files and morgues may index the travel articles they have used.

Most direct travel reference material, though, will come from magazines and books. The *Reader's Guide to Periodical Literature* lists most of the major consumer magazines and is both well indexed and readily available in libraries. When I went to the Amazon for a three-week writing trip I listed every article about Belém, Santarém, Manaus, and also Quito and Bogotá (for stops on the way back). I then made a copy of the articles for my grid and for all the extra facts and observations they contained. (Almost all libraries also have the computerized *Magazine Index* available in addition to the *Reader's Guide*.)

In-flight magazines (available on airplanes) usually aren't listed in the *Reader's Guide*, so I'll discuss them below in "Other Sources." Articles in thousands of other magazines, journals, and newsletters aren't listed in the *Reader's Guide* either. Most of these are academic and are listed in scholarly indexes available in college or university libraries. Almost every academic discipline has one: business, biological sciences, modern languages, literature, and psychology.

To locate books on your topic, check the card catalogue at your local library. For books not available locally but currently in print, check the *Subject Index to Books in Print*. You can get these books in one of four ways: check with nearby libraries, contact bookstores (which can order what they don't have on hand), ask the reference librarian to check larger holdings to see if the book is available through interlibrary loan, or check the bookstores on the Internet for availability.

Although interlibrary loan is very effective, it should be your last recourse because it takes too much time. Nevertheless, it can be a great asset. When I was writing my thesis in history, titled "The Mormon Battalion in the Mexican War," I needed a pamphlet that had been printed circa 1846 in Council Bluffs, Iowa. I discovered that there was only one copy extant, in a college library in Walla Walla, Washington. They "loaned" me the original (rather than merely a copy), which I received in five days! (Sometimes a copy is sent. You usually pay for the postage and, if necessary, the copying, plus a small sum for the service. A huge bargain!)

Even more effective, and forever helpful, are the "angels of the stacks," the reference librarians. If you do the base work—checking the catalogues, stacks, cross-references, and obvious sources—they will help you zero in from there. Tell them you're a writer to whet their appetite even more. (Later, a copy of the printed article with a note of thanks for their help in making it possible is always appreciated.)

Another quick way to find other sources is to check the bibliographies of the sources you do use. Your library even has bibliographies of bibliographies! And biographical information abounds. My two favorites are the *Biography Index* and *Current Biography*. Also check the many versions of *Who's Who*.

Larger public libraries and academic libraries usually have a map or cartography section—windfalls for travelers since the topographic and other maps available here are often far more detailed and useful than those you can buy. Better yet, you can usually make copies to take with you. Ask for town, historic, or cultural maps as well.

Probably the least known gold mine for travel writers is the "vertical file." More common in local libraries, this is a repository for the odd-sized things that don't well fit on the shelves: maps, menus, guidebooks, clipped articles, catalogues, photographs, and the like. I once found a woman's personal diary of a Ecuadorian train trip from Quito to Guayaquil that she had taken a decade earlier in a vertical file. Several years later I took the same trip! (Or tried to. When our train hit a burro and nearly tumbled into a canyon far below, we were ordered to escape immediately and carefully. We hiked to the Pan American Highway and took a bus several hours back to Quito, Guayaquil unseen.)

Finally, the most useful items for a coming trip, current guidebooks, may or may not be found in your library—or may have a waiting list months long! However, these are usually available in bookstores so let's discuss them next.

Bookstores

Whether you're a well-heeled travel writer or a footloose student, somebody has written a guidebook for you. The trick is to find it, then use it.

You might try the library first. Amazingly my library once had the very copy I needed still wet from the press! But most of the time you will have to buy your copy at a bricks-and-mortar bookstore or a computer equivalent.

The larger bookstore chains and amazon.com and others have travel sections that usually sell the better-known guidebooks, those by Frommer, Fodor, Waldo, and sometimes Fielding or Baedeker. Be sure to read the contents closely to see if the emphasis of a particular guide meets your needs. For museums, Baedeker is best; for low-cost housing, Frommer, and so on... Look for the most recent edition, of course. Most updates occur in the fall.

In this age of specialization, boutique bookstores are flourishing in fact and digitally. Most cities have a travel/map store replete with dozens, maybe hundreds, of guidebooks to everything from backpacking the Bavarian Alps to bussing over the Andes (a trip taken once!) to finding your way through Melbourne or Marrakesh.

Why are such guidebooks valuable for travel writers? Because they highlight the key attractions; give times, dates, and prices; list taboos; put some objective structure under the puffed prose of most articles you will read about the location, and can save you a bundle in housing and food costs. In addition and very important, in your query letter about a site yet to be seen, much of the information on which you base your proposal to the editor (and which slant you use for the magazine's readers) comes from these guidebooks.

At the bookstores you can also buy phrase books for the area to be visited, if the folks for some strange reason don't speak English. Some bookstores even sell newspapers or magazines from other states or countries. Buy these too!

Web Sites

Plucking information from the Web is both a blessing—it can be immediately accessible at home by computer 24 hours a day—and a bane. There are a pinch under two million items listed in the www.google.com search for "travel+writing," and a lot of it is utterly useless or the link leads to the ethers, the site long (and mercifully) gone.

You can lessen the hunt by first going to your search engine's compacted list. With google, it is a category given near the top of the first page of the broader listing. In this case it says "Arts>Writers Resources>Non-fiction>Travel Writing. " In the 14 items listed were specific, recent articles, sites with travel writing information and tips, market guides, and more.

The more specific you can make your search topic, the better. Using the plus sign to link the definers in the search field, you can quickly find train schedules in Spain, the best camera lenses for specific cameras and needs, what Copacabana means, and magazines using articles about the economy of Belize in the past three years.

The biggest drawback is that simply being accessible through the Internet doesn't guarantee that that the material accessed is accurate, unbiased, current, or even sane. It takes some cross-checking and often a phone call or e-mail follow-up (or several) to be sure that what you are putting in your copy is correct.

Other Sources

In-flight magazines contain excellent articles about the airlines' ports of call, plus events, calendars, cost comparisons, and other travel-related information. Alas, they are seldom found in libraries or listed in the magazine indexes. Sometimes they are found at the airline's web site. You might also ask the reservation clerk at the local airport (if it is served by that airline) to snag you a current copy. Or you might check the in-flight magazine section of *Writer's Market* for specific titles, then write to the respective editors and ask for copies.

The federal government has scores of books, booklets, pamphlets, and maps that simply await your request or purchase. The government publications section of a large library will have numerous guides to federal publications. You can also contact Consumer Information of the U.S. Travel Service (U.S. Department of Commerce, Washington DC 20230).

When I was a student in Bahia (Salvador), Brazil, we were provided with a booklet about that country prepared by the State Department. It was right on target and full of how-to details. Check both the Departments of State and Defense (the latter, if our military is or was recently stationed there) for these publications.

For parks and outdoor activities, the National Park Service (Department of the Interior, Washington DC 20240) is very helpful. Be specific about where you want to go and what you want to do.

State governments are eager to lure visitors and can provide detailed assistance. The same applies to cities, museums, historical societies, sports centers, and amusement parks. Write or call them or check their web site; the general number or address will get you routed to the right person.

Foreign countries are just as enthusiastic to help you tell others about their charms. Contact the travel promotion bureaus or the consulates in the larger U.S. cities (or the embassies in Washington, D.C.)—let your mail carrier bear the consequences! Request a current map at the same time, and a city map of a particular site, if needed. Glean the truth from this shiny, promotional public relations material—and double-check the facts before you use them in print.

Maps can also be secured in person or by mail from the auto clubs, like the American Automobile Association or the National

Auto Club. If you tell them the route you have in mind, they can usually put together a packet for you. Sometimes they handle a trip abroad as well. Maps are also readily accessible on the Internet.

Now that you have well researched your topic, you're ready to focus on the next steps: writing and selling your travel articles. You'll need to make writing and selling plans, both of which we'll discuss in the next chapter. And at the end of that chapter we'll look at an example of how to plan for the big trip, using the tools and guidelines covered up to that point.

Chapter Three

YOUR WRITING PLAN
AND SALES SCHEDULE

THE WRITING PLAN

From your research you have (I hope) extracted specific topics that (1) you think others would like to know about and (2) you want to write about. List these topics under the heading "Pre-trip Queries," and rank them according to your preference, placing the one you most want to pursue first. These are the topics you will actively market before you leave. Done right and with sufficient vigor, you should receive enough positive replies to ultimately cover your trip's expenses!

Now make a second list, under the heading "On-site Topics." Here you'll list potential articles to research while you're on-site; you'll query about these when you return, and write them for sale later. Although it's preferable to query about a topic in advance (especially for tax purposes), some topics cannot be queried at this stage. Usually there is too little written about them to create an honest query letter. Or the subject is so new that you're not sure there would be an article's worth of information when you arrive.

There can be other reasons too. Some years back when I was headed to Manaus and the Amazon I very much wanted to meet and write about a legendary jungle and river guide, the Bavarian adventurer Kurt Gluck. But I couldn't query for three reasons. One, almost nothing was in print in English or Portuguese about him at the time, though everybody on the Amazon knew tales of his exploits. Two, what I had heard about him as a college student in Brazil was about as believable as stories about Paul Bunyan, scant stuff on which to build a credible query. And three, guides have a way of being out guiding when you show up to interview!

So I put Gluck on my on-site topic list and sought him out the moment I arrived. I caught up with him just as he was about to take off—had I dallied ten minutes longer I'd have missed him entirely! We managed to squeeze in two days on the Rio Negro and the Solimões River some days later, I as his boat boy while he showed the jungle and critters to very nervous tourists. I had plenty of time to interview while we poled and putted about. I wrote query letters after my return, and many articles followed.

Some of the on-site topics will lead to exciting multiple sales. Others will be gossamer. Still others, nothing at all: rumor, factually wrong, or too dull. Given the last, pursue on-site topics until the first hint that no salable copy will result, then abandon them.

Pencil in a third list at this stage: "Newspaper Articles." Include anything that can be researched and photographed at the site. Newspaper pieces sometimes also take different slants to the go-aheads or on-site articles. You gather your newspaper copy at the locale, then write about it when you return and submit it with a cover letter.

The three lists comprise your writing plan. Articles based on the positive replies from the pre-trip queries pay the cost of your trip, so pursue those most actively now.

Newspaper pieces are where you make your profit, and on-site items can be bountiful, blessed bonuses for post-trip queries and subsequent sales.

THE SALES SCHEDULE

When do I sell my articles? And how do I coordinate the research, preparation, and mailing to magazines and newspapers of original articles, rewrites, and reprints?

You sell the trip in four installments: (1) within three weeks of your return, you send articles to those magazines that gave you the go-ahead before you left; (2) to those magazines that respond positively to your post-trip query; (3) to newspapers you submit articles accompanied by cover letters; and (4) you sell reprints—always after the item to be reprinted has actually appeared in print—and rewrites of articles already written.

Create a rough schedule for each trip that puts the selling opportunities (and other key steps) in a time flow. List the opportunities on the left and the dates or time periods on the right. (See the
"Tentative Travel Itinerary" near the end of this chapter,)

Opportunities include

(1) the feasibility study

(2) writing/sending pre-trip query letters

(3) the trip itself

(4) writing/sending go-ahead articles from the pre-trip queries

(5) writing/sending post-trip query letters

(6) writing/sending newspaper articles

(7) writing/sending rewrite query letters, and

(8) writing/sending reprint cover letters.

Follow this schedule as closely as possible. Sometimes this may
be difficult, especially when you don't have the luxury of, say, six
months' anticipation (as we do for the Big Trip imagined here).
You'll have to hustle to squeeze in research, planning, and querying
in the time you do have.

On the rarest of occasions the editor will want the copy rushed
to print from the site, to beat a tight deadline, so the traditional
three weeks after you return to prepare the manuscript won't work.

You have the most flexibility at the rewrite stage. Rewrites can
be done the moment you return. You simply give a different spin to
the material gathered for your go-ahead articles. You can query for
a rewrite as soon as you formulate the idea.

It's clear that most of what you write, from go-ahead articles to
rewrites, comes from the success of your pre-trip query letters.
These should receive your utmost care and attention, because they
are the seeds of your financial harvest. By knowing what you can
sell before you leave you can design the articles, pinpointing precisely what you'll need once you arrive to make the writing work,
and save hours of wandering-around time once you're on-site.

From these same pre-trip go-aheads you should be able to rework several rewrites and reprints, even pulling out many of the
facts for the newspaper pieces you'll write when you get home.

Most important, as we shall see in Chapter 4, pre-trip queries
lay the groundwork for later tax deductions. Simply sending queries

proves that the purpose of your trip was to write (keep a copy of each query letter and response to prove it was sent!). And by getting positive replies, you can prove that the intent of the editor was to seriously consider the article's purchase. Voilá!

Travel writers get one blessing that other writers don't: They can query well in advance of actually submitting their articles. In fact, they can begin querying as much as six months prior to the trip. The only stipulation is that they mention in the query (1) when they will go, (2) when they will return, and (3) when the editor can expect to have the copy in hand.

Sometimes departure and return dates are uncertain, so here you must approximate. Nobody will be at the pier or airport checking. But you must be exact about when the editor will receive the article. Since three weeks is a magic time in article writing (the length of time it supposedly takes you to do a masterful job), you simply promise to put the material in the editor's hands three weeks after you return. If you're not sure when you'll be back, make sure that promised date is three weeks after your *latest* possible return.

If you've already taken the trip, plan to have your copy to the editor three weeks from the date you receive a positive reply to your query—unless, very rarely, the editor wants it at another time.

Although we've touched on the basics of preparing a writing plan and sales schedule, these are complex tasks, mixed inextricably with the feasibility study and query letters. We'll address queries more fully in Chapter 5.

Right now I want to show you how to plan for a big trip. I'll pursue pre-trip queries and research those receiving positive replies before I leave. I'll also prepare a writing plan and a sales schedule. Then I'll be ready to go.

EXAMPLE

PLANNING THE BIG TRIP

I picked Santa Barbara, California, for this writing jaunt because I think it is one of the most exciting, unique, and geographically blessed tourist sites in America, is nonetheless relatively untainted by tourism, its weather is inviting all year, the local folks are friendly, crime is low, and there's something to do for almost every taste. Finally, I suspect that others want to read about it as much as I want to see it.

Which makes it a perfect target for a travel-writing trip!

What is my thinking at the pre-trip stage?

Time constraints dictate that this trip will be for ten days maximum, and I chose May as the time for my visit (October was my second choice) because most of the visitors fill the hotels from June to September (with a strong second thrust in the winter) and because the "rainy season," as it is, mainly occurs in December and January. May is dry, spring flowers are in bloom, and everything I want to see is open.

I can afford to spend about $2,000 and I would expect to earn at least $6,000 back. Let's plan this trip from Chicago (where I was born)—a central site that will keep the costs more realistic for many of you coming from other points in the U.S. That means I must include a round-trip ticket and wheels when I arrive.

As it turns out, that's doable directly from O'Hare Airport to Santa Barbara, and even possible from the Chicago's less accessible Midway Airport for a slightly higher cost. Many writers coming from smaller cities may find it far less expensive to fly to Los Angeles, rent a car, and drive about 2½ hours north on 405 to 101. A ten-day car rental, to my surprise, is about the same in Santa Barbara as Los Angeles. So for my trip I will fly directly to Santa Barbara and rent locally, saving the five hours round-trip driving but losing a great article telling newspaper readers the fun things they might see and do along that L.A.-Santa Barbara route.

When visiting a widely scattered site (like Germany in the earlier editions, where I had to travel from Frankfurt to Heidelberg to the Bavarian Alps) much time is spent driving and repeatedly settling in. In those cases I expect to spend about a day and a half to research and photo each magazine article. But in Santa Barbara 80% of my work will be within fifteen miles from the center of town, and the rest can be done in a long day wending north about 100 miles (and perhaps a short day cycling south), so I can figure I can research an article in one no-nonsense day, or nine magazine pieces in my 10-day visit, plus spin-off newspaper submissions later. The ideal is to send out about 13 different query letters, hoping for nine go-ahead replies. (I will start this six months before the trip and may send as many as five or six slightly rewritten versions of those stock 13 letters, one at a time in prioritized order, until I get a positive response to that topic.)

Can I do it for $2,000? Time for a quick budget estimate, which I can adjust later as article ideas take form (see Figure 2):

Figure 2 *Estimated Budget*

FIXED COSTS	
Airfare (round trip, LAX-SBA-LAX)	$ 240
Rental car	180
TOTAL FIXED COSTS	**$ 420**
VARIABLE COSTS	
Food ($25 per day x 10)	250
Lodging ($60 per night x 10)	600
Sightseeing fees	75
Local shuttle bus	2
Entertainment (feeding interviewees)	50
Rental car additional expenses (gas & parking)	60
Cycle rental (full day*)*	25
Other expenses	50
Pre- and post-trip expenses (film & processing; mailing)	50
TOTAL VARIABLE COSTS	**$ 1,162**
Multiply Total Variable Costs by 1.2 margin of error	**$ 1,394**
Add Total Fixed Costs & Total Adjusted Variable Costs	
TOTAL ESTIMATED TRIP COST	**$ 1,814**

As you can see, my budget is doable—if I can in fact dig up $1,814 to make the trip happen! The estimates are lean, but I probably won't need the $232 variable, since inflation seems to be in check at present. Food isn't cheap in Santa Barbara but there are plenty of fast food outlets and reasonably priced restaurants, and of course once in a motel I can also shop at the local marts and delis and eat for less. I assume that I may have to buy a meal or libation for a person or two (to get interviews with them), so I've included entertainment costs. I might find a new, local acquaintance who would gladly let me use his or her extra cycle and accompany me on my excursion, and save $24! The rest seems about right. (Souvenirs for your kids and a local gift for the spouse are extra.)

How do I know these costs are representative? From an Internet research for discount air and car fares, from cost sheets sent by the local Conference and Visitors Bureau, and from one phone call to a local cycle renter found on the web.

How might I expect to earn back far more than the $1,814 in costs? I figure I can get paid from four different sources. To make this clear I write up an estimated earnings schedule.

Estimated Earnings

Magazine Articles	Nine sold at $500 each, including photos	$4,500
Newspaper Articles	Six different articles sold an average of 2.5 times each at $100 apiece	$1,500
Newspaper Photos	Used with ten sales, at 1.5 photos per article and $15 per photo	$225
Reprints or Rewrites	Five magazine pieces sold at $250 each, including photos	$1,250

The total income from sales would be $7,475, for a profit of $5,661. That's a 412% income over costs ratio. Bingo, if I'm shooting for a three-times-costs return. (Desirable ratios are in the 300% to 500% range, with 300% the more realistic goal.) I could still reach my 300% goal on this trip by selling five rather than nine articles, or any other combination yielding $2,033 income less. How might I improve the 412% (or any) ratio? Be more frugal, sell more, and sell to higher-paying markets.

Will I hold rigidly to these plans? Maybe not. If I receive a go-ahead from a magazine paying $5,000 for copy and photos, I'll spend more than one day on it. Maybe four or five. Or if my query replies in one area seem to strike a hot vein, I might decide to zero in and create three different magazine pieces and a couple of newspaper spin-offs on clearly different aspects of that topic only. Say hiking excursions into the Santa Ynez Mountains. Given just so many days available, other proposed articles won't happen. Which ones aren't sacrificed? Those for which I have a solid go-ahead from a magazine.

The most important thing is that I have a general plan. Next I must send out query letters to test my plan and lay my tax deduction base. Ultimately, neither I nor Uncle Sam care precisely how I cover my expenses and earn a profit, as long as I succeed! I start with a plan, then I modify it as needed.

Researching the Big Trip

Since I've chosen Santa Barbara as the focal point, it is tightly confined between mountains and the sea, and I will arbitrarily limit myself in the distance I travel north and south to get related article information, my sites are easily researched.

That research will take me in five directions.

First I will contact the Chamber of Commerce to get as much information as possible, by mail or by Internet. I will explain my general writing plan (10 days on site; when I plan to arrive; goal of nine go-ahead articles plus newspaper, rewrite, and reprint spin-offs; a short orientation session desired with their contact person my first day there, etc.). The C of C is gracious but directs me to the Conference and Visitors Bureau and Film Commission, who handle outside travel visitors. They send me a fat folder, encouragement, and web sources.

I then visit two libraries where I live (one local, the other at a nearby major university) and a specialty bookstore.

My local library offers a potpourri of resource tools: a computerized card catalog that lists hundreds of entries mentioning or related to Santa Barbara on the shelves of one of the 24 town libraries in my county—but on its own shelves nothing more helpful than Frommer's Frugal Traveler's Guide *California From $60 a Day* (four years out of date); a computerized newspaper index (alas, without many of the newspapers; Sunday copies only of the *New*

York Times, for example, and those only a few years deep); access to a fairly comprehensive computerized magazine index, Infotrac (but only 26 of the cited magazines kept on stock, for five years); and the *Reader's Guide to Periodical Literature*, intact and current.

From the magazine listings I find ten full articles about Santa Barbara in the past five years, in publications like *Harper's*, *House Beautiful*, the national edition of *Sunset*, *Conde Nast Traveler*, and *Conde Nast House and Garden*.

The university library is far more complete but far more out of date. Yet they are helpful in two ways: they have the magazines with the articles I need to read plus a dandy map library with several large, detailed maps of the region and several more about hiking in the adjacent mountains.

My final expedition is to my local travel/map store, a hidden gem that can order what isn't on its well-stocked shelves. Here I find the newest travel books about Santa Barbara and two cycling books that include the Carpinteria to Goleta areas (through Santa Barbara).

I read and skim the assortment of books from the three locations, check the articles in print (copying what I may need later), and make reproductions of specific maps.

What do I do with this now growing pile of assorted data and maps? First I make a grid, then I put it into article-related folders.

I make my grids now on a computer, putting the page in landscape format (sideways), where I create a table with about eight columns and a dozen rows, which I can shrink or expand by row or column as needed.

Along the top row I list TOPIC in the first box, and in the following boxes the source of the information to be listed, most from books (with title, author, publisher, and date of publication), magazines (title, author, magazine title, and date of publication), and newspapers (article title, author, newspaper title, and date of publication). Additional information listed might come from booklets, travel videos, websites, etc. In the TOPIC column I list those topics the authors thought sufficiently interesting to include specific information of value. That information is summarized, and sometimes I add the page number where it was found.

Here is a much abbreviated, fictitious example:

Grid Sheet (example of format)

TOPIC	"America's Riviera" John Smith *Pacific Paradises* 6/17/01	Santa Barbara Visitor's Guide SB Conference/Visitors Bureau 8/12/01
S.B. Mission	Gives detailed tour Says to go on week-day - 17 Weak on artifacts	Full page, details Also some info about Lompoc, Solvang missions
Fine Dining	Lists 6 restaurants Gives city so-so rating - 14	Not objective Lists many restaurants and price ranges – 34+
Golf in area	Likes Rancho San Marcos and La Purisima Gives fee rates - 15	Lists private courses Mentions public links - 54 Little info

Once I have information about a topic I create a file folder. Into it goes fliers, articles, or photocopies of the printed sources. On the latter I note where the enclosed material came from: source, author, date, and page number.

The Writing Plan for the Big Trip

Time now to ferret out nine (actually 13) good article ideas that I can cover well in ten days, assuming of thirteen I can get nine go-aheads in six months of successive query submissions. I also note any newspaper slants I might want to develop in Santa Barbara and write about later.

From my library research and the press packet sent by the SB Conference and Visitors Bureau I see several dozen topics that I would enjoy writing that editors may well want to buy for their readers. The lucky 13?

Tentative Article Topics

(1) The "Red Tile Tour" to see the historic core of the city, a 12-block free walk that can last from 75 minutes to many hours. The "red tile" refers to the Spanish-style roofs atop the County Courthouse, the many early adobe homes, and the sprawling Presidio as well as the early colonial style of the arcades, plazas, and museums.

(2) Cycling: four possibilities. (a) an inner-city loop from the waterfront to a dozen key sites (like the Courthouse, Presidio, Botanic Gardens, and SB City College), ultimately passing the Mission into the higher Riviera region overlooking the city, (b) a more challenging ride from SB City College south to Carpinteria, mostly along the shoreline, (c) an even more challenging cycle, from downtown up to Foothill Drive, south past Westmont College to Montecito, then back along the coastline to the waterfront, or (d) the killer, from downtown to Montecito and up the challenging Romero Canyon Road to Gibraltar Road that crests the Santa Ynez Mountains atop the distant city, with a heart-stopping return down Highway 154, the narrow Lake Cachuma Road, returning via Foothill to the waterfront.

(3) Hiking: again, three possibilities. (a) a mild in-city trek from the hotel or waterfront to the Mission, the Natural History Museum, and up to the Botanic Gardens, (b) any of four clearly defined but decidedly vertical climbs through the woods that sit between Foothill Road and Gibraltar Road at the top, possibly enjoying the many hot springs along the way [swimming garb optional!], or (c) for the firmest of foot, any part of the Gibraltar Road-Camino Cielo Trail, from Toro Canyon Park in Carpinteria up Romero Canyon to Gibraltar Roads along the mountaintops, continuing on Camino Cielo West past the former Reagan ranch and down into Solvang, ending at Nojoqui Falls, some 63 tough miles in total.

(4) The Wine Country, driving from Santa Barbara past Lake Cachuma to Los Olivos, where the many wineries begin on Foxen Canyon Road, heading north through Sisquoc, Santa Maria, and as far north as Paso Robles. Article will explain the choices, with details: (a) doing it alone, (b) joining a group, (c) going with a guide, (d) combining the wine tasting with other sightseeing in the region.

(5) The Missions. A fun day seeing three quite distinct missions: spending several morning hours in Santa Barbara, touring the mission and walking the grounds, then driving the superb Highway 154

past Lake Cachuma and lunching in Solvang, with a quick visit to the Santa Inez Mission, the least preserved of the three. Then on to Lompoc and the only secular (now state-run) mission, the excellently preserved and extensive La Purísima, where visitors wander the grounds and hike to the still-operating drainage and waterworks. A drive back on Highway 101 provides a good round-the-mountain taste of the area. (If a launch is planned at nearby Vandenberg Air Force Base, a quick drive to the coast north of Lompoc will provide a car-rattling view!)

(6) Santa Barbara free? There are 101 things to do in and around the city that cost absolutely nothing, so a series of fun, free schedules might comprise the heart of an article for cost conscious readers.

(7) Cachuma Lake. So much to do here it would be hard to squeeze it into a day: the drive itself; Paradise Road to Red Rock, hiking paths, fishing, and the dam; fishing, swimming, picnicking, sailing, and canoeing at the Lake Cachuma Recreation Area; even a drive back to the Happy Canyon region and true backwoods camping and hiking.

(8) Nature day: Lots to see and do for these readers, starting in Carpinteria with its world-famous nurseries (listing those with public tours), Lotusland in Montecito, SB's well-designed Botanic Gardens, the Alice Keck public park and gardens, the local Museum of Natural History, the waterfront zoo and bird refugee, and the endless wild areas between Foothill and Gibraltar Roads.

(9) Golf: Santa Barbara has a dozen golf courses within easy driving distance, most publicly-accessible links with extraordinary views (and challenges) that could form the core of one or several selling pieces: Glen Annie, Sandpiper, Rancho San Marcos (near Solvang), Alisal (in Solvang), and La Purisima (in Lompoc).

(10) There's a unique find in downtown Santa Barbara called the Karpeles Manuscript Library Collection, open free every day of the week to the public, with such rarities as the original of Albert Einstein's Theory of Relativity, the original proposal draft of the U.S. Bill of Rights, and the Emancipation Proclamation Amendment signed by Lincoln.

(11) Art abounds in the area, with 25 galleries and museums. As abundant are the many antique stores both in the city and the sur-

rounding communities, including the block-long Brinkerhoff Avenue Landmark District in downtown Santa Barbara.

(12) The Beach, almost continually walkable (in low tide) for 18 miles, from Carpintera to Santa Barbara. Actually 18 beaches, all free, four with their own hiking trails. Where visitors can camp, the cost, parking, lifeguards, sharks, seals, rays, fishing, much more.

(13) The Waterfront in Santa Barbara, with its with open beach volleyball courts, parks, an Olympic-sized public pool (locally called The Plunge), a pier with restaurants and a maritime museum, the harbor, a zoo, the bird sanctuary, surfing, the cliffs, and a large art fair held every Sunday morning with much to see and buy.

Newspaper Articles

There is an abundance of potential magazine articles from Santa Barbara—I could list another dozen topics in addition to those above. For starters, though, I will simply pluck from what I find researching and visiting the 13 topics listed, restructure the central point, and from that create another half-dozen magazine articles, each clearly distinct. Most will be sent to newspapers after I have sold the magazine pieces most closely related.

Many of the nearby towns or cities also lend themselves to newspaper pieces, if I can find the extra time to ferret out those items that readers afar would enjoy reading. Certainly Carpinteria, the odd history of Summerland, Montecito and its hiding Hollywood stars, Ojai peeking down from mountains above, Solvang and its Danish heritage, perhaps Los Olivos for its quaintness, Santa Maria of tri-tip fame, and a combo of Lompoc and Vandenberg.

A broader piece would tie all of that together and focus on Santa Barbara County. Another would be the weekend escape north that brings so many from L.A., and what outsiders to Los Angeles would see and could do on the drive along Highway 1 past Malibu, through Ventura—even detouring through Ojai.

Strolling State Street at night is fun both to do and to write (and read) about, with the many theaters and live performances as worthy destinations. Where to eat, where do the locals go, what kind of fun you can have, concerns for safety, and more.

Since newspapers pieces are short (1,200 to 1,350 words is ideal), finding six more articles in this cornucopia will be easy. I plan the newspaper items least and last since they either flow out of the magazine research or they become obvious to me on-site and I gather what I need at the time.

So much for possible articles. The big question is if I can squeeze that much work into ten days and make it all work logistically. In other words, can I physically cover nine articles in ten days? Yes, but barely. It will fit snugly if done this way:

Tentative Travel Itinerary

Day 1	Arrive, get settled, walk downtown and waterfront
Day 2	Early a.m. interview at SB Conference and Visitors Bureau; begin downtown article research
Days 3-5	Continue SB research
Day 6	Cycle to Carpinteria, get local info/pix; do the same in Summerland and Montecito en route; photo sections of beach walk and local beach parks
Day 7	Drive north to Solvang and Lompoc missions and the wine country; stop in Los Olivos en route
Days 8-9	Wrap up local stories; visit Lake Cachuma
Day 10	Last day to get missing info, interviews, and photos
Day 11	Fly back to Chicago

The Sales Schedule for the Big Trip

Now I must figure out when I will foist these Santa Barbara masterpieces on the unsuspecting travel editors of America. And how I will get all the disparate parts of my master writing/selling scheme to work as a lucrative whole.

So it's time to develop a rough trip schedule that puts the selling opportunities (and other key steps) in a time flow, something like this:

Selling Itinerary

Opportunities	*Date*
Feasibility Study	December-May
Write/send pre-trip query letters	December-May
Trip	May 10-21
Write/send go-ahead articles from pre-trip queries	May 22-June 15
Write/send post-trip query letters	June 16-20+
Write/send newspaper articles	June 16-July 15
Write/send rewrite query letters	July 1+
Write/send reprint cover letters	After articles are in print

This is my sales schedule! And it seems like a lot of lucre to extract from ten days. A lot of reworking and reselling the same information as well. I'd better get hustling and find some super ideas for those major magazine articles!

Chapter Four

TAXES AND RIGHTS: LAW AND STRATEGY

TAXES

At this point it's a good idea to address taxes, *before* planning and taking the Big Trip. Your goal is straightforward enough: How can you take your travel writing expenses as a business deduction? The answer is no less complicated: Do it, but be sure you have full documentation to prove that your writing is indeed business related.

I'm not a tax expert so please resolve any tax questions with an expert or the IRS. (This is a disclaimer!) What follows comes from reading the experts, checking with the IRS, following my own advice and faithfully paying taxes for years, and receiving invaluable assistance from an actual but in these pages anonymous IRS auditor (who attended my travel writing seminar and now allows me to bounce tax questions his way). Also, using plain old common sense.

For starters, the IRS allows you to deduct business expenses, but generally does not allow deduction of costs to pursue a hobby. Should you be brought in for an audit concerning your writing-related deductions (which is highly unlikely unless your numbers are grossly out of balance or they spin the wheel and it's your turn), the first question will surely be: "Was this a hobby or a business?"

Make your writing a business. You can have a regular job plus any other job that your energy, skills, and time permit. Uncle Sam encourages many jobs. Report your primary income, for which your employer deducts withholding and other taxes, on Form 1040. Report your other businesses, including writing, on Schedule C, using a separate schedule for each business. (If they are closely interwoven, like writing and photography, they can be included on the same form.)

All writers, like all businessfolk, have certain obligations related to properly filing their Schedule C. You must report, and be able to prove, all the income and expenses generated by your writing. That means that since you will almost always be paid by check, you should keep the stub of each payment. If that isn't clear enough, write the date, amount, and item sold on it. If paid another way, resist the inclination to simply pocket it. Note it on a sheet of paper, with the name and address of the payer, and report it as well.

Expenses can generally be recorded in one of four ways. (1) When paying by check, write on the memo line in the lower left-hand corner how that payment relates to writing, such as "writing/research" or "writing/supplies." (2) When using a credit card, get a receipt at the time or, if unavailable, note at the end of the month on your bank credit-card reconciliation sheet those items related to writing, and how they are related. (3) If you pay by cash, get a receipt, even if you must prepare it yourself. Indicate on it the amount paid, what is being bought, and the date, then have the recipient sign it. (4) Keep a booklet with you or in the glove compartment of your car in which to faithfully note car expenses (include the date the car is used for writing-related activity, the mileage or odometer readings, and how it relates to writing) and those other expenses for which no receipt is possible: public phone calls, parking meters, coin-operated copy machines, and so on.

What kinds of expenses can writers in business generally deduct? Paper, pens, envelopes, stamps, other mailing costs, newspapers and magazines, typewriters and word processors if used primarily for business (you may need a log to prove this), the paper and software needed by the computer, a printer, camera and tape recorders, a specific and clearly defined place to conduct the business (if in your home, check the IRS pamphlet for details), phone calls needed for writing, travel, and anything else the business requires.

At issue is whether the expenses were necessary for writing and for the proper operation of the business. Keep notes on why or how each expense was necessary should it be challenged in an audit years later. Entertainment expenses are a good example. If you and a few writing cronies slip out for lunch and a libation, that may be fun but it's hardly deductible. But if you take a client out to dinner to discuss your writing a newsletter for his firm, note the details on the receipt and claim it.

An auditor will be interested in your accounting, your receipts, and the volume of business you do, to see if yours is a legitimate business or simply a hobby that you'd like your not-so-rich Uncle Sam to subsidize. To help satisfy the auditor, keep a mailing record on which you record, faithfully, every query letter or actual manuscript you send out, the response (noted each time there is communication sent or received), and any income earned, with the date. The income should be matched by the check stub. These communications should be provable with copies of your queries or manuscripts and editors' responses.

What is the auditor seeking? Proof that you generated enough business activity, in the beginning, to at least potentially earn back your expenses; later, more income than expense. The guidelines now state that you should show a profit three years out of five. The IRS allows tooling-up costs and doesn't expect a profit (or conceivably even an income) the first year. But businesses can't lose money forever. Good documentation, a serious attempt to become solvent and profitable as quickly as possible, and prudent business practices count heavily in determining whether you are in business or enjoy an unprofitable hobby.

As a travel writer you must prove that the intent of your travel is to produce income. That the travel is a necessary expense to do business and not just a scheme to deduct a few years of globetrotting. This is best done by planning your trip like other professional travel writers: in detail, in advance, and on paper, with plenty of proof as to why you are going, when, and what business results you expect.

Let's plot out a model trip now so you can take all your proper deductions. Start six months before the expected date of departure. Determine where you will go, create a realistic budget, then complete a full two-pronged feasibility study (see Chapter 5). The goal of that study is the preparation and mailing of query letters to editors of the magazines most likely to print articles about your trip.

Query letters are a double blessing. Whatever the response, the letter itself states, or at least undeniably implies, that your intent is to travel to write articles, with the rough dates of travel noted.

These letters clearly show that the purpose of your trip is business related.

Better yet, positive replies to query letters justify the expenses required to prepare the articles promised. Your goal is to try to get enough positive replies before you leave to cover your anticipated budget. Although editors almost never give assignments to new writers, their "let me see it," "send it to me," "send it on speculation," or anything similar and positive is, if followed up professionally, almost tantamount to a sale. You must incur travel costs to complete the promise. So by complying in good faith by submitting the manuscript or material promised in the query, the expenses involved are deductible, whether or not the articles are purchased.

How much can you deduct for each such positive query response? Deduct what the article costs to prepare, which can be determined either by exact costs or by taking the total costs of the travel and operational expenses and prorating them to specific articles or projects.

There are four more ways you can earn your trip. One is to develop stories on-site, query about them when you return, and write when you receive the positive replies to those queries. The second is to gather information at the site and prepare newspaper travel pieces from it when you return, since newspaper travel editors generally don't accept queries, preferring to see the actual copy. The third way is to either resell the queried articles written and sold, assuming the second or reprint rights are yours (more about rights later), or to rewrite those articles and sell them to different publications. And the fourth is to sell photos and illustrations to accompany the copy gathered on the trip.

All of which should result in far more income than expense, meaning that the costs related to the writing and photography are deductible—and the profits are taxable!

But what if you have no track record as a travel writer (or a writer at all)? Say you take a trip somewhere exotic and suddenly decide to become a writer, doing all of the professional activity after you return? You can deduct only what you earn, up to the total of the writing-related costs.

Why? Because you didn't clearly establish the intent of the trip first, then back it up with sufficient documentation (query letters).

Again: Plan in advance, send out good query letters, establish a paper trail proving that the purpose of the trip is to write, then write and sell. Four things will let you survive an audit: sales, documentation, your businesslike approach, and the obvious volume of income-generating activity. The bonus? You'll probably bring in far more money than you spent!

| EXAMPLE |

THE TAX PLAN

My purpose is to earn back at least three times as much as my costs. But there's a second benefit: I can also deduct the legitimate business expenses incurred traveling and gathering the raw data. I must simply convince my taxing Uncle that what I am doing is a legitimate business.

So my first task, well before leaving, is to get a bevy of sharp, successful query letters in motion. I plan to write nine magazine pieces, a heavy load for a 10-day trip, so to get nine positive go-aheads in reply I must write at least nine queries. Each will be about a different potential article and will be sent to one editor at a time. So nine queries will be sent more or less simultaneously to nine different editors. (Actually I'd probably send 13 different queries since from that number I'd more likely receive nine go-aheads before I leave.)

My querying goal is twofold: (1) to get each editor to say something positive indicating that he or she would buy or at least seriously consider buying the manuscript proposed, when submitted after I return, and (2) to at least equal the projected cost of the trip in potential income from those positive replies.

Why? Querying shows my intent: to travel to Santa Barbara to write articles. It promises the articles as a result of taking the trip and paying the necessary expenses to get there and secure the information (expenses like food, lodging, photography, and additional travel). It justifies the costs for a business purpose.

To make my tax plan clear, I diagram it (see Figure 4). The diagram defines my tax strategy, which is both perfectly legitimate and good business.

Figure 4 *Tax Plan Diagram*

PRE-TRIP GOAL		POST-TRIP		
Equal estimated		QUERIES		
trip costs from		New articles		
go-aheads from		or magazine		
pre-tip queries	**T**	rewrites		**TOTAL**
	R			**TRIP**
PRE-TRIP	**I**	**NEWSPAPER**		**GOAL**
QUERIES	**P**	**ARTICLES**		
13 different		6 different		Earn
magazine		post-trip		three
article		articles		times the
queries;		submitted to		estimated
goal,		many		trip costs
9 go-aheads		newspapers		
		simultaneously		
ESTIMATED				
TRIP COST		**MAGAZINE**		
$1,814		**REPRINTS**		
		Cover letters		
		sent		
		simultaneously		
		once original is		
		published		

During the trip I also intend to create additional magazine articles, which I will query about after I return. I'll send other post-trip queries for rewrites of the articles queried before departure, to sell them in a different form to other magazines.

When I return I also intend to send at least six different newspaper articles, each to many newspapers simultaneously. And, after the trip, I will sell reprints (or second rights use) of magazine articles to other publications once the articles have been in print (see below for a discussion of rights).

It's not enough, though, just to intend to do this. I must have sufficient documentation to prove that I did indeed execute a business plan. Therefore, I will keep a copy of every query sent plus a copy of each respondent's reply. And I'll do the same for all subsequent query and cover letters and replies to them.

As important as the number of items sold and money earned is the professional process by which the income is sought, to prove your business is legitimate and diligently pursued. To assist in this documentation, I keep a mailing record and files for each query/response. Although I list every query or direct manuscript submission on my mailing record, what follows is an abbreviated and excerpted form, with an entry for each of the five kinds of submissions (the kind listed in the fourth column).

Mailing Record

2/10	Query – Red Tile Tour	A1 Magazine	pre-trip query
6/17	Query – Karpeles Manuscript Library	B2 Magazine	post-trip query
6/21	Waterfront in Santa Barbara	Newspaper	newspaper
7/15	Hiking Special: SB to Red Rock	C3 Magazine	rewrite
11/6	Red Tile Tour	D4 Magazine	reprint

The mailing record shows, respectively, the pre-trip query, a post-trip query, a newspaper article, a rewrite of the pre-trip query (after its resulting article has been in print), and a reprint of the article (from the pre-trip query, written, and sold).

On my actual mailing record I would have many more entries between most of these dates, and under each unrejected entry would be more information: date and kind of reply, date of manuscript submission, information about the number and type of photos sent, other correspondence or exchanges, the date accepted or ejected, and the amount paid. For example, over a period of many months the first entry might look like this:

Specific Mailing Record Entry

2/10	Query – Red Tile Tour	A1 Magazine

   4/7   — let's see it / remember: lots of pix,
         readers low budget
   6/9   — ms, photo info sent with captions
   6/21 — more info requested about 2 photos
   6/30 — accepted ms with 3 color photos
   8/1   — check arrived, $780
   11/10 — article in December issue

The second part of my tax plan is to keep a daily accounting of expenses on the trip, plus all related costs before and after. I will keep receipts for each of those expenses in a large envelope, plus local driving and incidental expenses in a notepad in the glove compartment of my car.

RIGHTS

Let's talk about rights as they pertain to travel writing, leaving further exploration of the legal pastures to those books written specifically about them, like Bunnin and Beren's *The Writer's Legal Companion*.

Copyright first. When you write something it belongs to you. In a common law country when you create property (say a book or an article) the rights to that property are yours. But only that property: the actual words in the order in which they are written. You cannot copyright an idea, only the way you express it.

Moreover, if taken to court you will be required to prove that you wrote it first, if that is what is challenged. This will be easier if you register your work with the Library of Congress. To do this, you can access the needed information and fill out the TX form at http://lcweb.loc.gov/copyright.

You will be asked to submit two copies of the manuscript with a registration form and $30 to register your opus. Do as indicated for scripts, books, tapes, software, music, and lyrics. However, you may not want to bother with this for your articles. They are seldom worth the cost of taking a thief to court, frankly. And if you keep a clear paper trail—query letter, response, mailing record, and copies of the published article itself—you are in good condition anyway.

Can others use your words? Without your permission, they can use the facts and opinions you express, but not in your exact words in the order you wrote them, except in small amounts (usually a paragraph is about the limit, but less if the original work was itself shorter, such as a poem or lyrics). And the source—you—must always be acknowledged. But ideas and impressions can't be copyrighted: they are in the public domain, for all to use. In fact, you probably used others' ideas and facts to help write your article!

Other rights attach to travel writing as well: all rights, first rights, and second or reprint rights.

These rights are defined as a contractual relationship between the author and the publisher that define what the publisher is buying. If a publisher buys your article on an "all rights" basis, for example, that means that the publisher can use your piece in that exact form (with some leeway for modest editorial rewriting) as often as he or she wishes, forever.

Although that sounds terrible, in truth it isn't bad. For one thing, there are few all rights buyers any longer, and they usually pay better. So sell it to them, then rewrite the piece! All they bought were the words in the order in which they were written. Do a major rewrite and resell the facts and ideas elsewhere. Two tips: Come at it from a significantly different angle the second time, changing the title, lead, and conclusion. And don't sell it to the original buyer's chief competitor. Hawk it to other fields!

Most publications buy first rights, meaning that they have the right to use that article first in their publication. You may not sell it again until it appears in print in the publication that purchased first rights. On rare occasions your manuscript is not used. In these cases you must have the rights returned to you by the publisher before you can sell first rights again.

Once your article has appeared in print, you are free to sell it to any other publisher on a second or reprint rights basis. (The terms are used interchangeably and mean the same thing.) Second rights means that it has been in print before and you are offering, on a nonexclusive basis, the opportunity to other editors to use the work on their pages. You can send a cover letter attached to a copy of the printed article that (1) promotes the contents of the article; (2) offers the article for sale, stating three points that the reprint buyer needs to know: who bought the first rights, when the article appeared in print, and that you are offering reprint or second rights; and (3) offers for purchase the photos that accompanied that article plus any other photos not bought or used by the original editor.

How specifically might these general guidelines on rights affect travel writers?

In the magazine field, the process is straightforward. Sell all or first rights to the best possible market, then sell reprints to all those who will buy them. The latter are almost always those who pay on publication.

Newspapers are usually interested in circulation or distribution rights, presuming that you will handle your own minisyndication and thus will not sell to other syndicates in the United States. Newspaper distribution usually extends in roughly a 100-mile circle from the city of publication. Generally you can sell to any other newspaper outside that circle, with the exception of the national newspapers. (See Chapter 12 for a more complete discussion of newspaper submissions.)

Of course you can always write different articles about the same site or trip and sell each to a different market. Just keep them clearly different. And to avoid undue confusion, don't ever sell the exact same article to a magazine *and* a newspaper. Trust me, you'll see why as we go along.

Newcomers labor unduly over rights, spending tortured nights and queasy days afraid that their gilded words will be lifted and converted into billions of purloined dollars. Or that they will be sued if they use any two printed words in tandem. Forget all that. Follow the simple rules just outlined. And worry instead about turning out words so good that editors will want to print them and others will fight to steal them. By then you'll know that 99% of these fears are baseless. And all of the energy so spent is unprofitable.

| EXAMPLE |

RIGHTS

The *Writer's Market* indicates the kind of rights each publication buys, so I act accordingly.

I query, then sell them what I promised in the letter. Let's say that one magazine stated that it bought all rights. That's it. I can rewrite that piece but the original is theirs. Say the rest bought first rights. If the subject lends itself to it and there are other interested markets, I will try to sell those articles as reprints once they've appeared in print.

I don't quibble over rights. I'm much more interested in what publishers pay! I don't quibble there either, until I've been on their pages enough that some expenses should be picked up. Then I'll simply make a straight request. If they don't pay enough I don't query them at all, no matter what rights they buy.

Chapter Five

QUERY LETTERS:
THE MAGIC KEY
TO MAGAZINE SALES

Magazines are your best markets for travel articles. They pay more than newspapers, buy both slides and black and white (b/w) photos, and often help with travel expenses after you have written for them for a while and earned their confidence.

Whether the publication is a travel magazine, one more broadly directed at consumers, or a specialty/trade category, the key is approaching the editor the right way at the most advantageous time.

Beginners usually write articles and send them in final form to magazine editors. That's like a father sewing a dress for his daughter, without consulting her at all. It doesn't work! How much wiser to discuss it with her first, do some measuring, and share ideas about the style, length, and fabric. The same strategy applies to editors. You've got to find out what they want.

Remember, amateurs write, then try to sell. Professionals do just the reverse. They sell the idea first, take the trip, gather precisely what they need on-site, then write an article to the editor's needs upon return. Well in advance of their excursion these writers send a one-page query letter to an editor that sells their travel story idea and themselves as a writer. An editor's positive response is usually specific: "Be sure to mention the bus system"; "Keep it very detailed: price and dates"; "Remember that our readers expect to spend $300 a day!" Or, by simply responding positively—"Let me see it," "Send it on spec," or "Sounds good, let me have a look"— but without further stipulations, the editor assumes that you know what the magazine uses and the size and style of its articles.

IT STARTS WITH A QUESTION

Query letters sent to a magazine editor are built around an inquiry, "Would you be interested in an article about...?" But to which editor do you write? Often the *Writer's Market* specifically states, "Send query letters to..." Or the editor of the section where the article would be used is named and titled, like Ms. Mary Jones, Articles Editor.

If it's not clear from the write-up, query the top person if it's a small to middle-range publication; if it's on every supermarket checkout counter, query the managing editor.

Make your query letters positive, clear, and no longer than a page. On that page bring the topic alive, demonstrating by your style how you will write the article. In addition, provide other necessary information: why readers would be interested, what your expertise is in the field (if necessary), what you've published of a similar nature, when you will take the trip (if in the future), when you can get the manuscript to the editor (three weeks after you return), and anything else that helps sell your idea.

Let me comment on the one-page stipulation. It's not rigid, but it is based on what most editors tell me: "If they can't sell me in one page, they sure can't do it in two..." Yet when I spoke on a panel in New York City about querying for the American Society of Journalists and Authors, an editor of *Vogue*, also on the panel, said that she wanted two full pages to grasp the whole idea and to sample the person's writing. Another editor in the audience agreed. So the length is up to you. But one page has always worked best for me and those professional writers I know well. However long your letter, it should be neatly typed (or printed out with a computer) in a business-like fashion on clean, business-size paper, providing easy-to-read copy.

While the one-page guideline was designed for snail mailed query letters, the same idea holds true if the query is e-mailed, though the page length is really determined by the size of the recipient's monitor, and who knows how big that can be? But the point doesn't change: keep the query concise, fast, and stimulating. Shorter is better. Too short means you are afraid to show too much of a shaky skill. In e-mails, think five or six paragraphs as maximum length.

NEXT COMES A FEASIBILITY STUDY

Before you write a query letter you must process the idea through what I call a feasibility study, which is, in fact, two studies. The first asks whether it is feasible to write the article; the second, whether it is feasible to sell it.

A query letter asks if the editor would be interested in an article about .... So if the editor replies positively, you must be certain that you can in fact write about the subject you've proposed. Therefore, as described earlier, you must conduct a limited amount of research before writing your the query, to know with certainty that you could comply and also to gather enough information about the topic to write a solid, accurate, and exciting letter.

Given this, you don't want to spend weeks researching at the pre-query stage. For one thing, editors don't respond favorably to every query. You would be wasting too much valuable time exploring to exhaustive depth what an hour or several could reveal. For another, all you really need to know is if the subject proposed can be written about in the style the letter suggests, and if so, where you can find the needed information after you receive the go-ahead.

"Is it feasible to sell?" requires a different kind of research, one best gathered through a three-step process: (1) Ask yourself "Who would be interested in reading about this topic?"; then list potential audiences from the most to the least interested, (2) Ask "What do they read?"; then next to each of your target audiences, list the magazines each might read. (3) Rank the magazines in that list by priority.

You can approach step one, finding the most likely readers, in three different ways. Using your imagination is the best. Close your eyes and think about the topic. Ask "Who cares at all about this?" Write down the types of people—professionals, students, hobbyists, homemakers, and so on—who might buy a magazine in order to read about your topic. Remember to include people in the travel trade. An article about a certain kind of hotel not only appeals to potential guests but also to those working at that hotel, other hotels, or in the travel business in general.

A second way is to look at the table of contents of the current *Writer's Market*, which lists well over one hundred publishing categories that, with some more imagination, can suggest even more kinds of readers.

Deduction is a third way. Check your topic in the *Reader's Guide* or the computer equivalent (found in your local library) to see where it has appeared in print before. By looking at the audience of the magazine in which it was previously published you can assume that it might work well again for that audience, as well as for related audiences.

The question posed in step two, "What do they read?," is easier to answer. Check the current *Writer's Market* to see which magazines are listed. Then check other guides and library periodical holdings to see what else is published about your topic. Put all you find on a list.

Which brings us to step 3. If you could send a query to every magazine listed you wouldn't need to prioritize. But you can't, mainly because each buys some form of exclusivity and you can't promise all rights to all people.

So you must put the best market first, from your perspective, then the second best, and so on. What do you use for criteria? When they pay, what they pay, how much freelance material they purchase, and how often they publish. Where do you find this information? In the current *Writer's Market* or, if the magazine isn't listed, write a letter directly to the editor (find the name and address in its masthead), asking whether they buy from freelancers, when they pay, the range, and other relevant information. Also ask if they would send you a "guideline-for-writers" sheet, if they have one. This usually contains all the answers to your questions as well as provides you with the information found in a typical *Writer's Market* write-up.

Magazines pay in one of two ways: on acceptance (their check may accompany their letter of acceptance of the manuscript or be sent on their next pay date, usually within 30 days) or on publication.

The latter is froth with "if's"—if they pay if they use it, if they remember, if they haven't folded, if you remind them that they forgot (if you can still find them!). So you don't want to query or send original work to a magazine that pays on publication.

Taking your prioritized list, draw a line to divide your markets into two parts. Put those that pay on acceptance above the line and query them in order of priority. Place those that pay on publication below the line and sell them reprints.

Reshuffle those above the line by how much they pay. It makes the most sense (and cents) to put the highest payers first. The worst they can say to your query is no. Why talk yourself out of a top sale by not trying it first?

How much they pay, as well as how often the publication is issued and what percent is written by freelancers, should be explained in either the *Writer's Market* or the guideline-for-writers sheet.

If the payment is listed as a range, say $300-550, rest assured that at the beginning you will be earning closer to the bottom than the top. The more they buy from you, the quicker you will move up. Some editors will include expenses after you're a valued member of the family. Photo payment is usually in addition to that base amount or range, and can exceed it. But if the listing says they pay "for the package," that means copy and photos.

Finally, find out how often the magazine comes out and what percent of each issue is freelance written. A magazine buying 99% freelance is more desirable from a selling position than one buying 2%, as is a daily publication that uses 300 times more copy than an annual. These features will cause you to move a magazine up or down on your list, all else being equal.

QUERY ONE PUBLICATION AT A TIME

Let's say that for one of the likely audiences you find five magazines, which you have prioritized. Your immediate inclination will be to write one query, modify it a bit for all five, and send a letter to each editor, and take your chances, assuming that at most one would probably be interested anyway. Don't do it!

Why? If you query many magazines simultaneously and find that two or three want to see the article, you are in a tough spot. You can only send the manuscript to one, on the assumption (probably 99% accurate) that it will want to buy all or first rights. So you must then ignore the other interested respondent(s) while you await a reply from the first editor. The editors who are ignored will simply not be interested in future queries from you—and you might not even sell your article to the first editor anyway! This is why you must query only one magazine at a time.

It makes no sense to lose editors through greed or impatience. There are few enough of them to start with! Try the first editor on your list. If he or she says no, try the second, and so on, until you have sold the item or exhausted your list of those who pay on acceptance.

That is not to say that you can't query others simultaneously about somewhat related topics. If you are writing about Brazil, don't query an all-you-ever-wanted-to-know article about Rio de Janeiro to several editors simultaneously. Use this query for one, try another about Copacabana Beach, a third about Sugarloaf Mountain, a fourth about Maracanhã Stadium, a fifth about Tijuca Forest, and still another about the Imperial Palace. All share a Rio background yet each is distinctive. That way you can write an article for every query that brings a positive reply.

Why not just pick out four or five ideas and write a sharp paragraph about each in the same letter, asking the editor to choose which article he or she would like you to submit? Some writers do that and it works for them. But they almost always have long, successful selling records and are known by the editors. I don't advise it early in the game for one simple reason: It's too hard to sell a full article to a paying editor by saying so little. One paragraph is not enough for little-known writers to demonstrate their ability.

In the beginning it makes much more sense to focus on your best idea, using the query letter to develop and sell it, and by extension sell yourself as a writer. This is not to say that in the same letter you can't spin off a second or even third angle based on your main idea. You might suggest a general article about Wales and then suggest later in the letter an alternative (or a sidebar), say, a highly focused piece on early Celtic castles in and near Cardiff. The postscript is ideal for this; make it a solid, selling paragraph.

When you have determined that it is feasible to write and to sell the article—when you have sufficient information about your topic and you've got a prioritized market list—it's time to write a query to the editor of the first magazine on your list. Before writing you may want to look at several issues of that magazine to learn its style, taboos, and expectations. This knowledge will help you write an effective query letter, tailored to the specific magazine.

SLANT AND CONTENT

A Sales Letter

The query letter is a sales letter. It should make the editor say, "My readers want to know more about that subject. I'd be a fool not to look at that article." The query must indicate what the editor can expect: a well-researched, sharply written manuscript done in a style appropriate to the topic. If the angle is humorous, the query must be written with the same degree of humor to show that you can do it. If serious, sobriety must prevail, but not to the detriment of the lively, vital exchange of information.

Since you will take the trip before you write the article, remember the three stipulations mentioned for the sales plan: You must indicate when you will be at the site, when you'll be back, and when you can have the final manuscript (with photos, if promised) in the editor's hands—usually within three weeks of the date of return. (If you have already taken the trip, simply deliver the manuscript within three weeks of receiving the go-ahead from the editor.)

QUERY BY LETTER, FAX, PHONE, OR E-MAIL?

A decade ago how you sent query letters was a foolish question. Even fools knew that they were mailed: a stamp, envelope, the letter, and an SASE.

Today, nothing is absolute. For e-zines, you e-mail. The rest, you check the current *Writer's Market* (or the guideline-for-writers information sheet mailed to you at your request or posted at the publication's website) to see how the editor wants to be sold.

A sample check of the "Travel, Camping, and Trailer" section of the 2002 *Writer's Market* found these preferences for the 47 publications listed: 42 accepted snail mail queries (three wanted manuscripts only, without queries, and two, e-mails only, one in Greece and the other in distant Michigan), 30 accepted e-mail, fax was fine for 19, and three would accept query phone calls (but three more specifically stated, "no phone queries"). About half accepted snail and e-mail or both plus fax.

The lesson is obvious: you query the way the editor wants to be queried, so find that out first.

Two more lessons aren't as obvious. One, unless you are as thoroughly prepared when you query by other means as you would be by snail mail and you include the same selling hooks (great idea, clearly explained, why the reader would want to know more about it, and when you can deliver), your danger of rejection multiplies with the haste of your query.

The second is that however eloquent your plea by phone, about the best you get is an irked suggestion that you put that idea in writing and mail it in (like you should have done in the first place). And like your competition has already done by mail, e-mail, or fax.

What do I hear from the trenches and see in practice? Snail mail queries get the best reception and have the highest response rate. Faxes are rare so nobody had a comment, and e-mails are by far the most ignored. Save the phone call for an editor who has already bought five of your best articles, loved them all, and is starting to think of you as part of their publishing family. And even then, send most of your stuff with a postage stamp.

THE REPLY

However it arrives, you can expect one of three basic replies to your query: no reply at all, the answer no, or a qualified yes.

If you don't receive a reply within two months, send a copy of your query letter to the same editor, with a note attached. Your note might say (1) the query attached is a copy of a letter sent to you on such-and-such date; (2) perhaps it got lost in the mail; and (3) if the idea is still as exciting now as it was then, should we share it with your readers?

If the editor still hasn't replied a month later, the magazine has probably folded! Go to the next one on your list and write a new query to that editor.

How do you avoid the no-reply response? Keep your *Writer's Market* current by checking the "Markets" section each month in the new issue of *Writer's Digest Magazine*, put out by the same publishing house. Cross off all magazines that have folded, update current listing as necessary, and photocopy any new listings and append them to your book. (Keeping your *Writer's Market* current this way can help it last two years instead of only one.)

If the editor says no, thank God you didn't waste time writing a whole article for those pages! Blessed are editors who let you know quickly—and kindly. Simply go to the next publication on your market list and query it.

The nicest reply is yes! Alas, it's almost always a qualified yes: "Let's see it," "Send it on spec(ulation)," or "Let me take a look." Not much wind for your sails, that tepid a reply. Yet in reality that's about as close to a sales commitment as you'll get, particularly when you're new to the editor.

When the editor sends you a qualified yes, your topic and name are written on the editor's calendar, probably for the issue that hits the stands two to three months after you promised to submit your manuscript. The editor wants you to submit top-grade material to adorn the magazine's pages. All that separates you from print and pay at this point is your writing.

YES? STUDY YOUR TARGET MARKET!

Top-grade submissions come from studying the target market closely after receiving an affirmative reply. Get the last three issues and find at least one article in each as close as possible in subject, style, or tone to what you want to write about. From these articles deduce what the editor is seeking for those pages, and thus what you need to provide from the site to bring your manuscript alive and make buyable.

Again, I'm going to borrow from my book *How to Sell More Than 75% of Your Freelance Writing*. Called "How to Study a Printed Magazine Article," this 12-step process shows how to analyze editors' needs and preferences by what they buy. (It works as well for newspaper travel articles.)

How to Study a Printed Magazine Article

(1) Read the article closely, then ask yourself what basic or working question it answers. Write the question out. It may also answer secondary questions, so write those out too.

(2) Now read the entry for that publication in the *Writer's Market* for the year of (or preceding) the article's appearance. Given the working question in (1) and the indications in the *Writer's Market* of what that magazine was seeking, try to put yourself in the writer's shoes. How did the writer slant the subject to appeal to the magazine's readers? Why did the editor buy it? Study its length, illustrations, position in the magazine.

(3) To see how the writer carries the main theme through the article, underline each word that relates directly to that theme, then outline the entire piece. Study the writer's use of facts, quotes, and anecdotes. What is the ratio between them? How is humor used? Is it spread and balanced to the same degree throughout? Do other articles in this issue use facts, quotes, anecdotes, and humor in roughly the same way and in the same proportion?

(4) List every source used, including direct references and quotations. Where would the writer find the facts, opinions, and quotes that are not clearly identified by source in the article? If you are uncertain, indicate where you would find the material—or where you would go to find out.

(5) Focus on the quotations. Why is each used? How does it carry the theme forward? Note how the source of the quotation is introduced, and how much the reader must know about the source to place the person and what is said into perspective.

(6) Is the article written in first person (I), second (you), or third (he, she, or it)? How does that strengthen the article? Does the person change? Why or why not? Are most other articles in the same issue written in the same person?

(7) Set the title aside and concentrate on the lead. How long is it, in words or sentences? How does it grab your interest? Does it make you want to read more? Why? How does it compare with other leads in that issue?

(8) Most articles begin with a short lead followed by a longer second or third paragraph that ties the lead to the body of the article. Called the transitional paragraph, it tells where you are going and how you will get there. It bridges the attention-grabbing elements of the lead to the expository elements of the body by setting direction, tone, and pace. Find the transitional paragraph and study it. Organizationally, after the lead it is the most important item in the article.

(9) Now underline the first sentence in each paragraph. They should form a chain that will pull you through the piece. Note how the writer draws the paragraphs together with transitional words and phrases. Circle the words that perform this linking function. Often the same words or ideas will be repeated in the last sentence of one paragraph and the first sentence of the next.

(10) Earlier you outlined the article. Now look at the transitional words and the underlined first sentences and see how the structure ties the theme together. Is the article structured chronologically, developmentally, by alternating examples, point by point? Or if the article was written to answer the working question you isolated in (1), did the answers to the secondary questions stemming from that working question provide the article's organizational structure?

(11) How does the article end? Does it tie back to the lead? Does it repeat an opening phrase or idea? The conclusion should reinforce and strengthen the direction the article has taken. Does it? How?

(12) Finally, look at the title. It may have been changed or rewritten by the editor. Nonetheless, does it correctly describe the article that follows? Does it tease, quote, pique one's curiosity, state facts? What technique does it use to make the reader want to read the article?

While you have the articles before you, check the editor's photographic needs as well. What kind of photos accompany the articles: b/w or color? Are they horizontal or vertical? Do they include people in every shot? Doing what? Were they taken by the editor? Do they use captions with each photo?

This isn't busywork. It tells you specifically the kinds of information you need to gather before the trip and at the site, as well as the type and quantity of photos you might need to provide. A careful study in advance can cut your working time on the trip by as much as 75%—and virtually assure you of a sale. Conversely, gathering material at random for some imaginary publication to be found later requires far more work and no assurance that it will even be enough or will result in a writable article for which a market can be found.

The chemical composition of a travel article is facts, quotes, and anecdotes, to which photography is a valuable addition.

As suggested earlier, the more you can gather before the trip, the less risk you run of coming up short at the site. Read all you can about the destination: encyclopedias, books, recent articles in magazines and newspapers, travel brochures. Remember to ask yourself what earlier writers found sufficiently interesting to write about. Develop the grid as discussed in Chapter 2, creating your own "must see" list. See travelogues, live or on TV. Rent video-tapes about the area. Record every fact that you think you might need for your articles, keeping track of the source of each. Put these facts on a legal pad or index cards to bring with you, so you can verify the most important at the site.

Don't rely on being able to find or use libraries for fact gather-ing on the trip, even if you can read the native language. You'll use your time far better if you gather the core of information before you go and work on-site observing, interviewing, and photographing.

While you're gathering facts also note, on a separate sheet, the name of every person quoted, plus anything about them mentioned. Editors almost always want live quotes; beginners rarely get them. The more informed and reliable the person quoted, the better. See whom the professionals quoted earlier. Then if you can't find a knowledgeable person with whom you can speak when you arrive, you at least have a list of previously interviewed people you could seek out. Even if you can't find them, the locals are likely to direct you to others of similar stature or reliability.

Anecdotes bring articles alive, so write down any you find in your source materials. You will likely add more anecdotes acquired on site, perhaps from your own activities.

Finally, see what others have photographed. It's a good idea to take more shots of the same thing but from different angles or in different contexts to fall back on should completely different photos be impossible or not come out as desired.

Remember, every hour you spend at home preparing the trip frees up that much precious time at the location. A well-researched base makes the days on-site less anxious, less harried, and just plain more fun. Isn't that really what your travel is about?

WHAT IF IT'S A NO?

The answer no is not fatal, but it sure is depressing. You could quit writing, of course. Or send a foul retort by special delivery, guaranteeing that you'll never have to worry about appearing on those pages at all. Or you could read the rejection to see what the editor really meant.

Rejections come in all forms. The most discouraging appear to have been reproduced by the millions on leaky, hand-cranked mimeograph machines, sliced into irregular forms, and piled up awaiting your self-addressed, stamped envelope. They say something like

> Thank you for your submission. It does not meet our present editorial needs. Good luck in placing it elsewhere. The editor.

In fact, that's precisely what they do mean. The idea wasn't appropriate—and didn't excite the editor enough to generate a personal reply, which is what you would prefer (other than a booming acceptance!).

Sometimes the editor will return your query, or a copy, with *no* written across it in a firm hand. Not much to build on there, either.

Still, editors need good writers, and they can spot them through sharp, interesting queries. So even if the topic proposed doesn't work, you are really looking for two kinds of addenda to your rejection, typed or handwritten: "Not this time, but send another good query (or idea)" or "Can't use it now but try me again in (five) months."

The first says that you can write well enough, or so it seems from one query, but the topic missed. Find a better topic and query again, as well as you did or even better. Try to follow up on this immediately.

The second means that the editor just covered that area or subject—they can only use so many articles about turtle-racing in Tennessee—but in five months, or whenever indicated, it would be seriously considered again. If you can't sell that idea before that date, mark your calendar and send the query again. No editor asks to see a query twice if they aren't seriously interested. On the other hand, they are giving you a chance to sell it elsewhere, so their interest isn't rabid. And they have it off their desk!

Before getting a positive response, beginners may write six, eight, even ten queries, one after the other. Even hardened professionals, to whom queries are as familiar as their morning coffee, are pleased to sell to a third of the editors they query.

You must write each query fully intending to get the sale from it. I've seen at least 20 of my students hit pay dirt on their very first try. Even if it is rejected, learn from it and try again, and again. Querying success comes from skill, tenacity, and sheer mathematics.

Unless you shouldn't have queried in the first place....

WHEN NOT TO QUERY

As I mentioned earlier, you submit the final draft for newspaper articles directly to the editor, no querying involved (more on this in Chapter 12).

Certain kinds of articles don't lend themselves to querying either. For instance: full-gusted humor. What would you say? "Would you like to read the funniest article ever written about the Cumberland Gap?" To which the editor would reply, "Send it to me and we'll see if it makes me laugh." Instead simply send the article. (Keep humor pieces short and spread the humor to the same degree throughout.)

How do you tell the difference between a *humor* article and one that is *humorous*? The "funniest ever written" is a straight humor piece, the purpose of which is to make you laugh, whatever the subject. Dave Barry or Woody Allen stuff. But humorous writing shares information humorously. The point is the information; the style is humorous. Therefore you do query—humorously, to the degree of the humor in the article you're proposing. Humorous travel pieces sell well. You simply must not alter the truth, too much, to make it funny.

You also don't query for "fillers," those one-page-or less items that contain less copy than the query itself would. These are often used as inserts, to fill up space. Simply write them and send them.

The pay is low and slow, since editors usually pay for them when they are used.

A few magazines don't want to be queried ever, and they state so in the *Writer's Market* write-up. I usually ignore these publications, since researching and writing takes too much time to gamble on an editor's interest. Later I send these magazines rewrites of articles already sold.

Some highly-subjective, first-person pieces are also hard to sell without being read, since their flavor can't be imparted in a query letter. I almost always send articles like these to newspapers.

> *Query letters are the difference between the amateur and professional in the magazine writing world. They are the key to the magazines' coffers.*

EXAMPLE

QUERYING FOR THE BIG TRIP

Time for business! It all starts with a selling query, so I must get to work.

Is an article about an historic downtown, 12-block "Red Tile" self-guided walking tour of Santa Barbara feasible to sell? I ask myself, "Who would eagerly read several thousand words, enhanced by brilliant photos, about well-preserved adobes, a super fort being rebuilt, quaint arcades, a much-photographed Spanish-Moorish County Courthouse, and a whiff of the not-so-distant Mexican past?" If done right, anybody with a speck of wanderlust, sense of adventure, or spark of curiosity would enjoy the vicarious, verdant trek back into the romantic early West past.

For the broader city-core article I shoot straight for the larger travel magazines, using the current *Writer's Market* as my guide. I find six likely magazines, five paying on acceptance, one on publication. I set the last aside now (I'll send reprints later). I list the remaining five in preferential order, with the best payer first. These comprise my market list and I will query them in order. If one says yes before I hit the bottom, the rest will either get a different query about a different subject or a query with a rewrite angle after my return.

What do I know about the first: *A1 Magazine*? The *Writer's Market* description tells me who to query, the address, that it buys first rights and uses 85% freelance, that it's a monthly sold to about 500,000 subscribers and newsstand buyers, pays between $500 and $700, prefers articles of about 1,800 words, seeks top-level digital color transparencies that add depth to the prose, and wants "the reader to be transported to the site and mood."

I've read this first-rate glossy often so it's not necessary to trot over to the library to see how it actually looks and reads. (I'll do that later if I get the go-ahead so I'll know precisely what they want in their articles.)

My slant? Let the places visited bring back the early Spanish-Mexican flavor as best I can on one query page; then I'll do it even better in the article after I've seen downtown Santa Barbara in person. I must paint some mental pictures in the query.

I Send the Query Letter

Five or six paragraphs are all that separate me from gold and glitter. Will this be the query letter that pays, in part, for my California excursion? (See Figure 5.)

Figure 5 *Pre-Trip Query Letter*

P.O. Box 6405
Santa Maria, CA 93456
(805) 937-8711
February 12, 200_

Mrs. Janet Wolfe
Managing Editor, *A1 Magazine*
7388 Belvens Court
New York, NY 10010

Dear Mrs. Wolfe:

It's hard to look from the base of his statue on the parade grounds of Santa Barbara's oldest building and not wonder if Carlos III isn't kicking himself in his grave for being so stupid. It was 1782 and the last Spanish *presidio* (fortress and administrative seat) he built in the New World was a zero-hour effort to hold on to his distant, empty territory. Too late. How could he have let this gilded gem, the Riviera of the Pacific, slip away?

Today the state historic park sits plunk in the center of the narrow city of 85,000, stretched between the Santa Ynez Mountains and the sea. Its shimmering walls, festive chapel, and trenches of archeological digs are the strongest tourist magnet in one of California's favorite resort cities.

Let me take your readers on an unforgettable 12-block "Red Tile Tour" that ties together the city's earliest adobe homes, plazas, flag-draped store arcades, the Guard's House, its first (and still active) theatre, gardens, Col. John Fremont's headquarters, the site of the Mexican Assembly's last meeting in 1846, two superb museums (of art and history), and its most photographed hub, the County Court-house, a Spanish-Moorish masterpiece where its 85-foot high four-direction observation tower begins or ends the 75-minute (or many-hour) free stroll through history laced with salsa and sun.

At every corner the old touches the new. A coat of arms on the modern library, a statue of Franklin sitting on the same bench with a blushing Oaxaca maiden, Gucci's and McDonalds on the arterial State Street near the Hill-Carrillo Adobe, with the city's first wooden floor. Plus weekend mariachi bands, docent tours, scores of restaurants, movies, shops, and benches. Twelve blocks uphill sits the stately Santa Barbara Mission. Downhill, closer, is the park-lined waterfront, Stearns Wharf, volleyball, and whales.

I'll be in Santa Barbara from May 10-21 and could have the completed article to you on June 15, with 100 digital photos for your selection. The article will be tailored specifically to your readership, much as I've done in the 1,700+ pieces I've put in print over the past 30 years. I could also add a fact sidebar on the city: how to reach it, local telephone numbers and websites for information about lodging, dining, weather, other key sites, and the calendar of events, much as you use on your pages, if interested.

Will you let me know soon?

Gordon Burgett

The Editor Replies

Off goes the query, to be read, sniffed, and pinched by the editor. "Soon," for the reply, is a loose term in the editorial world. It can mean instantly or whenever. So, much to my delight, 18 days later comes a reply (Figure 6).

Figure 6 *Reply to the Pre-trip Query Letter*

7388 Belvens Ct.
New York, NY 10010
March 22, 200_

Dear Gordon,

Let me see your "Red Tile Tour" article about Santa Barbara when you return. Any time in June is fine. If I use it, it will be in the winter. Which month is drier, November or February? Slant it for the drier of the two and include the average temperature.

Since this is our first contact, it must be on spec. Keep it to 1,800 words, 2,000 with the sidebar. Use last month's box about Cairo as an example. Go beyond the tour: something about the Mission, the beach, nightlife, three best restaurants, how to see Lotusland, and so on.

Photos that pop off the page increase your chances. Long shot on a cover too (an extra $500), always a vertical. Captions required. Set your digital at 1600 x 1200 for the cover; 1024 x 768 are okay for the rest. No b/w's.

Expect about $550 if accepted, plus photos ($100 each, when used).
Have a good time!

Best,

(Mrs.) Janet Wolfe

Looks good! Chances of her buying the piece? Almost 100%, if
it's as good as the other articles in her magazine, if I can capture
those eye-catching photos and I bring the place alive.

I'm already ahead financially since this will allow me to deduct at
least $500 on my taxes, as long as I follow through and submit the
manuscript. It's a great "letter of intent."

Still, there's work to do now to get the actual cash later. Off to
the library to scour the last three issues of *A1 Magazine*, listing
everything I should gather onsite. I zero in on at least one article in
each issue closest to what I'll write. I then analyze them to see how
those writers put together their articles that successfully appeared
on the magazine's pages, so that I can do it too!

For example, I see that quotes are used less in these articles than
usual but that adjectives (word paintings) are abundant. The articles
supply precise costs, streets, times. Lots of subheads break up the
copy—one for every three or four paragraphs. They quote tour
guides; every quote tied to full name and Mr./Mrs./Ms./Miss.
Short paragraphs (two to three sentences). The articles also indicate
how long things take: tours, meals to be served, hikes. Very little
humor.

This and everything else I find and need goes on my notepad, to
be included later in my Red Tile Tour/ Santa Barbara/*A1 Magazine*
file. Nothing is left to memory or chance. When I'm sitting in a
taqueria on State Street laying out that day's attack on the fort I
want every weapon on that list!

Chapter Six

PHOTOS

Just as the year 2000 bopped in, travel photography was turned upside down. Three words tell all: Film or digital?

Suddenly there were two remarkably different ways to do the same thing. We could visually capture a place, person, or thing with our old reliable 35mm camera on film or we could do precisely the same, with a similar new camera, using 0's and 1's. With care, the results would be shockingly similar. But which is the editor buying? That, Ollie, is the rub.

So let me do this. Let me upgrade the 1994 edition as if digital refers to fingers, to define the old system—film, f-stops, slides, prints, negatives—so that those planted in this camp have tested, reliable submission guidelines for as long as film remains commercially viable.

Then I'll look at digital photography: who is buying it now, how to know when specific editors will prefer it in the future, the advantages and disadvantages it offers, and some of the evolving submission protocols currently in favor.

But the basics first. Like, how important is photography to selling travel articles?

If you are writing about the desolate northeastern backlands of Canudos, somewhere near the fringe of the known world, where the messianic madman Antônio Conselheiro held off the entire Brazilian Army in an epic battle more than one hundred years ago, you'd better have a photo or two of the place, fifty is even better, to give credence to your words.

But if you're talking about Chicago's Loop or the Eiffel Tower, you don't need to take your own photos. You can obtain them for free if you need them at all. (I'll tell you how later.)

No form of writing is so interwoven with photography as travel. And nowhere can you so quickly double your income with a camera.

Photography gives your prose that extra dimension of immediacy. It adds a tangible fullness that lets vicarious travelers skim across thunderous waves on a surfboard or creep into the cavernous bowels of a mountain.

But is it absolutely mandatory? No. Word painters can survive on adjectives alone. But why not make use of the visual and prosper from it?

The danger with beginning travel writers and their cameras is they too often overdue it. They forget that good copy is crucial, and good photos are an extra, though a valuable one. Never forget that the paycheck comes from the printed word, from the artful blend of facts, quotes, and anecdotes. If the copy sells, photos simply fatten the pot.

How much money can photography add to the kitty? A newspaper usually pays between $10 to $25, sometimes more, for black-and-white (b/w) photos. A magazine usually pays between $25 to $150 or more for color. A cover photo can bring between $200 and $800. Both *Writer's Market* and *Photographer's Market* explain a publication's wants, needs, and pay range.

What follows is not a step-by-step guide for professional photographers, nor will it tell you how to point the camera. To be honest, I'm still not quite sure what happens when I hear the shutter click yet I've sold at least 450 photos with my articles! So if you're seeking the definitive word on zoom lenses, storage cards, or the aperture setting to best capture rocket launches, this is the wrong book.

On the other hand, I can tell you how a true amateur can actually sell a lot of color and b/w shots to magazines and newspapers, and how you might do the same (even if, like me, you wonder if the film is really going anywhere when you crank the handle or what is happening when you push the button). I can tell you how to submit and how to do the basics, profitably.

SOME GOOD ADVICE FOR THE AMATEUR

Nothing is more basic than the advice I got from a true professional after he reviewed some of my early photographic attempts. He told me in the firmest voice possible: "Take a lot, I mean a *lot* of pictures." On the remote possibility, I guess, that some of them might actually come out!

So that's my advice to you: If you're using film, take lots of shots. The same digitally. A true pro might be pleased if 1 out of 100 was acceptable. My eye isn't nearly that discerning. I hope for 1 out of 15. It takes plenty of honest tries to get a dynamite picture to mate with good copy to create a super article.

Another comment I heard reinforces the many-shot film philosophy, "It's a hell of a lot cheaper to take an extra roll than to fly back to Rome to get what you shoulda got!" Given this advice, what kind of photos do I usually take?

COLOR VERSUS BLACK-AND-WHITE

For magazines I always take color. (Although you will occasionally see color photos in newspapers, they're almost always from some travel editor's photo supply, travel bureaus, or from photo stock companies.) For newspapers I usually take b/w's. Occasionally a magazine will use these too, usually for the later pages.

Color shots can be either vertical or horizontal since the longer magazine deadlines allow the art editors the time to do fanciful cropping. I mix my color up according to the subject itself, often shooting the same shot vertically and horizontally. I also try to get some reds and yellows in every slide, to complete the color spectrum, knowing that outdoor photos (the kind I generally shoot) already contain nature's usual abundance of browns, greens, and blues. Where do I find red and yellow? Often in the clothing of those I photograph, unless I can stand them behind a tulip patch. Color variety, however, is less important than clarity and brightness.

Newspapers prefer b/w verticals at about a ratio of three verticals to one horizontal. I usually submit an assortment of 16 shots, 12 verticals and 4 horizontals, so the editor has a choice. The newspaper's low-resolution print begs for high contrast and sharp, tight shots. Rather than a murky, global photo of the Grand Canyon, I shoot the mule train climbing out of the Canyon, with the head muleteer atop a mule, a second mule and rider at the edge of the shot, and the Canyon in the background.

If at all possible, get people in your photos. Preferably attractive people, unless you find a type who fits your copy to a tee. A grizzled, warty old varmint with a gold pan in hand is what I want for a prospecting story. But, at the risk of being called sexist, I'd rather feature bikini-clad women in a piece about sunbathing in Santa Cruz—and I think that's what the travel editor and readers would like to see too.

Avoid obvious but unexplained (or inexplicable) contrasts, like midgets and giants casually strolling down the street together. Or bums and big-bucks sipping the same beer. The purpose of your picture somehow gets lost.

The people you're photographing should be doing something active related to the article, not simply staring at the camera or obviously posing for it. A mountain climbing piece calls for a person, or several, either climbing or fastening equipment or checking pitons or perhaps scouring a map, with a landmark mountain in the background.

CAMERAS WITH FILM

What size camera should you use? At least 35mm. I carry two film cameras with me at the same time, one for slides, the other for b/w's. Since one is an automatic and the other requires a light meter, I use the latter for b/w's since they are generally harder to take well.

The standard camera lens size is 50mm. If your model has a single-lens reflex, what you see through the viewfinder is roughly how the final shot will appear. You will probably want at least two more lenses: a wide-angle and a telephoto, for close-ups. Zoom lenses are particularly useful for outdoors or nature photography.

Take time buying what you need. A good, used 35mm camera from a reputable store is the place to start. Find a salesperson who knows cameras well and explain to them how you will use yours. Ask questions. Take two or three rolls and experiment before you travel. (I shot the entire first roll on my just-purchased 35mm camera with the lens cover doing what it does best!) Two key questions before you buy: Is the camera comfortable in your hands? And can you see clearly through the viewfinder, particularly if you wear glasses?

Don't buy a fancy camera case unless you plan to carry it with you 24 hours a day. A backpack or small, padded duffel bag works just as well and doesn't attract light-fingered attention. And remember to put your camera in the case, or at least keep the camera out of the sun or the subzero cold as much as possible. Dust, sand, salt water, and snow are its natural enemies. You can shoot in the rain but dry the camera off as quickly as possible, and always keep the lens dry.

As a minimum guideline per article, I take three rolls of 36-exposure b/w film and two rolls of 36-exposure color slides. But if I have a go-ahead from a magazine, that two-roll minimum very quickly becomes five, eight, or even ten rolls. For color slides, Kodachrome is my all-purpose favorite film. For b/w's, Kodak Tri-X has a high enough ASA to include anything I shoot. Always bring more film with you than you think you can possibly use.

DIGITAL CAMERAS

Although many printed magazines still use and prefer 35mm slides, digital images are being accepted as well. Online publications prefer them. Many newspapers have gone exclusively to digital work for their staff photographers, and although they still accept slides and prints, they are well equipped to receive and use digital images.

How can you find out which format the editor buys? Sometimes the current *Writer's Market* will tell. The *Photographer's Market* is much more explicit but not all of the same publications appear in both. You can check the publication's website, particularly the photography section of the "guidelines-for-writers" sheet. The best way is to ask the magazine editor—but only after you have received a go-ahead from your query. For newspapers, it's a roll of the dice. You can ask but since you submit after the trip and manuscript preparation, that's a lot of shot-in-the-dark, pre-trip asking. The website might tell, but I'd lean to film if I were unsure. It's much more likely they can use film if they've switched to digital than the reverse.

What are the advantages of using a digital camera for travel writers? Beverly Schulz, in her online "Discover Digital Photography" class (check http://www.eductiontogo.com), says it best,

> Digital cameras allow you to see your work immediately, giving you the option of shooting again if you didn't get just the image you wanted. Since going back to a site isn't always easy, this helps send you home confident you've got great images to sell. You also have the ability to download images to a computer and e-mail them back to a publisher while on the road.

Also, with heightened security measures, film is more vulnerable and often times you won't have the option of hand inspections. Digital media generally survives much better and eliminates drawing attention to yourself at security checkpoints, which can result in extensive delays and searches.

Even if the editor prefers digital, you need to know the file size, resolution, and format they require. These are easy to comply with by using an image-editing package, such as Photoshop or Photoshop Elements (their less expensive version). There are many software packages on the market, and they'll continue to change, but the basics of sizing images should be available in most.

To insure that your digital images are the best quality, shoot in a resolution that is at least 1024 x 768, preferably higher. You'll get fewer images on a card than shooting at a low resolution, but the quality is worth the space. Images shot at a 640 x 480 resolution do not have enough detail to produce quality prints. By shooting at the higher resolutions, you'll be able to use your images both online and in printed form.   Many publications will ask for the images as TIFF files, but you don't have to shoot them that way. They can be taken in the smaller JPEG format and converted to TIFF before submission, saving you some space on your cards.

Depending on the length of your trip, you may want several storage cards or an additional way to download your images. Laptop computers work very well for downloading images and reusing the cards. If you're not traveling with a computer, there are storage devices designed simply to download and store your images until you get home. Alternatively, some digital cameras use mini-CDs as their storage media, allowing you unlimited storage without expensive cards.

Most digital cameras have rechargeable batteries, but you'll still want to travel with several sets. Electricity may be limited in some areas and you'll want to be able to keep shooting even if one set of batteries wears out.

FIND A FRAMESETTER

Whether shooting on film or digitally, find a "framesetter," a photo that tells all in one picture. When you do, take a dozen shots of it each in color and b/w. For example, if in Holland I encounter a healthy, ruddy-cheeked lass dressed in Dutch costume, a bouquet of tulips in one arm, a giant piece of chocolate in the other, wooden shoes on her pink feet, a windmill behind her left shoulder, and a dike behind her right—it shouts "Holland"! I'll shoot her straight on, from the left and right, from low and high, and vary the background—then do it again with the other camera!

When you have that special shot, the one that tells all, "bracket" it. To do this, set your f-stop to the ideal shutter speed and lens opening and shoot. Then move up one f-stop and shoot again; then down one and shoot once more. One of these shots will be perfect, one may be acceptable, and one won't be in focus. Great odds.

Still, most shots aren't this eye-catching. So you must ask yourself, What am I seeing that others would go out of their way to look at? If it adds to the substance of the article and can be captured photographically, fire away.

PHOTO RELEASES

Do you need a photo release of the people appearing in your shots? Rarely, unless they will be used as advertisements, appear on a cover, or will run in company or in-house publications, particularly if the publication includes the product in its title, like the *ABC Sausage Company Magazine*. (*Writer's Market* indicates which magazines require releases. These publications will provide a sample release, or you can copy the release from *Photographer's Market* and alter it for your own use.)

Except in the rare cases mentioned above, photos taken in or from public places don't require releases or permission of any kind, nor do those used to communicate "news" or of public figures.

On the other hand, it makes sense to get a release signed at the time when you focus on a specific model, or at least to get the person's name and address, in case you need a release later. This can be tricky, but let me show you how it might be done.

I was writing an article about the "Other Highway 1," from Marin County to Leggett, California, north of San Francisco. I needed a shot to symbolize the many pocket beaches along that route. But since the water is so cold there I figured I'd better start as far south as possible, at Muir Beach a bit north of the Golden Gate. Alas, when I showed up at 9:00 a.m. the beach was sunny but empty— and a beach shot without people isn't likely to be used.

I walked about looking for views I thought would best capture the scene, hoping that a person, attractive and beachlike (also dressed in red and yellow!) would appear. Even better, with a dog!

Up screeched a Volkswagen, out bounded a pooch that looked like it had just escaped from Orphan Annie, and shortly behind skipped a beautiful young blonde woman in a maroon sweatshirt and golden shorts. God listens! I approached her and said, "Hi, I'm Gordon Burgett. I'm writing an article for a newspaper on the East Coast and I was hoping to include some photos of people on the beach. Whatever you're planning on doing, would you mind if I took a few shots? I'll send you a copy of your picture and the article the moment it appears in print."

She agreed and I took several shots of her chasing the dog (toward me) down the beach. Then I asked if she would mind petting the dog at a spot I thought had the best chance of being used, a rock formation on the beach that allowed me to include the water, sand, and green mountains behind. I took most of the slides and b/w's there, explaining to her what I was doing and why.

When I finished I asked her name (I spelled it letter by letter so it was accurate) and address, so I could send her the photo and article. (Always do this afterward, when the person has a vested interest in sharing the information. Had I asked her first she might have released the dog and locked herself in the car!) Afterwards *always* send something to people who agree to pose: the actual photo in print, if used; a print and the article; a slide; or a photo sent by e-mail, with a note thanking them again for their help.

After I've gotten a name and address I usually ask subjects for a bit more information for the caption (that line or two of type below photos, usually used in newspapers, that explains about the picture), like their age, vocation, and why they are there. In this case, I also asked the dog's name. Even if your subjects are reticent to offer details, you already know enough for a simple caption: at least their names, the name of the site, and other circumstances.

Does this always work? Almost always, if you do it in a matter-of-fact, friendly way and keep professionally busy. Sometimes it works too well: The models want to stick with you for the rest of the day!

If you want to photograph people or groups, just ask. Seldom will they say no if they understand how the photos will be used and if you are unobtrusive.

Many years back I was hiking through the narrow, copper-colored canyons at Turkey Run State Park, near Marshall, Indiana, when I encountered a group of Mennonite teens. Like the Amish, the boys wore hooked jeans (no buttons or zippers), the girls, flowing pastel dresses and bonnets. The color contrasts were shocking, and lovely.

So I approached the oldest boy and told him what I was doing. Would they object if I simply followed along and took photos as they climbed and cavorted? The whole group drew together and talked about it, at length. Finally the spokesperson, another boy, came back, looked me hard in the eye, then smiled and shook my hand. He said that while they didn't read worldly magazines, if it made me happy I was invited to join them and use my camera. But please, he said in a lower voice, don't show it to our parents!

I didn't think I had a chance at all—and those photos were among the best I ever took or sold!

KEEPING TRACK AND PROVIDING CAPTIONS

How do I keep track of the photos taken and the people posed? For those shots on film, I put a number (for b/w's) or letter (for slides) on each film can. In my camera case or back pocket I carry a small notepad. Then every time I take a batch of shots I indicate the number and/or letter of the can and record the information I want to use. Coordinating the shots and the caption data later is easy.

When I return from a trip, I have the slides developed and mounted in paper holders. To each I adhere a paper name-and-address tag. Later I will send the best of these slides to magazine editors in clear acetate insert holders.

What do the caption sheets contain and how do they look? In a sentence or so you must explain what each slide shows, remembering that the editor has absolutely no notion of what he/she is looking at. To make things easier on the editor I put my slides in a loose narrative order, grouping those about the same site or topic together, and place them in the insert holder that way. On the caption sheet I identify them by row and number and offer an explanation of each. I identify the article and myself on each caption sheet as well.

When a photo is particularly important or requires a more complete caption, err on the side of giving too much rather than too little information. Make certain that the writing is good and the facts are correct.

Sometimes the photos you submit aren't ones you've taken. When this is the case indicate on the caption sheet those that need to be credited to another person or entity. In correspondence with the editor later, ask that those slides you want credited, either to your or to others, be included in the photo credit section of the publication.

It's wise to make a copy of each caption sheet. At least a dozen times an editor has asked me for more information about a specific slide, row, and sheet, so you may need a copy for your own reference.

SUBMITTING TO NEWSPAPERS

The process of submitting photos to newspapers differs in detail from that just described for magazines. It's best seen in action, however, so I will refer you to the example in the chapter on newspapers (Chapter 12), where we follow the process step-by-step. At this point it's enough to say that newspaper shots must be clear (uncluttered) and person oriented. (In Chapter 12 I'll also show how those submissions differs for film and digital photos.)

MAILING YOUR PRINTS OR SLIDES?

You can send most of your prints or slides by regular first class, priority mail, or some courier system (like UPS or Fedex), but not registered. I've never lost a photo in the mail nor failed to have them returned. But if I take once-in-a-lifetime b/w's (roughly that often), I have duplicate negatives made. And for extraordinary, irreplaceable slides, I make copies and send those for review. If they are selected, I *do* send the originals by registered mail, telling the editor in advance so the package won't be rejected by the publication. Remember to include a self-addressed, stamped envelope so that your slides or negatives are returned.

HOW DO YOU SUBMIT DIGITAL PHOTOS TO MAGAZINES?

The editors are usually quite specific about how they want digital images sent, so asking before sending makes huge sense. Most want them sent electronically as e-mail attachments. If there are many to review, many thumbnail miniatures let the editor pick out those full images they want to download and review more closely. (Internet providers often include the option, at no additional cost, for web space to post thumbnail presentations, with full-image download capacity.)

You can also send the images on a CD by snail mail, or you can print out a thumbnail sheet, like a proof sheet, and send that with the final magazine manuscript, for the art editor's use in requesting the full images that might be used. If you have a web page, you can also load the images on it and indicate to the editor the secret page address of those pluckable images.

IF YOU HAVE NO PHOTOS

If you have no acceptable photos or no photos at all, somebody else probably has just what you need, and maybe for free!

See what the current *Photographer's Market* says about the availability of photos in the area of your concern. Also check the *Literary Market Place* and the *Stock Photo and Assignment Source Book.*

If your topic touches businesses, organizations, or any group that would benefit from publicity, see if their public relations department can supply you with what you need, free.

Nearly free are items from the U.S. or state governments. The U.S. Government Printing Office will tell you what's available, including items from the National Archives and the Library of Congress. In addition, tourist bureaus in the United States and abroad want to help you draw people their way, as do museums, historical archives, and places of diversion and amusement.

And don't forget your colleagues in the press. News services or newspapers have thousands of photos, used once and ready for re-use, usually for a token fee.

SOME FINAL THOUGHTS

Unless specifically stipulated, photos are sold on a one-time rights basis. To avoid misunderstanding, write on the caption sheet "All photos sold on a one-time rights basis." You can also add the copyright symbol, the date, and your name, which gives you some legal protection. If the photos will be used in a newspaper, most of which are not copyrighted, you can also request that they use the symbol and information with every photo selected and printed.

Pray that some editor wants to buy all or some exclusive rights to your photos. That means much more money, if you want to sell them.

For magazines, even though I'm selling my shots for one-time use and I could use the same photo(s) anywhere else at any time, even simultaneously, I would probably *not* use them elsewhere until they'd seen print. Editors get testy if a photo they had bought appears on a competitor's pages before it appears on theirs. For newspapers, keep it initially exclusive in the circulation or distribution area only, which for regional newspapers means about 100-miles radius.

Two final questions, one at a time. What if you only took color prints rather than slides? Well, that's still a lot better than nothing. Some magazines might use them as is; others can convert them into slides, but quality will be compromised. Some newspapers might be interested if the prints are truly exceptional, but the conversions will lose even more sharpness.

If you took color slides only, can they be converted into b/w prints? Yes, since color slides are positives (rather than negatives) they can be duplicated as color or b/w prints. They won't be as sharp, though, and duplicating them isn't free. Some newspaper editors will absorb the trouble and cost, but most others probably won't. (Of course you can take both on a digital camera.)

If you have only one film camera and can use only one format, take color slides. Your b/w's will never grow color (you hope!) and slides sell for a lot more money. But look digital the next time you have some spare change and are thinking camera. It's only a matter of time…

A FINAL OBSERVATION

Be careful and be prudent.

Once I decided to get a breathtaking shot of a creek plummeting hundreds of feet straight down onto a sandy riverbed in Ohio. I leaned over the edge of a jutting rock, where the water pushed me forward. I almost lost my camera *and* my footing—only a tough root and an alert passerby kept me from becoming a statistic.

Almost the same happened to me again, at Fôz de Iguaçú, the spectacular waterfalls where Argentina, Brazil, and Paraguay meet. Wading a fork of the Iguaçú River to take a shot at the edge, the current pushed faster than I could wade. Fortunately, a tree branch prevented me from being swept over the falls.

Prudence is required too. Walking through the major public park in Quito, Ecuador, I saw what looked to me to be a perfect Sunday afternoon scene. So I took a picture, unaware that a gambler was throwing dice a few feet ahead, which was illegal. Thinking I was the police he lunged for my camera rather than running away! So I ran too, as fast as my camera bag would let me at 9,500 feet of altitude. We had a merry chase for at least six blocks until it must have occurred to him that I wouldn't be running if I were a cop.

The moral here. Be aware when taking photos of the physical dangers and perhaps of the social implications. Don't get yourself killed for just one good shot—you won't be around to reap the rewards!

At this point I redirect you to books about travel photography or just plain old photography, which you can adapt to travel use. Also check local educational institutions to see if workshops or seminars about travel photography are being offered.

We are presently muddling through a transition from film to digital cameras. Soon enough new provision protocols will evolve. But one thing will remain the same: Somebody must point the camera (or whatever technological wonder) at a spectacular sunset with lovers walking hand-in-hand under the palms. And some editor will pay for that photo (or the result from the technological wonder). So it makes sense to learn to see, to judge, to point the camera, and take the picture. And to keep asking questions about that day's preferred means of submission.

| EXAMPLE |

PHOTGRAPHING THE BIG TRIP

We're Santa Barbara bound! Usually I go to my closet and dust off my favorite film cameras, clean their lenses, make sure all of the parts work (by moving them and taking some filmless shots), then carefully pack everything in my duffel bag.

But the digital world has caught up with me so this time I will rely on my new filmless CD Mavica Sony camera with 8 cm CD-Rs or CD-RWs, which holds 100+ images both in normal, fine quality format and a smaller e-mail form. (I'll bring a second battery just in case.) When that CD is full, I'll just pop in another.

I'll bring one film camera and three 24- or 36-exposure rolls each of color slide and b/w film, but only as an emergency back-up should the digital camera malfunction or get stolen.

Which lenses should I bring? The 55mm, of course, and a wide-angle. The digital camera has a decent zoom feature and I don't see much use for the telephoto (for the film camera), but I'll put it in the bag and most likely leave it at the motel unless necessity dictates otherwise.

Crucial is my notepad. In the field I use two, one carried in my back pocket for photo data, the second, a stenographer's notebook, for interviewing and all other note taking. I put two of each in the duffel bag, plus a couple of extra ballpoint pens. Finally, a half-dozen pleated sandwich bags, great on-site for hauling CD discs, the spare battery, emergency film, raisins, whatever I want, dry and available.

WHAT SHALL I PHOTOGRAPH?

Every time I receive a positive response to a magazine query, I study the last three (or at least the most recent) issues, to see not only how other, similar articles were written but also how they were photographed.

I keep good notes on what the art editor buys: color or b/w photos, vertical or horizontal, what people are doing in the pictures, wide-angle or close-up, proximity to focal point, kind of caption, and so on—all of which tells me the kind of things to seek out when I'm shooting for those pages. I'll usually follow this assessment closely.

Studying my notes when I begin my downtown trek in Santa Barbara shows that the editor of the *A1 Magazine* wants eye-catchers, big building shots, some with lots of people doing every-day things—unposed. Uses vivid reds and yellows, and in each article there is one close-up of something unique to that location. Every shot seems to be tied to an item or locale mentioned in the piece.

The cover on *A1* also comes from one of the articles in that issue, and since the cover photos usually earn $500 and up it's worth spending extra time at the site seeking verticals that will beg to be purchased. (I'll also take some black and whites of the best shots with my digital camera—simply by switching the setting—since the buildings visited will figure prominently in many of the newspaper articles I will write about the city. Some of the b/w's might also find their way into some magazines.)

There are times when I have a definite photo plan. Usually I make such a plan when I know that I need a particular kind of shot or shots to show the readers back home what I am describing in words. In those (rare) cases I hunt out the visuals required and add whatever else looks interesting.

Otherwise, and especially if it's my first visit to the site, I let my eyes dictate what to shoot based on the most interesting thing that I plan to mention in the article. Whatever that is, it should be photographed, if possible, or something related to it. That is the core and I move out from there. I always hunt for the framesetter, the one shot that tells all. If I find it I take lots of photos.

And, as I said earlier, I always try to get people in photos, if possible, as long as the people don't undermine the point of the shot.

How Do I Submit Magazine Photos?

The process for submitting photos to magazines used to be fairly labyrinthine. (It is explained in detail in earlier editions of this book and in the report "A Travel-Writing Trip to Germany.")

It's far easier with digital photos.

Since I have a website, I simply isolate the best of my shots for each article on a special page, a dozen or two in either thumbnail or relatively small format, with a one-line caption for each. I direct the editor to that page, let him or her pick out the most interesting shots (which they can expand to see in far greater detail), and invite them to download directly for use or to tell me which they want so I can send them those photos as e-mail downloads.

In addition to the one-line caption with the photo, I include a more detailed caption page at the end of the same website page, which they can also download. I also offer to send even more complete captions for the shots chosen.

Let's look at the first page of how this might appear on the website (see Figure 8.) The actual page can be seen by computer at http://www.sops.com/TWG02pix.htm.

Figure 8 *Website Photo Display* (1st page)

RED TILE TOUR of SANTA BARBARA (California)

[Full captions after last photo.]

Gordon Burgett / (800) 563-1454 / Gordon@sops.com

1. Santa Barbara Courthouse 2. Sunken Gardens 3. Entrance to Courthouse

4. S.B. Downtown Library 5. Coat of Arms at Library 6. Old Guard House

7. Downtown arcade 8. Ben Franklin rests! 9. Lobrero Theatre

How do I prevent several editors from using the same shot? It's seldom an issue since almost all are buying one-time rights. But if they want exclusive rights (usually for a cover), I let them see the web page first and tell me which they want exclusively, which I then remove from the page before showing it to others. (How do I know they buy exclusive rights? I ask.)

An alternative way is to e-mail a page of thumbnails directly to the editor.

How does that expanded caption sheet look on my webpage? On the top it says RED TILE TOUR of SANTA BARBARA, (California). I put a one-line identifier with each photo, then more complete caption information at the end of the photo display. Near the top of the page, in red, I mention that the full captions are at the end, plus I add my name, phone, and e-mail address at both the top and bottom of the photo display since the editor will copy the page and I want to be identified with the photos. How does the text on the caption sheet read? See Figure 9.

From here on I let the editor take the lead photographically, assuming that if they want anything more—photos or captions—they will ask. I usually know what they decided upon when I get the letter of acceptance.

Figure 9 *Caption Sheet for Photos*

EXTENDED CAPTIONS

1. The Santa Barbara County Courthouse appears regularly on TV as a backdrop in ads. It is the city's best example of Spanish Colonial Revival architecture and sits on the site of two earlier courthouses, the first built of adobe.
2. The Sunken Gardens, behind the Santa Barbara County Courthouse, show the foundations of the earlier courthouses and today are the site of many outdoor musical and dance presentations. The gardens, the city, and the Santa Ynez Mountains are seen here from the 85-foot observation tower on the building's roof, atop its historic mural room.

3. The Santa Barbara County Courthouse still fully functions, and offers an interesting mural room. This Spanish-Moorish portal is its main entrance, facing the library.

4. The city's first-rate library also features several art exhibits in its Faulkner Gallery. Santa Barbara is a hub of small press publishing.

5. The festively colored Coat of Arms is now found over the unused but former main entrance to the earlier library, now incorporated into the larger building.

6. Virtually every block of Santa Barbara's 12-block Red Tile Tour reveals an earlier adobe residence either connected to the Presidio (fortress) or built by early soldiers as a small settlement grew. This is an early Guard House.

7. Between the adobe structures and the Presidio a vibrant downtown section of Santa Barbara thrives. This is an early morning photo of one of the many arcades.

8. While the real Benjamin Franklin was an old man tending to the creation of the new United States when the first fort in Santa Barbara was founded (in 1782), here he is at last taking a deserved morning repose in another of the downtown arcades!

9. The state's oldest theatre, the Lobrero, still draws top performers and operas to Santa Barbara.

10. In 1836 the Historic Adobe, seen in front, headquartered Col. John C. Fremont after the Americans took Santa Barbara in December, 1846. Next door (not seen here) in the Casa de Covarrubias, where the last Mexican Assembly met in July, 1846. The well-stocked Santa Barbara History Museum is seen in the rear.

11. Adjacent to the many arcades is the shop-lined Paseo Nuevo, with open-air restaurants, movies, and street performers.

12. Santa Barbara was the fourth and last *presidio* (after San Diego, San Francisco, and Monterey). Begun in 1769 and housing 55 soldiers (many with families), it was built against invasion, to pacify the Chumash Indians, and to house the regional government. The city and thousands of volunteers began in 1963 to rebuild the site into a living museum around the last two standing structures, the *cuartel* and a house. It is now Presidio State Park and free for all to enjoy.

13. King Carlos III ruled Spain when the last of the colonial *presidios*, in Santa Barbara, was built and officially founded in 1782.

A newly-independent Mexico soon took over, and 61 years later it was part of the new State of California!

14. The buildings were built of native materials. The walls were of adobe brick on stone base, filled with mud and whitewashed, with roofs of red tile atop beams and cane bound with rawhide. This loom, rebuilt from an original drawing, shows that most of the early settlers were involved in survival handiwork. Some of the product was sold to the rare ships reaching the harbor or the occasional cowboy.

15. The Presidio's chapel was the town's first Christian church, and today is brightly painted as it originally appeared. It is used regularly for Catholic services.

16. Padre Junípero Serra began the Santa Barbara Mission some 12 blocks higher up the mountains. The three bastions of early Spanish occupation were a *presidio*, mission church, and a settlement. It took many years for the population of Santa Barbara to reach 500. Today it is 85,000.

(All photos sold on a one-time rights basis.)

For more information, please contact Gordon Burgett at Gordon@sops.com,

(800) 563-1454, or P.O. Box 6405, Santa Maria, CA 93456.

My job is to put sharp photos in the editor's hands so he or she can quickly see and decide. It's so much easier digitally. But the photos still have to be top quality however they are sent.

PART THREE

During the Trip

Chapter Seven

WHAT TO DO
WHEN YOU'RE THERE

Have fun!

But... if you're traveling halfway around the world just to make money, stay home! You can get paid for writing about the things you know well right in your own backyard. And it's far less expensive to get there.

On the other hand, if you have a burning desire to experience the exotic, the foreign, the faraway, *and* make money, then get packing! You can travel wherever you want, write about it and get paid, deduct the writing costs from your taxes, and have fun all at once. Just don't forget the fun once you arrive.

The best way to do that is to plan and research thoroughly at home, gather enough query go-aheads to cover the basic costs before you leave, and stay well organized during the trip itself. You can get some of your organizing done before you depart or even en route.

For example, make a list of the three kinds of articles you might write as a result of your trip. The query go-aheads are the most important because they will justify (and, you hope, earn back) the costs. The post-trip queries are article possibilities you will explore on-site, querying about when you return and then writing them up if the editors are interested. You will do research and take photographs on-site for newspaper articles you'll write later.

Let's get the business out of the way first. We'll outline the above three approaches to time use. Then we'll loosen up for a moment to find those fun "extras" to write about when you're on-site. After that back again to business, showing you how you keep track of all your notes, interviews, and other paperwork.

PURSUE THE QUERY GO-AHEADS

The query go-aheads have top priority since you have promised to send editors copy when you return. Set aside approximately four hours a day (usually the first hours of the morning in my case) to work on go-aheads, until you have all the information, quotes, photos, and facts you need to provide solid, well-researched, balanced, and exciting pieces. Bring file folders or buy them there, designate one for each article, and write on the outside of each what you need to make the respective articles work. To keep track of your progress, check off each item as you gather it or its equivalent in copy value.

New writers never do enough interviewing, but editors virtually demand it in a final manuscript. Sharp, on-site quotes from people who are well informed bring almost any article alive and give it immediacy.

Either draw on the names from the list of people quoted in other articles about this topic that you prepared before you left (see Chapter 5 for "How to Study a Printed Magazine Article") or find locals in a position to know, then zero in on your topics. If there are people you *must* see in order to write a successful article, set an appointment time for the interview as soon as you arrive. Then you can plan the rest of your activities around those hours and days. (We'll discuss the interviewing process more fully in the next chapter.)

CHECKING OUT POST-TRIP QUERIES

Your post-trip queries will come from three potential sources: topics you knew too little about to write an intelligent query letter before you left, topics you weren't certain you could cover while on-site, or topics you didn't know about until you arrived.

In the first case see if what you suspected would make a good article before leaving is as promising now that you are there. Who would buy the article? What do you need to write it? What kinds of photos are necessary?

If it holds high promise, get to it, gather all you can find about it, take the shots, and hope you can sell it by query when you return. The problem with this approach is that you have no idea who will buy it and thus what slant you must take. To deal with this problem collect far more material than you do for a query go-ahead (where you've studied the publication before the trip and can tailor information gathering to the needs of the article).

You're in the same quandary with the topics you weren't sure you could cover. Usually your uncertainty comes from not knowing if a person needed for an interview will be available or if a temporary condition, like a drought or political situation, will still prevail when you arrive. Now that you are on-site, you can see. If an article is possible; if you will be able to sell it for sufficient profit when you return; and if you have the time after working on your pre-trip query go-aheads—write it up.

As for stories you discover at the site, they usually come from one of two activities. The first, from keeping your eyes open while touring and gathering other article information. The second, from asking what there is of particular interest locally that the tourists don't know about or don't see. Let's explore that more in "What to Do the Rest of the Day."

Sometimes new travel writers simply don't know what others want to read. So Chapter 19 provides you with 365 "starter" ideas, in the form of questions travel readers might ask, which you can apply to most areas or cultures.

If you gather what is needed to fully answer one or several particularly applicable ideas from Chapter 19, you could query about them when you return. If the response to your query is positive, you're 90% home to a sale! Or you might prepare an article from that material and sell it directly to newspapers (as we will see in Chapter 12). As you gain more experience, you will learn to work the material both ways, into two clearly distinct selling angles, one for magazines and one for newspapers.

DON'T FORGET NEWSPAPER ARTICLES

You'll write newspaper articles after you return. There are several possible sources for these articles. They might come from material gathered for query go-aheads, though in final form the newspaper article must be markedly different and should not be sold until after the original magazine piece is in print. They might come from material gathered for post-trip query articles, as mentioned above. Or they might result from new items you find on-site.

To determine the angle I will use for my newspaper pieces I apply a reverse proportion tool: The more important the city, the smaller the focus can be. If your topic is Fortaleza, Brazil, your newspaper article covers the whole city, since very few U.S. readers know what or where it is. But if your topic is Montreal, London, or Mexico City, your newspaper article would likely focus on a well-preserved quaint corner or suburb, or a fun new activity at that locale, or even off-season bargains and special treatment when the crowds are gone. For well-known places you don't have to spend valuable copy space getting the reader's geographic sights in focus. They know where London is, they may have been there, and they now want more detail.

While you're traveling fill your days and nights with activity. Some of that activity will be bacon earning: gathering information, impressions, and photos for the query go-aheads. Some will be extra gravy: any other material that will result in post-trip sales that earn above the basic trip costs. And some, just fat old nonwriting fun, which can range from lying immobile on a beach bathed in rays and soft breezes to dancing and hooting madly in clamorous abandon. (Often enough some of that nonwriting fun even sneaks its way into print!)

SET NO-NONSENSE WORKING HOURS

The temptation, once you're unshackled, far away, financially flush, and not due back for a week or two, is to treat yourself to 7 or 14 days of liquid, ribald madness, claim the flu or an even more exotic malady, and dismiss travel writing as an impossibility invented to sell books (like this one). But if you succumb to this, you'll make some editors very unhappy—and you'll have to pay for the trip yourself!

I've found that about four hours of daily discipline creates the core of a dependable income and leaves at least eight more hours for dervish fancy. Or more income creation. Or some of both.

Why four hours? Because that's about what you will need to gather the essentials for the query go-aheads: the facts, interviews, photos, and observations.

Remember, you already know what you're writing about, have probably outlined the needed article, have noted what the editor uses and studied the kinds of photos that appear on those pages, and may have already scheduled the interviews before you left. What remains is connecting the dots and filling in the blanks. Crucial stuff, worthy of full attention and close double checking, but not overly time-consuming.

I plan six hours of field work per query go-ahead, so that's a day and a half per article of "hard time." An editor is waiting for solid, vibrant, informative copy. That's what I must gather in those six hours. A poor base for liquid, ribald madness, unless you do the hard work in the morning and play after lunch.

Of course, some queried articles need more time to develop in the field, and some of the work will have to be done in the afternoon or evening. On the other hand, some are wrapped up and ready to go in just a few hours total. It gets down to the preparations you made before you left, your diligence during the working time, and a bit of luck.

Also, because you are working hard and pinching time doesn't mean that you must display a dour and rushed demeanor. A gentle humor and soft sincerity work best while gathering facts, interviewing, or just taking notes. Take your time, just make every minute results directed.

WHAT TO DO THE REST OF THE DAY

For a travel writer, the rest of the day is in fact the whole day. It's what you do from the moment the rooster crows until your eyes refuse to see. It's every minute, every smell, every sound, every sense, everything heard or read, it's everything that enters your awareness from the moment you step off the plane or ship to the moment you step back on.

Plus everything in between your house and your ultimate or many destinations, for the act of traveling itself is also a prime subject for travel articles.

It's even the four hours of query go-ahead time. Some of my best articles were spin-offs from query go-aheads: different slants to the same queried topics, tied together with parts of interviews taken especially for those queried topics, plus bits of scattered facts and photos, plus other off-hours interviews or digging, all sewn into a new cloth and sold through a post-trip query.

It's a storefront glanced into en route to a query go-ahead interview, then visited later for a newspaper short. It's a question mentally asked about why everybody keeps their refrigerator on the front porch as I walk to gather some other fact for a queried piece, then finding out that same afternoon and writing about it months later.

How do I find out? By research! Which means I simply ask people, in a friendly way, "Why do people keep...?" (The answers, from northern Colombia? "The refrigerator is on the front porch because it won't fit in the kitchen, the only plug is in the front room or from the porch light, or so the neighbors know I have one—and they can use it without waking me up!").

People confront new cities differently, so let me share my approach. I suggest that you create your own, using what you wish of mine.

I like to get a map and start near the center. The cathedral, the city hall, the park. I head first toward the oldest part of town, on foot. If it's a metropolis, I might go by bus or tram or "tube," anything that keeps me among the city's inhabitants. I like to hear what they say, see them interact, watch them laugh.

My notepad is out of sight until I see something I definitely want to revisit, which I will write down: its name, what it is, the address, and how I got there. I might note general observations every hour or so, sitting on a park bench or in a cafe. At that point I make my notes as complete as possible: exact routes, actual costs, distances, times, precise attire, color of hair, the weather. Sometimes I unleash my camera and take a picture. Usually I try to remain as unobtrusive as possible, soaking up all I can.

A waste of time? Not a moment of it. I've captured the key items on my notepad; that night some of these will find their way into my synthesis (which I type up), as ideas for articles or as background information for articles already in motion.

When I'm touring a town I dress as similar as possible to the locals. My notepad and camera aren't readily visible. I usually carry a local paper. I'm not the focal point. And I prefer to go on foot. (I use taxis as a last resort, to reach appointments on time or for last-minute reconnoitering.)

Most days I run. So when I'm on tour, I do the same (except that I wear my glasses while trotting about, since I'm not on familiar turf and I want to be able to see new sights in order to record them). Before I leave the hotel I have memorized a route or at least chosen a direction. I also write the hotel name and its address on a piece of paper and put it in my pocket. These days runners don't create undue attention. If I get lost, I just ask and folks invariably point me in the right direction. Sometimes other runners join in or walkers stop me to talk. Some of my most interesting stories have come from simply doing elsewhere what I enjoy doing at home.

But you must think twice. In Edinburgh, Scotland, New Years Eve is a particularly special night, and the following morning the streets are cold and empty. On one such New Year's morning I decided to run through the main downtown park and back, past Robert Louis Stevenson's childhood home.

When I found that a key gate through a castle yard was locked, seemingly inadvertently, I scaled a sturdy statue and flipped over a high picket fence. No sooner had I begun to lower myself from the King's metallic foot than a Bobby with a rifle pointed and asked, "And where is it that you're thinking of going?" When I explained he blinked twice and suggested I return, promptly, the way I had come. I later discovered that the treasury and crown jewels were in the building directly in front of me—and I was, plain to see, dropping in!

How does this wandering or running around convert itself into paying articles? In this case, immediately, into a visit the next day to see the crown jewels.

But in a larger sense, I ask myself, What are locals doing that American readers would like to know more about? I see a score of surfers down at the beach, I think of a "surfing-in-somewhere-exotic" article.

If I see a small funeral procession moving slowly down a street and a huge cross on a peak above a massive church nearby, I wonder whether these folks make regular religious pilgrimages to the top of that mountain. When? Can Americans join them? Another article.

Everything I see provokes questions. With whom do U.S. stamp collectors speak at the post office to buy special issues? What craft items are really made locally, and where can they be bought? When can you hear native music actually played by natives? How can a visitor see the countryside inexpensively? What is the single most impressive sight in the city? The best museum? How can visitors find out about the university concerts and activities?

Some of these potential articles will pop up on their own. Others must be dug for by asking local folks who know: hotel personnel, cab drivers, Americans living locally, students, or Peace Corps volunteers familiar with the local scene. Even by reading the local newspaper that I make a point to carry.

A Hawaiian busboy gave me solid advice decades ago: Ask the waitress, the busboy, or the concierge, in that order. Then tip them if the advice is good.

One question that has consistently brought me solid story material is, simply, "What's really worth doing here that the tourists don't know about?"

The "drunk boat," I was told in Manaus, one thousand miles up the Brazilian Amazon. This river craft ascended the Rio Negro, cut through a canal, and descended the Solimões River, dropping off revelers and picking up milk for the morning market. It left after the 3:00 a.m. rain and would return in about five hours, for the sum of $3.

What a spectacular way to see the howling jungle before dawn, man-sized *pirarucú* fish harpooned from canoes, darting parrots, thousands of iridescent blue *morpho* butterflies, freshwater dolphins, and hundreds of Brazilians awakening to a new day. I called the resulting article "The Milk Boat" and sold it widely.

The point is that the more you see and absorb, the more likely you are to find that one peculiar item or the felicitous combination of many that a travel editor would want to put in print. It can be as obvious as a statue of Buddha or the Portuguese ship ballast that is now the stone mosaic of Rio's historic streets. Or as rare as indigenous attire from Tierra del Fuego or the baby teeth sold in Chinese apothecary shops.

The newspaper travel articles that I enjoy most take me by the hand and lead me into a fun adventure, describing, painting, and sharing what I want to know through the local participants' words.

At the same time enough details are given for me to do it again in person. So that's usually how I write for the newspapers.

Your own tastes are usually a reliable guide for others. If something particularly interests you, pursue it fully, then sell it when you get back.

SHOULD YOU WRITE
NEGATIVE TRAVEL ARTICLES?

In a perfect world with a free press and a fully tolerant readership, the question wouldn't make sense. But travel pages are supported by travel ads and the amount of positive copy far outweighs the negative. That says something.

You simply can't be dishonest. But you can stress the positive, look to the bright side of travel, and let the negatives, occasionally, fall where they may.

Rather than saying "never go to Big Joe's Restaurant" and then elaborating at bilious length, I'm more likely to say: "Rather than going to an earlier favorite, Big Joe's Restaurant, I'd try..." Or simply not mention it at all. Balance the good with the bad, if there's much of the latter.

Actually, the problem seldom arises because I enjoy writing about places, activities, and travel events that are already positive and fun. Most of my solution comes from my subject selection.

And if I do have a real stinker to share? Like traveling third class by wood burner to Majagual, Colombia? Those become my humor pieces—so bad you couldn't help but bite your tongue, endure, and laugh. Heavy criticism is usable if put humorously.

KEEPING TRACK OF YOUR PROGRESS

Keeping track of your progress and of the information gathered can help put each element of the trip in clearer perspective. There are several ways to do this.

The Master Chart

Some prefer a master chart drawn up at home or en route, then added to on the trip. That would include every pre-trip query, the possible post-trip queries you want to explore on-site, potential newspaper articles to be researched and written later, and open space for new items to be developed at your destination. At the top of the chart are those "must-do" interviews, to be scheduled before you leave or as soon as you arrive.

A master chart helps you see where articles overlap and where one set of photos or an interview can be expanded to meet two or several needs. You can also quickly check off items, leaving the things to do in clear view.

File Folders

As suggested earlier, file folders can provide the same sort of visual progress sheet, with the steps to be taken and people to see noted on the front and crossed off as done.

Notes

Since articles must be accurate and interviews a careful reiteration of what was said, I find it helpful to put notes in usable prose at least once daily. For me the most convenient time is before I go to bed. (Others, dedicated partiers, prefer to do it the next morning.) For each article I worked on that day I slip a fresh sheet of paper in the typewriter, write out what I have gathered, and indicate the source of the material.

I note where interviews took place, with whom, others present (if any), and the time and date. Then I repeat the questions asked and the responses given. When finished, I slip the sheet(s) into the respective article files and cross off the corresponding items on the "to do" list on the front of the file or on the master chart. When an interview can be used for more than one article I slip a note in the other file(s) telling where the original is and how it might be used for that article.

For the other assorted material that isn't tied to a specific pre-planned article, I list ways it might be used or the slants I could take with it and see if it will provide support material for another piece.

Backup Documentation

One more thing remains to be accounted for: the backup documentation. There are two methods to choose from.

You can use tape recorders for interviews or to make comments and observations instead of, or in addition to, a notepad.

For interviews use two different ways to clearly note each person who speaks on the tape: record the information orally on the tape itself and in writing on the tape label. Number each tape and record the number in your nightly typed notes. You will later want to keep that tape on file should there be any question of accuracy. A strong case can be made for keeping each interview on a separate tape.

Other interviewers prefer a notepad to a tape recorder (I use a stenographer's notebook). Since the comments will be in your own shorthand, make sure that you give the interview a clearly written title saying who is being interviewed, when, and where. Ultimately you'll remove this material from the notepad, staple it and file it appropriately as evidence that the interview took place and as a document of what was said (the latter will be approximate except for actual quotes, which must be accurate; more about this in the next chapter).

Two final thoughts: You too might confine your four-hour fact gathering and photographing for query go-aheads to a particular portion of the day. As I said, mine is before noon. That way traveling companions can plan their personal activities to coincide with your working period. (But you must be flexible too. Some people cannot be interviewed during your assigned hours, and some articles will keep you hustling from dawn to dusk, with the next day totally free.) Set up an ideal schedule and be prepared to adjust it.

Keep in mind that while gathering impressions, photos, or facts during other hours, you might get your companion(s) to join in the fun. Make them the photographer for those off-hours articles (and give them the earnings later). Or let them talk with others while you are interviewing, to gather even more information. Use their senses. Ask them to describe places and moods to you, ask them what they think other Americans would most (or least) enjoy about the site.

Give them a true sense of involvement and you will benefit from their wisdom, vision, and presence.

And finally, as I said at the outset, have fun. Set aside nonwriting time, putting away your notepad and camera, and become a total tourist (or pseudonative) for at least a while. Isn't a bit of freedom one of the reasons you took the trip in the first place?

$$\boxed{\text{EXAMPLE}}$$

WORKING AND PLAYING ON-SITE

I put Santa Barbara at the center of my planning for a straightforward reason: It's where my plane lands, and if all else fails the trip should pay for itself with just that material. Trips a bit south and farther north for secondary articles still bring me back to Santa Barbara that night, and can be scheduled in.

Coordinating the Preplanning

In the months prior to my trip I did research on Santa Barbara and environs and from that drew up a list of things I think that readers (and I) would like to know more about.

Some of those were so promising and provided enough material already in print that I queried editors before leaving. Based on their positive replies I know that I need five of the articles proposed: (1) the Red Tile Tour, (2) a general piece including the city, waterfront, and activities, (3) a cycling trip, (4) a combination hiking and nature piece, and (5) the "Wine Country." A sixth was less precise, but wanted me to tie the old Spanish culture into the three missions, I think. And a seventh, in response to a promise of an electric article about the artistic side of town, said that if I could get a couple of interviews with famous Hollywood types who live in Santa Barbara that could be woven into that theme, I had a sale.

So I batted about .500 on my 13 queried topics, with the seventh a tough task that I will discuss with the Convention and Visitors Bureau folk.

I will nonetheless pursue three more: a beach walk piece, the nature article, and a mountain hike up to Gibraltar Roads at the crest. I won't focus on golf, will weave Cachuma Lake into the Wine Country jaunt, and will save Karpeles for either a newspaper piece or as part of a rewrite.

Newspapers? A destination, "all you ever wanted to know about Santa Barbara" piece on this tourist gem, pulled together from all of the items above, with special emphasis on the city itself and its visible uniqueness.

To make all these magazine and newspaper articles particularly salable? A ton of breathtaking photos, mostly color, a few black-and-white.

All of what I have gathered and thought about for each of these potential articles exists in files that I bring with me. I made a rough outline, in Chapter 3, of what I'd have to do at each of the areas: downtown, the greater city, south to Carpinteria, and north to Lompoc and the Wine Country. I also figured out the time needed for the trip and the expenses I might incur so I have that list too. What I must do now is create a master chart.

Creating a Master Chart

The term "master chart" sounds so formal, but mine is simply a rough timetable of what I must do in each of the four areas, then assign days to do it. This I write it in my notebook and check off as each item is done.

For example, of the ten-day itinerary divided into ten separate pages, my first full day (May 11) might look like this:

Figure 10 *Sample Page from the Master Chart*

May 11

If up, at 7:30 visit the Alice Keck Garden and giant children's park across the street.

Interview at SB Conference and Visitors Center, 9 a.m.

With whom can I touch base for more info while I'm here?

Is my schedule doable? Any way to tighten it or do more in time set?

Is it possible to speak to three Hollywood notables for "art" article?

Do you have any specific contacts I can interview for ___ pieces?

Is it possible to get comp or press passes for the museums, etc.?

If one or another photo doesn't develop properly, do you have a pool of available p.r. photos? How or when could I look at them?

Other advice?

Visit Karpeles Manuscript Library to see what it contains. Speak with director or p.r. person: printed fact sheets, etc.? Earlier articles?

Lunch

Take the self-guided Red Tile tour from the Courthouse. Park in library lot. Spend afternoon. Get four interviews, lots of photos.

Supper

Walk the waterfront from East Beach to SBCC area, checking restaurants and night activity. Get a dozen good night shots: focus on Stearns Wharf and the harbor. Try to get three interviews from locals.

Then Do It!

A master chart, or any to-do list, is one thing. Doing it is quite another. Sometimes a giant "other," because you're bushed, it's raining, nothing is as pretty or as exciting as you thought, or you're just plain petrified.

You can kick back, open up a paperback safely snugged in your room or on the sand, and forget about it. Or you can kick yourself in the pants and get moving. It's really up to you.

If you're bushed, get to bed early the first night, or take a nap (anywhere will do), or lessen the stress by breaking the schedule into even smaller parts and do each bit at a time, much like the marathoners (at least my kind) who finish by running from power pole to power pole or block to block as they near the end.

Rain you can't control (although you can plan your visit during the dry season, as I have by visiting in May). I could easily switch days. After the interview on May 11, if I needed vigorous exercise I might climb the mountains or cycle to Carpinteria that day, and shuffle the rest of my May 11 schedule into the times I had allocated for those adventures. Or if it did rain on May 11, when I planned to make the Red Tile Tour, I might hit the Art or Natural History Museums that afternoon instead.

As for things never being quite as they are billed, it happens. Adjust your expectations, find what is worth pursuing, and zero in there. Half the time it's your attitude that's sour, not the site itself. So nap, eat, hike, do something you enjoy, and then get back at it.

Petrified is how many travel writers feel the first time they tackle a big trip. Which is why small trips close to home with clearly defined objectives are the ways to prevent or at least greatly reduce that fear.

Petrified of what? That you won't sell a word when you return? Not likely if you've queried, received positive replies, and can gather good information and photos.

That nobody will talk to you? People love to talk. All you must do is guide conversations so they're useful in print later.

That you'll lose every dollar you've invested in the trip? At least you'll have a fun trip to show for it. And you can't lose, unless you simply do nothing and prepare no copy.

The cure is work: notes, interviews, photos, and plenty of the good old common sense that drove you to think that others would want to know about the places you will visit. They do. They want you to succeed. They want you to travel for them, report back, and share the joy and excitement and honest appraisal of places and people and events they can't see in person.

I'm sharing these thoughts because I've had every one of them. Early on I would hibernate for hours on end, letting lunch drag into a long afternoon. I was full of doubts that anybody cared a whit about London at Christmas or Praia Branca (a fair distance from Rio). And some places, gleaming in the travelogues, were truly awful. Luckily my curiosity would somehow be piqued so I would dig around and, surprisingly, always find something interesting to report. Almost all my fears were self-created. The worst thing I could do was nothing (and the same will be true for you).

Putting my doubts aside and with my master chart in hand, I've got to go to it!

Chapter Eight

INTERVIEWING

Facts are the bones of travel articles, the basic structure to which all else adheres. But quotes, whether live or second hand, bring people into the equation, and readers love to read what others think, say, or suggest.

Editors also want quotations, actual words, in your articles. These make the piece relevant, keep the focus human, and let the publication's pages talk to its readers.

Well-chosen quotes are a godsend to writers. One sharp interview can make an otherwise humdrum article leap from the page, give it depth, and inject humor. The words of others help you express your own feelings yet keep your copy in the third person—and they provide a welcome respite from the endless adjectives otherwise needed to create word pictures.

But you can't just buy interviews in the market like fish. Occasionally you'll find ready-to-use quotes in research material, from a reliable, maybe even famous, source. Other times the person sitting next to you on a bus begins speaking in perfect English expressing the very thing your article needs said. And sometimes fish do fall from the sky. Just don't count on it.

Usually, to get the kind of quotable copy you want, you'll have to set up interviews on-site. Good interviews almost always take planning, time, tact, a recorded trail, and follow-through. We'll discuss each element in this chapter.

A final thought here. Just because somebody will speak with you doesn't mean that they know much, or anything at all, or that what they think they know is accurate. Or that they aren't trying to lure travelers into their brother-in-law's lamb house by bleating its charms. Or, the worst, that they aren't jokers trying to pull two legs at once. All interviewees aren't equal.

Having said that, getting good, live interviews is far easier than you imagine, but it requires some sleuthing and some preparation on your part.

WHOM DO YOU INTERVIEW?

First you must know why you want the interview. If you're writing about a rugged backpacking adventure from Mt. Whitney to Yosemite's El Capitan, you'll want to interview veteran survivors of that trek, rangers in charge of the parks you will pass through, and others in the know.

If your article is about glassblowing along the Ohio River, a glassblower or two, a plant manager perhaps, and maybe an expert on quality buying will add some depth to the local handout material on the subject and area.

Determine what people want to know about the topic and find articulate spokespeople with knowledge or appropriate credentials. If you're discussing the historical Yuma Federal prison, don't interview other tourists baking in the desert sun. Find an historical ranger. Find quotes in print from Yuma's prisoners. Make every word speak with authority or unique flavor.

The easiest way to find names for interviews is to see to whom other writers have spoken when writing about the same or a similar subject. If the person they interviewed is *the* expert, that person, or someone nearly equivalent, should be on your list. If those interviewed came from a larger source group, go to others within that group. For example, if you are writing about RV's and exploring the unpaved backlands of Arkansas, go directly to the RV manufacturers to see what they say. Then to the RVers themselves.

Sometimes the article takes both sides of an issue: mountain bikers versus no-bike hikers on some narrow, remote trail, for example. Let's say that you know the name of the spokesperson for the mountain bikers but not that of the opposition. To find it out ask the mountain biker spokesperson! He or she will know, better than anybody else, and 90% of the time will share the name with you.

Other times you'll have a super subject and simply no idea where to begin. Find the travel industry or association most closely related to your topic (by identifying the products or services involved) and ask them for names.

Other writers can also be very helpful. Travel or sports editors at nearby newspapers who have rubbed elbows with every kind of creature can usually point you to the right cage. Your local reference librarians frequently can offer solid suggestions as well.

ARRANGING THE INTERVIEW

Interviews are held in person or by telephone, the latter usually for interviews before or after your trip.

Sometimes the interviews are on-the-spot occurrences, and you'll scurry about for the most qualified or appropriate person or two on-site to give your article "live words."

But usually you will have an idea of who you want to interview well in advance of arriving at your location. If you're certain of your arrival dates and times, it is best to make an appointment in advance, setting aside anywhere from 15 to 60 minutes for the interview itself. Even if you don't know whom you want to see until after you've arrived, it's still best to call first, before showing up on their doorstep.

Once you have the key interview, or two, you can fill in with other, instant interviews at the site.

Most of my interviews at home have been by phone. Some after-the-fact travel articles have been enlarged and improved by a call or two after I've returned from my travels.

However, even when interviewing by phone I call to arrange for a telephone appointment later, which I almost always limit to 15 minutes. Be ready to interview during this first call. At least 20 times I've heard, "Well, why don't we do it right now?"

Which is best, by phone or in person? You can look the person in the eye when interviewing in the flesh, and it's usually a bit more spontaneous, after the first nervous moments. Since so much humor is visual, you gain a lot by meeting in person. But you do have to take time to get dressed up, get there, and get away.

The phone is far quicker and sometimes much more to the point. If I need sharp answers, no dallying, I choose the phone. But I sense more suspicion on the phone too. Your interviewees can't see you and aren't quite sure the whole thing is legitimate and positive.

I've found that women are less inhibited on the phone and thus more expansive. It's the other way around for men.

No time for an appointment because you need the information yesterday? Call or show up anyway, beg forgiveness, explain the circumstances, and see what happens. No interview and no attempt results in nothing at all.

If the interviewee is savvy, he or she will want to know which publication you are writing for and what specifically you are writing about. The latter is easy; the first is tough, particularly if you are just taking your chances in the hope that some editor will buy your article. Don't say "I don't know."

As bad is the reply that you are a freelancer or, God forbid, a journalism student completing a class assignment. (The more professional your interviewee, the less likely he or she will have time for an interview that's not assured of publication.)

The best reply is that you are on assignment from *X Magazine* or *Z Newspaper*, if true. The least you should have at hand, or tongue, is the name of a publication that would likely use your piece—and hope they don't probe too deeply. You queried *LMN Magazine*? I open up the conversation with "I'm preparing a magazine article for *LMN Magazine* and ..." It's true. They might even buy it!

WHY WOULD THEY SPEAK WITH YOU?

In the travel world most of the people you will interview benefit from seeing their name in print. You are doing them a favor.

Some are the owners or managers of profit-based firms, so by having their ski chalet or ferryboat mentioned, they profit. Others are experts. Being in print continues to validate their expertise and by extension sometimes gets them the perks that expertise brings: free equipment, meals, clients, consulting. Still others are in public relations and are speaking for their customers.

There are also those who don't directly benefit. Often they're just flattered to be asked. Or they believe strongly in something and want to share the good news with your readers. Still others want to see their name in print.

Don't worry about why they would speak to you. If they are the right person for your article, simply ask.

Beginning writers often wilt at the thought of talking to "big names" or "famous people." True, some folks with fame are hard to reach or get to agree to an interview. The hardest, I've found, are academics, who are extremely suspicious of whatever you are doing, and lower echelon business executives who are afraid to say hello for fear it's a trade secret and will put their jobs in jeopardy.

Yet most people if approached correctly will gladly speak with you for a few minutes, and some for longer.

I've spoken with presidents in South America, ambassadors, U.S. politicians of all stripes, movie stars, sports personalities, academics, businessfolk, and plenty of people just like us and hardly a one said no or failed to give me enough to significantly add to my article. Ask. The worst they can say is no. If you don't ask, the result is the same.

SHOULD YOU PAY FOR INTERVIEWS?

I don't pay for interviews. Sometimes you're asked by a potential interviewee, "What does this pay?" To which I smile and say, "Eternal fame, I guess. A chance to help others. Something to show to your grandchildrens' grandchildren." And smile again and tell them why I think the subject is important and how I'd like the article to contain the most accurate information, and that's why I chose them to interview. "But if it's a problem...."

Rock stars, I hear, want cash on the line or no interview. But in the travel world I've never been turned down.

Having said that, since I have to eat on the road and prefer good company at mealtime, as often as not I'll pop for a lunch or supper, sometimes a libation, during which time I conduct the interview. So I guess that's payment, of the tax deductible variety.

Be warned, though, that interviewing while eating or drinking is much harder to do. You must still get to the heart of your need in the interview, between ordering, sniffing, small talk, and other interruptions and distractions.

PLANNING THE INTERVIEW

Since by this time you already know whom you want to interview and roughly the kind of information you need, you must research both elements before actually speaking with the person.

You must know enough about your interviewee so that you don't spend precious talking minutes seeking the biographical facts that you should have already gathered.

For example, you must know how to spell and pronounce their name, the current position they hold, why they are qualified to answer your questions, and if applicable, how their position concerning the issue relates to others' positions. Finally, you must know how to get in touch with them after the interview, should you need to.

Where do you find all this information? Much of it comes from previous, published interviews with these people, from their affiliations with groups whose position or stand are familiar with, or from their writings or speeches.

If they work for a company or an institution, see if that group has a public relations office that will send you biographical and other material. If they are entertainers or such, contact their agents. If they appear in *Current Biography*, *Who's Who*, or have been the subject of an article in a major newspaper or magazine, look there also.

When a person is only known locally, check with the town newspaper to see what it can offer. Some papers will let you see their clippings or morgue material. At others the editor is the entire filing system, and he may give you a "few fingers of prose" about the person in question, plus often a name or two of other locals who might provide more information.

Ask yourself before calling: If I could get only one thing from this person, what do I most want to know? Is it information, a strong quote, anecdotes, their expertise? Put that first on your list, then do the same for subsequent items, up to about five.

THE ACTUAL INTERVIEW

You have a limited amount of time and a specific need. The success of your interview will be determined by (1) whether you can actually get the interview, (2) whether you get the information you need, (3) whether you can do the interview without abusing the interviewee's time constraints, and (4) whether you establish a bond sufficiently strong that you can contact the person again with follow-up questions or clarifications.

Think in terms of the basic 15-minute interview, which will probably go longer if you do your part right. Then order your needs in a logical fashion, convert each into a question, and make the one thing you absolutely need to get your *second* question—I'll tell you why in a moment.

Let's say that you are interviewing Bill Denneen, a retired biologist and highly regarded Sierra Club tour leader in the Santa Maria and San Luis Obispo region in California. You want to talk with him about the rigorous hike in the mountains and sand dunes along Pt. Sal Beach. What might you ask him and how might you say it?

Sample Interview Question List

(1) "The hike is described as rigorous, Bill. What does that mean? Would you describe the terrain to me? Who shouldn't participate?

(2) "I've heard that the experience is really unforgettable. Why? What's there that's so special?"

(3) "They tell me that you've led this trip hundreds of times. Why do you keep going back?"

(4) "Have you had any odd or particularly funny things happen over that period of time? Have there been any serious accidents?

(5) "I'm sure that most hikers bring cameras. What do they usually photograph?"

I've put the five questions above in the order I want to ask them. Although question (2)—"What's so special there?"—is the one that interests me most, I put it second for two reasons.

First, I want to put the interviewee at ease. Question (1) gets Bill talking, lets him paint a picture for me and share some of his expertise. (If for some reason I don't find out, say, who shouldn't participate, I can ask that later, or last.) Question (1) is also a fairly logical segue to question (2), because Bill can move from describing the terrain to revealing what is unforgettable about the trip.

The second reason I place the most important question in second place is that I definitely need an answer to it—it will give me the core information needed in my article. Thus I place the question early, but not first. If, as sometimes happens when the interviewing process becomes more comfortable, the interviewee answers the question well and then begins to ramble, I still have gotten the answer I need.

The third question is really an extension of the second. It allows Bill to further explore why this hiking trip is special.

The fourth lets him tell some war stories, the funny and odd things that will liven up the article. And the fifth lets me focus on the visual highlights. Since I'll likely take the trip myself, it also lets me know what others think is worth keeping photographically. But if I don't get to question (5), it's not fatal, because when I go there I can see for myself.

If Bill wants to talk longer, I've opened up five avenues I can continue to explore with questions. Or I can just let him talk and see where that takes the interview. By the end of the fifth question I have plenty of information to use. I've gotten the answer to my core question, and the rest is pure bonus.

Do I ask the questions exactly as I have written them? Almost never. I memorize the first two questions and the gist of the rest. I'll ask the first, let Bill talk, and then use the other questions, rephrasing to fit the conversational flow, as prods to get the information I seek. For me, the best interview is one that flows smoothly from one point to another, with the interviewee doing the talking.

I think of the first question as getting the cattle moving in the direction of the second, and every other question as a gentle prodding into a slightly different but related pasture.

Why not just read the questions as written? Sometimes I have, particularly if the speaker was hostile and resented the whole experience. Reading keeps attention focused on the mechanical aspects of the interviewing process and helps to defuse some of the hostility, so that I can get the information I need. But 95% of the time I don't really want the person to know precisely what the question is, for a very good reason.

Veteran interviewees learn to spot the key questions and develop pat answers to them, answers that sound good but don't say much. Politicians are masters at it. So I try to have the questions flow from the context, as if they are simply expansions of points already being made. That doesn't trigger the automatic responses, at least not as often as set questions do. It leads to much more spontaneity and openness, and far better articles.

What if the interviewees want the questions submitted in advance? The rarest of requests in travel writing, but common abroad in the political realm. Send them—in clearly understandable, straightforward English, without slang.

How do I keep notes during the interview? I seldom use a tape recorder, since they inhibit most people (and afterwards I have to transcribe the whole thing onto paper). Usually I write the key comments in partial sentences, using mostly verbs and nouns, on my stenographer's notepad. I simply add the question number when we address it.

You will probably want to directly quote one or two important comments. If you can't keep up with the speaker, ask, "Would you phrase that another way so the readers will better understand it?" As the speaker is saying it another way, continue writing the original comment down. Listen to the second and capture as much of it as you can too.

You don't need to write whole sentences to repeat what was said later. Just pay attention, ask questions if you don't understand, and capture the essence on paper, recording the key words, precise verbs, and memorable adjectives. Then sit down and transcribe those key elements that night or shortly after the interview. You'll find it coming back, as much by context as memory.

What if you don't get the quotation word for word? Of course you've got to try, but a close approximation is usually acceptable. You just can't change the meaning or the spirit of what was said.

Be sure to listen for asides as the person talks, little throwaway comments. Often they change the meaning dramatically. "He was as honest as you'll find ... usually." Note these comments and raise questions on the spot or later. Ask, "When he isn't honest? In what way?"

Sometimes you can get even more information by purposely misunderstanding. I recall a person telling me that an admission cost was increasing to $35 per person in the near future. That seemed very high to me, so I said "$65? Isn't that a lot of money?" When he corrected me it gave me a chance to ask why, what response did they expect, and from there we moved into the whole area of cost and profit, which the speaker had artfully avoided until then.

The biggest problem new travel writers have is keeping quiet. They want to tell the interviewee about themselves. Or they are so nervous they feel they must talk. Smile, relax, be pleasant, ask questions, laugh or groan or do what an honest response requires, and just let the other person speak. Silence isn't toxic; the speaker will fill it. If the silence is prolonged ask, "Could you explain that more?" Or go to the next question.

Avoid yes/no questions and those answered with one-word. If the interviewee simply says yes or no, ask why? Or why not? Dig for information.

What do you do if the person doesn't know the information you hoped to learn from them? Ask them if they have any idea who might. Sometimes they can even provide addresses or phone numbers.

What do you do if one of your questions is likely to be considered offensive and will end the interview? Ask it last! And precede it by saying, "I don't mean this to be offensive but I'm sure our readers would like to know if... Could you shed some light on that?"

I have a standard closing question that has been passed down from writer to writer: "Is there anything else I should have asked?" Sometimes they have something they want to say: a message. I dutifully write it down and thank them very much. That seldom sees print. But at other times interviewees have volunteered absolutely vital information I had no idea they knew. And kept me interviewing another 40 minutes...

Anyway, it's a sensible way to thank them and get away before the whole process becomes tedious and unpleasant.

But before you actually leave, one last bit of business remains. Would they mind you contacting them if a question comes up or a point needs clarifying while you're writing the final article? Most agree. Get the phone number if you don't have it. Check it with them if you do: "Should I call (the number)?"

KEEP TRACK OF WHAT IS SAID

How long do you have before the magic words turn to mush?

In my case my memory is good for about a day for details, specific comments, and impressions. If I pay close attention during the interview, capture the key points on the notepad, and catch word for word the one or two most important comments as they were said (even at the time repeating the quote back to the person, when appropriate, to be doubly certain I had it right), I can then duplicate almost all of the rest on the computer or typewriter if I do it that day.

Most people have blind spots in their memory. Mine is what a person looks like and what they wear, while numbers stick like glue. So when I interview a person whose physical appearance and attire are important, I write that down either before we speak or immediately after, while they are still in sight. If I don't, people with blonde hair become red-headed, those without glasses acquire spectacles, and God knows what they covered their bodies with—if they were covered (if not, I probably *would* recall that!).

FOLLOWING UP

What do I do when interviewees want to preview the article while I'm writing it? I say, "Sorry, that's against the magazine's policy." It may be, but it's also against mine. My obligation is twofold: to tell the truth as they gave it to me and to write an honest, selling article. I won't alter what they said to make it salable. But I also don't want them to interfere with my writing. I've never had a person complain. Guess it's too hard to buck magazine policy.

After the interview, a thank-you note is due, and expected. Later I always send a copy of the article plus another note thanking them again for their help in making it possible.

There's more than courtesy involved in sending a thank-you note and article. Nearly half the time I'm able to interview the same person again for another piece, the second time more likely by phone.

Once in a 20-minute call I gathered information for five articles about gray whales from the same expert oceanographer. I explained who I was and what I wanted, then named the publications. "Let's get to it—I'll be famous!" he said, laughing. I agreed and suggested an easy format: I'd ask about the specific details I needed to know for each publication in that order. Like shooting fish...oops.

I later sent that scientist a copy of each article, plus a letter to his department chair noting his much appreciated and very professional assistance, to be added to his personnel, or promotion, file. The point: if interviewees are particularly helpful, let their superiors know. But ask the speaker first before you do it—and get the right names, titles, and addresses. Sometimes I even ask how the letter might be phrased for maximum help.

If you keep the lines of communication open, are courteous, and show true concern for the speaker from the first to last step, you'll create good articles and make repeat interviews possible.

EXAMPLE

INTERVIEWING ON THE BIG TRIP

I plan to conduct three or four short interviews about the Red Tile Tour and will probably speak to three or four more people (while walking around) whose comments I might also include somewhere in my articles about it. Plus I may get some quotes from written sources in print or from the media quote sheet most Chambers of Commerce press packets blessedly contain.

As mentioned, my first interview will be at the Convention and Visitors Bureau in Santa Barbara the morning of May 11. I don't yet know with whom. So when I arrive later in the day on May 10, I will call and reconfirm the appointment. Once there, I'll explain that I'm a professional travel writer with a commitment to write nine magazine articles about the area, plan to add a few more to that when I return, and will also sell a half-dozen or more spin-offs to newspaper travel sections.

I appear promptly at 9:00 A.M. the next morning with my master chart, notebook, query go-ahead replies (should they ask for some verification, which they almost never do), camera in clear view, and a pleasant smile.

This will be less an interview than a probe. I explain what I have in mind, the three key things I must explore, the time schedule I've set up, and ask, first, Am I going about it sensibly? Should I be able to do what I wish in that time? And what would they suggest I do differently?

Then go over each item on the master chart in detail.

After we are finished I plan to visit the Karpeles Manuscript Library Collection. Is there anything there worth sharing in a general article? Who would be most interested in it? Do you know the director? Is he or she the person I should speak with for more specific information?

After lunch I'm talking the Red Tile Tour. Is there more good information about any specific part of that tour available to the public? Do you have it? Where can I get it? I'd like to interview three or four people about the tour in general or about specific locales on it. Who would you suggest? How can I contact them? Of all the things I will see what are the two or three most important? Is there any news element I can tie into a newspaper spin-off? Has anything just been completed or renovated? Will there be changes in the near or far future? Do you have copies or know of any particularly good articles about the tour written in the past few years?

Tonight I'll walk the waterfront and pier after supper. Anything I should particularly see? Is it safe? Where can I find the most activity?

You get the idea. Why reinvent the wheel?

Up to now I've been asking logistics questions. How to get from here to there. The answers will save me a lot of time, and I'll usually get at least a good local map as a result, plus free entrance tickets to things they want me to see.

But I have other questions too. Are there well-prepared tour guides I may want to hire for a half day who will fill me with a ton of information I'd take a week to find elsewhere? Every city has one or several local historians who love to be interviewed and who know much not readily available. Does the local newspaper have a columnist who handles travel or local lore?

And even though it's May as we speak, I need to know of special events that take place in or around Santa Barbara during the rest of the year, particularly in the coming months around which I might tie the topics for a timely release. (Magazine articles written in May often appear in print in August or September. All the better if there is a city Art Festival that September and you are writing an art article. You wrap your research around that event, including an in-depth interview with the festival director and the list of events.) But how will you know unless you ask? Can your contact give you the details? Are slides or prints available of these events that I could also submit with my photos?

And of course, with whom should you speak if questions arise at final draft time? Their phone number and extension? What days and hours do they work?

And more. Sometimes a person in the visitor's center is in fact an expert on some facet of the city. Or knows one. Or will accompany you on part of the trip. A probing interview of this kind often unearths much of value you would never learn about in any other way, and certainly not as quickly. That's why I've scheduled it before I dig in.

The purpose is to get all the needed and readily available information possible about the key topics.

Interviewing the Tour Guide

Sometimes there is a tour guide at a location. How can you make optimal use of that learned soul's knowledge?

Often my relationship is nothing more than standing on the outer fringe, copying in my notebook the key points the guide is making, writing in the margin places to return to photo later, and occasionally asking a question if I'm uncertain or I need another fact. I read the guide's name tag to get the correct spelling, shake hands afterward, express my thanks for an (excellent, very informative, humorous—you supply the adjectives) tour. I then mention that I'm writing an article for *A1 Magazine* about this topic, I'd like to send them a copy when it appears in print in several months, and they wouldn't object to my using their comments, would they?

About 95% of the time they are flattered and want to know more about me! In those cases I ask them where I should send the article, which normally gets me their address. I double-check the name spelling at that time, sometimes adding the first name and even Mr., Ms., or Mrs. If they are particularly open, I ask whether they would mind if I called them should I have a stray question begging an answer once I return. If they are agreeable I need to get their number and the best time to reach them.

The other 5%? Smile, leave, and use what you heard anyway. Just don't tie their name to it. "The tour guide..."

Incidentally, sometimes I do use a tape recorder for just these purposes. If they speak loudly enough and they don't mind being taped (I ask), I turn it up full, stand near the guide, and take other notes—what the place looks like, comments others make outside the recorder's range, thoughts about other information or photos needed, and the like.

When you interview people, do you need their permission to use what they say? Nope. You must report it accurately, that's all. I simply try to keep the conversation alive and to get access to them if I need even more.

One last note: If others are tipping the tour guide, which is common in many places, be sure to tip too (a bit generously is even better).

Interviewing Other Tourists

I mentioned earlier that I expect to include comments from three or four others at some point in my articles, beyond tour guides and experts or people directly related to the focal topics.

I will do a lot of mixing with people while taking notes and photos of the *cuartel* or the Casa de la Guerra. Frequently I'll ask questions, just to get them talking. "What kind of architecture do you suppose that is?" "What kind of lesson would kids get from seeing this?" "I just got here. What's the prettiest or most outstanding thing to photo?"

Some will look at me like I was just dropped in from Bobo City, particularly if they are from another country themselves. But most people are friendly, clever, and humorous and they say repeatable things. And occasionally I encounter a real expert who can give yards of depth in a few inches of prose. I never know unless I ask. And there are other people I don't even have to ask, I just need to listen.

I will drop some of those comments into the articles without attribution. "A father said to his son..." But others—ones of substance that do provide valuable information—will require a source. I make sure to introduce myself to the person responsible and ask if

I can use their remarks in my article. I then get their name and affiliation, job, or background.

And Later that Night...

I put in an hour or so of true drudgery, typing up what I captured in the notebook or even the gist of what's on the tape recorder, then separating it (or creating cross-reference notes) for the respective files that I have created for each article. The last things I do are check off the work done that day, take a quick look at what I have to do tomorrow, suffer bodily and dental ablutions, and sleep like the dead.

More interviews tomorrow.

PART FOUR

After the Trip

Chapter Nine

THE TRIP BACK AND THE CRITICAL THREE WEEKS THAT FOLLOW

The work you do in the three weeks after your trip is critical. You've got to get the promised articles and their photos to the editors in that time. These articles have priority. Next in priority are, respectively, post-trip queries, newspaper articles, and resales or any other sales you can squeeze out of those golden days and nights on the road.

If using film, as soon as you get back you should have your slides and black-and-whites (b/w's) developed (remember to have proof sheets made of the b/w's). But you can't wait for your photos to be ready before you begin writing your articles.

Between the fact gathering and the submission of the final manuscript, most articles go through three developmental stages: blocking, roughing, and editing

BLOCKING

Unless you're too exhausted from the fun and hustle of your trip, an ideal time to pull your material together and block it is on your way home.

Blocking isn't the actual writing. That will come later. To block you simply take a sheet of paper and list the article's components in the order in which they'd best be used. The purpose is to create a road map that will make the actual writing faster and more purposeful.

Sometimes articles are most easily broken into segments that will use subheads. Other times they come together best by just organizing the components.

If a quote would make a good lead, note it first. If a short transitional paragraph would come second, followed by a fact, then an anecdote, add them to the list. Keep this up, sketching the article out or outlining it in detail from the material you have on hand. If something is missing, note that too so you can find and insert it later.

Start a new page for each article you block. When you're through place the page(s) in the appropriate folder.

Blocking helps you develop a logical plan or design that carries the text forward and puts all of the support material where you need it. You turn an organizational eye at what you have to work with and how it can be molded into a selling piece.

Incidentally, seasoned writers sometimes block articles before they take the trip, after closely studying other pieces in the targeted magazine and seeing the formats most preferred by the editor. Then they work to fill in the gaps on-site, leaving some flexibility for new, compelling material to be added.

You might say that blocking really begins with the work you did pre-trip. You began to create the article then, when you discovered what the editor and readers expected from your writing. During the trip you modified those expectations by what you actually found on-site. Now you put it all on paper, in block form.

Once home, the bags unpacked and the pets fed, open each pre-trip query article folder and take out the blocking sheet(s). Now you're ready for the roughing stage of writing your articles.

ROUGHING

Rough all the pre-trip queries first, then edit (or rewrite) them one at a time.

Professional writers learn one thing early: It's far easier to rewrite than to do the original writing. So they get the first drafts down without delay or fanfare. They simply dust off their laptop or typewriter, pull out the blocking sheet(s), spread out their facts, interviews, and other elements from the trip, and dig in, converting the rough data and words into organized text as outlined in the blocking, without much regard for spelling, punctuation, or grammar. That's why it's called "roughing."

When they finish with one article, they move to the next. Roughing may take an hour, perhaps two, per article. The only editing professionals do at this phase is the occasional "V" mark indicating where new or unavailable material might later be inserted. They might add a handwritten note to the typescript about unused items or additional thoughts, to be considered later when editing. Time is of essence here. Get it down and move on to the next piece.

EDITING

When all of the pre-trip query articles have been roughed, get to the more time-consuming task of editing. This is when you turn a crude stone into a polished gem. Editing usually takes you two to three times longer per article than roughing does (we'll cover writing and editing in more detail in Chapter 10).

At this point you take another hard look at the target magazine. Review what you think that editor wants, the stylistic and content parameters, the taboos, the kinds of people who read those pages, and what the write-up in the latest *Writer's Market* calls for.

Does the roughed article meet those desires and demands? Does it make sense as composed? Is it interesting? Do the sections flow well? Do you have enough authoritative quotes? Is there a proper blend of fact, quote, and anecdote? If humor is used, is it spread to the same degree throughout the text? Can your text be comprehended quickly, without the benefit of some inside knowledge? What is missing? What would make this text even better?

When you are satisfied that the general order and contents work, focus on the words themselves. Is the tone consistent? Is everything clear, concise, and topic-directed? Are the words you used the ones that the readers would best understand? Is the text visual? Does it infuse the reader with a full sense of the place or theme? Can they see, smell, hear, feel, taste it? Do the quotes sound real? Is it grammatically correct? Are the words properly spelled? Does the article read as well as or better than other articles in the magazine?

Look at the adverbs. Why aren't you using stronger or better verbs or nouns instead? The same with the adjectives. Can't you paint a cleaner picture with fewer words? Is it obvious what every pronoun refers to?

When you're satisfied on all points set the piece aside and start on the next one. Let the edited manuscript sit for a day or two, before going back and reading it again, first to yourself and then aloud. Where does the piece bog down? Where does the energy ebb? What points could be clearer? Make the changes, then read it aloud again. When it is as good as you can make it, prepare the final draft in manuscript format (more about this in Chapter 10), print it out, put your name tags on each page, and get the manila envelope ready for mailing.

CHOOSING ILLUSTRATIONS

All that remains is to select the photographs and get this Pulitzer prize-winner on its way. Since the article is for a magazine, review the appropriate slides. Set aside all that are fuzzy or otherwise unusable. Where you have duplications or near-duplications, choose only the best. Label each slide mount with your address tag, insert it into a clear slide holder, prepare a caption sheet for each holder, put an address label on the caption sheet and make a copy, and add the slide holders and caption sheets to the manuscript. (See chapter 6 for details, and how this deviates for digital photography.)

Few magazines use black-and-white photos, but should the editor request them send uncut proof sheets with the manuscript and slides and ask which shots are preferred, so when you get the proof sheet back you can send either negatives or prints. If the editor wants prints, be sure to ask what print size is wanted. (In Chapter 12 you'll see that the process for sending black-and-whites differs for newspaper submissions.)

SEND IT IN!

The last step is a quick cover note reminding the editor that enclosed is the article about such-and-such place requested in their query reply of such-and-such date, with illustrations, and that you are looking forward to a response at their earliest possible convenience. Should they have any questions or if you can help them further in any way, please contact you at (your phone number or e-mail address). Place the cover letter on top, the article next, and the illustrations last, perhaps with some cardboard behind the illustrations for protection. Remember to include a self-addressed, stamped envelope with enough postage to get the whole package back, God forbid.

No time to brood or muse. You've got another article to edit!

$$\boxed{\text{EXAMPLE}}$$

PREPARING THE ARTICLES

Blocking the Article

Sometimes I do my blocking while still on the trip, to see if I have holes that need filling. That's a good idea if you're new at the game because it's one hundred times less expensive and easier to grab that last fact or quote while on-site than to try to get it later, many time zones away.

Usually, though, I do the blocking in the airplane. I pull my files out of my carry-on and silence my seat companion with an idiot nod or a quick comment in another language. I proceed to go through the articles one at a time.

What does blocking mean to me? Determining before I write the text where its building blocks go. Positioning what I want to share so it best meets the readers' needs.

What does the reader of *A1 Magazine* want to know about Santa Barbara? And how do they want to know it? They want to know what it is and why it's worth seeing; they want a visit painted in words reinforced with photos for those who will never get the opportunity to go there—all done with verve and excitement, completely honest.

What does the editor want? According to my notes on similar articles in *A1 Magazine*, Mrs. Wolfe wants a grabber lead, short paragraphs, five or so subheads, plenty of tied-in quotes, a box of bulleted specifics, and no B.S.

To block this article I take the information and impressions I've accumulated and begin their conversion into smooth, readable text. Rereading my notes I close my eyes and picture the readers of *A1*

Magazine. Then I try to formulate what I'll say to them to snag and keep their attention.

Of course I'll speak to them in paragraphs, and for a 1,800-word article at about 12 words a sentence and three sentences a paragraph, I'll need about 50 paragraphs. With a subhead every ten paragraphs I'll need about five segments for the article.

Sometimes a lead jumps out at me while I'm blocking, but that's an exception. I used to spend hours mulling over leads. No longer. Now I just get writing, and when I've got the piece headed in the right direction with the parts in approximately the right places, I go back and find or create a lead that shows where the whole article is going.

So to get writing now means I must create five or so segments first.

What I initially put down is this:

Preliminary Blocking

Lead

TOUR: Start at the County Courthouse: tour, mural room, observation deck, gardens

Focus on Spanish Revival Architecture as walk south on Santa Barbara Street

PRESÍDIO: Go straight to Presidio: explain significance, what's there, plans for next two phases, what's in buildings and grounds, how this is pivotal spot for town history

Go south to Santa Barbara Historical Museum: key displays

OTHER SPANISH BUILDINGS: Go through the patio to the Casa de Covarrubias and Historical Adobe: explain uniqueness of each

Go up Anacapa Street, see City Hall, plaza; cross to Casa de la Guerra, and into the Passeo to see stores, Spanish theme

Cross to Lobrero Theatre, up to Hill-Carrillo Adobe and Guard House

Cross over to Paseo Nuevo to see style, stores, restaurants

Return by S.B. Museum of Art, cross through arcades to Library

SIDE TRIPS: Take a short side trip to see the Karpeles Manuscript Library

Where to go from here: uphill 12 blocks to the S.B. Mission, Museum of Natural History, Botanic Gardens or downhill 10 blocks to the waterfront, Stearns Wharf, East Beach, the zoo, the harbor, beach walk

One-day side trips: (1) by cycle to Carpinteria, (2) by car to Wine Country, Solvang, and missions in Santa Ynez and Lompoc

MORE ABOUT CITY: Restaurants of all kinds: the "best" three

What's up at night: where to go to see the action (as it is)

Rich theater, musical selection in city and nearby

SIDEBAR: What's up in November-December

Websites/phones of key contacts for information, prices, lodging, etc.

To complete the blocking I must fill in the segments. That is, insert the facts, quotes, and other material I will use in each section. Let's take one of the segments above as an example:

Expanded Blocking Segment

TOUR: Start at the County Courthouse: tour, mural room, observation deck, gardens

Focus on Spanish Revival Architecture as walk south on Santa Barbara Street

Use quote about Courthouse

Explain how to find parking lot by Library

Tie the arched carriageway into County Courthouse across street into three recent ads

Inside door, speak with the docent and get Red Tile Tour map for 25 cents

Explain thumbnail of guided docent tours of Courthouse

Tie in washrooms on first floor before walk

Can return later to see courts in session!

Go upstairs to mural room: tie in anecdote about early council meetings

Take elevator to four-direction observation tower.

Explain what they see in all four directions: note the red tiles throughout city

Tie in Mission in north, waterfront south; explain the foundations of
  earlier adobe courthouse in Sunken Gardens to east
Quote about importance/uniqueness of architecture they are seeing
  and will see

In other words, I break the article into segments (in this case, the
material between subheads), then I write in what I have available
for that copy. And then it's on to blocking the next article.

Roughing the Article

I'm now back home, rested after a hectic flight and the great bag
grab at the airport (this time I got mine first!). I finalize the digital
shots in my camera, my computer sits where I left it, and it's now
time to turn fun on the Pacific into financial freedom at home.

I take the blocking pages for the *A1 Magazine* piece and scatter
around my desk the interviews, notes, quotes, map, travel guides,
and even some quick photos printed on my computer to help refresh
my memory. Looking at all this starts me writing, and I get the
words down from first to last.

Successful writers don't compose final copy at one sitting any
more than sculptors create final forms in one blow. It takes a con-
cept, adding words, refining, reading aloud, moving text, checking
the thesaurus, reading again, and then again. Even after all this you
may want to change a word or two. You move from hammer to
chisel to file to sandpaper to the touch of your hand.

Let's follow one paragraph, the lead, through this process.

I write down everything I want to tell the prospective reader.

There is a huge statue of King Carlos III at the Presidio that
captures the haughtiness and despair of a monarch trying, too late,
to hold on to a New World. All he saw was his land slipping
away—and those pesky Indians and the English poking up the Pacific Ocean (thank God the French and Dutch were contented to
nibble on the Atlantic).

I could build on Carlos III. Americans are enchanted by kings. I
must work in the year 1782, the year the site was officially founded,
but don't have time in the lead to show that the year was important
in the formation of the new United States as well.

The heart of the tour that I want to share in print is the *presidio*, the fort around which the town was built. It is the most unique element, is fun to visit, has many archeological digs around it, and offers an interesting 15-minute video about its history. So that building should also be mentioned early. Maybe a contrast between the vulnerability of the site then and how valued it is now. The term "the Riviera of California" says it all, though it surely would have troubled Carlos III's thin, beaky head. Why he wanted a fortress in Santa Barbara is critical too.

But I also must work in the purpose of the article, the "Red Tile Tour," and anything a reader should know about it: free and self-guided. What will one see on the tour? History from the three rulers: Spain, Mexico, and us (or U.S.). When can the tour be taken? Every day of the year, including relatively rainless November.

I just keep writing ideas down, following the outline of the blocking.

I know that every line I write needs work. That doesn't bother me at the roughing stage. The idea is to let the words flow, get them on paper, and later find the precise terms, the best images, and the most harmonious combinations of sound and meaning. For now, getting it on paper is the first and toughest step. The rest, the editing and polishing, takes longer but for me is much more fun.

Do I rough all of the pending articles one after the other, or do I edit each the moment that the roughing is done? It depends on how close I am to the deadline. Since I have several weeks I'll go ahead and rough out many of the articles I find in Santa Barbara. Then I'll come back to each with a fresh perspective. Usually I find other ideas I dig up later work as well, modified, in my first roughs.

Editing the Article

I'm back! A few days have passed and it is now time to go through this roughed version of the "Red Tile Tour" article with a lot more attention. I figure that if I spent two hours roughing, and since the editing and final manuscript preparation can run three times that long, I might be looking at six more hours of work. Although sometimes editing zips right along....

The lead needs work. For one thing, it has too much information for one paragraph. So I'll work on creating two, with the transitional component in the second, the bridge that links the lead to the body of the piece. I'll go over each sentence and indicate the kinds of thoughts that come to mind. I'll create the final lead later:

My first thought is that Carlos III had no idea that when he put a presidio in Santa Barbara it would later by a tourist attraction. Duh. Who is Carlos III? A king. So it's King Carlos III of Spain. But work the Spain in so it can just be King Carlos III. This is the last colonial presidio (whatever that is—refer to it as a fort later).

When did it take place? 1782. Why did he put the fort here? The place was empty, foreigners (non-Spanish) were sailing in these waters, the Indians were a potential threat, and anyway the king wanted to send somebody to keep watch over this land. So he'd send some soldiers too, and they had wives and kids.

The problem is that Carlos III was way behind the swing of history. Independence was in the air: the U.S. had thumbed its nose at England just six years earlier, France would be next in Haiti, and rumblings wee rampant throughout the inefficiently ruled Spanish empire.

But it's not too late for us, who can go and see what the Spanish (and, later, the Mexicans) built and left. Best yet, it's a free, self-guided tour plunk in the heart of the downtown that we can take every day of the mostly sunny year!

Maybe, "King Carlos III would be surprised to see that where he put his last presidio turned out to be a sunny city of 85,000." What city? The "California Riviera." Insert "colonial" before presidio and italicize and put the accent in *presídio* to show it is a foreign word, since it is more accurate and explains Carlos's role. But surprised? How could he know? Why not delighted? He would love to have 85,000 loyal tax-paying citizens of Greater Spain instead of half-a-hundred soldiers.

So why not "King Carlos III would have been delighted to put his last colonial *presídio* in the heart of a sunny California Riviera of 85,000."

What was the site like then? "The city was so desolate then it invited invasion." But what city? When? Why would anybody want it? So a rewrite might say, "In 1782 Santa Barbara was an empty port inviting invasion so he needed a fort."

I continue to rework every line, moving words around, defining, trying to come up with the best version. I come back to it again and again, tweaking, adding, but mostly substituting and cutting, trying always to paint word pictures that are easy to see by those who have never been within 1,000 miles of the subject. What is the final result?

> King Carlos III would have been delighted to put his last colonial *presidio* in the heart of a sunny city of 85,000 now called the Riviera of California. But in 1782 Santa Barbara was an empty port inviting invasion so he needed a fort. He also wanted to subjugate the local Chumash Indians and have a place to house his administrators and 55 soldiers and their families.
>
> Now he's probably kicking his royal self in his grave for dragging his slippered heals. Too late! But not for us to walk the free, self-guided, 12-block "Red Tile Tour" through the city's heart to see and touch the well-preserved Spanish and Mexican buildings and architecture. When? 365 snow-free days of the year.

Every paragraph gets the same close treatment. When I have what I think is a well- balanced piece, I again visualize my readers and ask, Will this help them? Will they understand it? Will it grab and keep their attention? Is it 100% accurate? I read it and reread it; I set it down again to read it a day or two later, then I review it once more, paragraph by paragraph.

When the editing is done, I proudly type up my newest creation in acceptable manuscript form. But before I send it to Mrs. Wolfe I've got to assemble the appropriate photos.

Selecting the Photographs for the Article

From the 100 or so digital color shots I must choose 20 or 30 I will post on the website that best illustrate this article.

First I reject the losers by not even putting them in my computer's memory (though they are still on the CD disk where the camera stored them). If I mention a particular site or feature in the article I try to find one, two, or many photos that best show it from different angles, times of day, or focal points. Then I choose other, super shots that are related to the piece.

I group the photos by logic and geography on the website, keeping the page narrow enough on a monitor that either all of the photos can be seen directly or that all at least touch the screen and can be easily seen by moving a bit left or right with the mouse (see Chapter 6).

I must remember to keep some photos aside for newspaper use. Thank goodness I took lots of photos whenever I found a particularly exciting view.

Sending a Cover Letter

Do I need a cover letter with this submission? Many months have passed since I queried so I probably do. In fact, I always send one with articles that come from pre-trip queries. (But seldom to accompany go-aheads if I send the queries after the trip.) Here I include one that is brief and positive (Figure 11).

Figure 11 *Cover Letter for Submitting a Manucript to a Magazine*

P. O. Box 6405
Santa Maria, CA 93456
May 25, 200_

Mrs. Janet Wolfe
Managing Editor, *A1 Magazine*
7388 Belvens Court
New York, NY 10010

Dear Mrs. Wolfe:

I'm back from Santa Barbara, bursting with enthusiasm about the trip, and am particularly pleased with the information and photos I got for the article, attached, that you asked to see in your query reply of March 22.

I took over 100 usable photos which I have divided into three categories: (1) 18 that I think are the very best shots (or covers, when vertical), (2) another 24 vertical shots I want to propose for consideration for the cover, and (3) the remaining 50+ that are visible in true thumbnail format that will open up to full shots at the touch.

All are visible and accessible by computer. To see them, please open http://www.sops.com/___ for the 18 best in (1).

Additional cover possibilities, in (2) above, are also visible at http://www.sops.com/_____.

And the remainder (3) are at http://www.seephotos.com/_____.
I can also send the photos on CD-ROM divided into the indicated three sections. If you have any questions or I can be of any help, please e-mail, write, or call.

Would you let me know about the article and photos at your earliest convenience?

Respectfully,

Gordon Burgett

Chapter Ten

PUTTING THE WORDS ON PAPER

If I could really tell you how to write—what words to put precisely where—I could perform miracles. This is not the case. Too much of writing is in your creative juices, in that mind-to-ear part of your soul, to ever successfully codify and put into a never-fail formula.

Yet I can suggest what seems to work best, what is usually done in travel articles that sell, and some thought patterns that might make the writing process easier. Actually, it's simpler to tell you what not to say or do.

STYLE

Articles share information. They are paths to knowledge. The fastest paths are the straightest and least adorned with obstacles or distractions. Most readers don't want tedious hurdles between what they want to know and what you have to say. They don't mind you lining the path with flowers, for purposeful adornment, or lightening up the journey with a bit of anecdotal or analogous variety, but they mainly want you to get the message home.

That usually translates into nouns and verbs conventionally arranged in relatively short sentences. Adjectives used as needed, pronouns with clear antecedents (exactly who "it" is), and adverbs employed only when absolutely necessary—don't "speak softly," whisper; don't "run quickly," dash or sprint. Avoid the word very as much as you avoid packing your piece with superlatives. In truth, how much restaurant food is "absolutely scrumptious"? None is "very, very scrumptious," or none that any self-respecting travel editors would share with their readers.

VOICE

Articles are written in first person (I), second person (you), or third person (he, she, it, or "Mrs. Smith"). You must pick one and stick with it.

Beginners are enamored with first person, on the conviction that everybody would just love to relive every second of a hike the writer took eons ago as a child, up a trail to some half-dry reservoir. This predilection of first-time writers is the very reason that travel editors plead no "Me-and-Joe" stories please! Diaries should be adored, and kept, at home.

There are times, however, when first-person articles are called for: when the action described is singular or hard-to repeat (high adventure falls into that category), when it absolutely requires personal comments or observations ("I was trapped overnight in King Tut's tomb!"), or when the subject is highly subjective or intimate (third-person love stories lose something).

Second person—you would enjoy this, do that—isn't as commonly used as one might imagine, in part because it's hard to find a perfect "you" to whom it might universally apply. It can also sound too bossy or preachy. Still, many newspaper items take this tone, and personal accounts in magazines sometimes also take the voice that one uses in a family letter, the unstated "you."

To the surprise of newcomers, most articles are written in the objective third person, impersonal, one step removed. This is how newspaper copy is written. When in doubt, employ the third person.

I recommend a simple rule of thumb for deciding which voice to use. Read the publication where you want your article to appear and use what it uses. My articles on travel in the Midwest for *Better Homes and Gardens* were in the third person because that's what the magazine always used. My high adventure pieces, mainly gold hunting on the Upper Amazon, were sent to publications that only used first person hair-raisers. My newspaper advice items ("Ten Fun Things to Do in Bahia, Brazil") were second person since newspaper travel normally accepts all three voices and advice works best with a me-to-you approach.

PUNCTUATION

Several marks of punctuation cause problems for new writers. One is the semicolon

Use it sparingly and always correctly. A high school grammar text tells you how.

Also use dashes appropriately and indicate them correctly in your copy. A dash on your typewriter is two hyphens, with no space before or after. Hyphens are singular, no space either. On your computer, for a dash use an em dash. Go to Alt/Insert/Symbol and find the em dash in the Special Characters—(there it is; it's usually listed first.) Note, again, that there is no space before or after the em dash. (For speed, once you have found and highlighted the em dash, you can press the Alt key, hit I and S, then the enter key twice, and it will appear!)

Never end a typeset or printed line with a hyphen, even if it looks odd to carry the whole hyphenated composite over to the next line. Carry it over, with the typesetter and editor's blessing.

Then there is the question of how to punctuate items in a series. Choose the series comma: "Bill, Betty, and Babs" (the series comma is the one before "and").

CONTENT

THE LEAD

Every article has a lead, which consists of the first paragraph or occasionally the first two paragraphs. No combination of words that follows is as important.

Editors call these openers "hook leads" because when properly done, they pull the reader in. If the first words don't create interest or curiosity, if you don't entice the readers to look through the door, you will never get them in the room.

Keep your lead short. A sentence or two is fine, three is probably one too many, and four is a funeral oration.

You needn't write your lead first. Just write copy and worry about the lead later. Better yet, write five or ten leads before or after the rough body of the text is completed. Then pick the best and bring the rest of the text in line. It takes only a few verb changes, a new transition, and off you go.

When I taught journalism the students learned the seven most frequently used lead types the hard way: I had them take home their shiny new article, just written for class (a few, I suspect, written moments before), so they could write seven different openings for the next class session.

Not all worked equally well, of course, but by knowing the various types they could select the best one in the future.

What are the seven types of leads?

The Seven Most-used Types of Leads

1. The *summary* lead. For hard news, the most common. This approach lets a strong and interesting subject sell itself by getting straight to it: "Ricky Larf was captain of the basketball team, a straight-A student, and father of three sons, all by different teenage girls, when he disappeared from the face of the earth."

2. The *narrative* lead. Hard to do, but very effective. Put your readers in the story by making them identify with or become the protagonist. Used often for travel adventure: "Larry Danton's sinewy 6'7" frame, shiny new rifle, and razor-sharp fillet knife were as useless as an ice cube on the Amazon as he stared into the opening of the blow gun nervously pressed to the Auca Indian's mouth."

3. The *descriptive* lead. A favorite in travel because, through adjectives, you bring the subject or site into instant focus: "Tex Bennett's face was a Technicolor diary: his gray right cheek sagged from an Apache bullet, his nose a red beacon from back-creek moonshine, his last tooth a bright yellow stump."

4. The *quotation* lead. The quote must be sharp, short, and directly related to the article that follows: "'Thar she blows!' shouted the skipper to scores of camera-pointing landlubbers hugging the side deck as a spout of water shot 20 feet into the air."

5. The *question* lead. Editors don't like these because they're too easy and too often misleading. But precise questions can work well in travel: "Why spend more than $100 to tour the Galapagos Islands for two weeks?"

6. The *direct address* lead. Uses the word *you*, thus pulling the reader immediately into the text. Will only work in second-person articles and is hard to do well. "It happens. You're carefully

brushing back the hard-packed sand at a Turkish dig and you see the fresh bones of a child's hand..."

7. The *trick* or *teaser* lead. Any gimmick that will get the readers' attention, to tease or trick them into reading the lead. Usually funny, always to the point. I started an article about Mason City, Iowa, which was "River City, U.S.A." in Meredith Willson's *Music Man*, with the lyrics:

> You got trouble, friend,
> Right here, I say,
> Trouble right here in River City!

The Transitional Paragraph

The first hook is really the title, followed by the second hook, the lead. These are the eye-catchers. Their function is to attract readers' attention and then lure them into your article. Most of what follows is the body, the information you want to share. But strategically hiding between the hooks and the body is a paragraph or two, sometimes three, that is a verbal map explaining where the article is going and how it will get there.

Many readers don't know this. They aren't aware of the transitional paragraph(s). Nor are some writers, but these paragraphs play a vital role. Following the lead, they explain the theme, indicate the article's destination and method of arrival, and establish the tone of the article.

Most frequently, transitional paragraph(s) tell if the article will be structured chronologically, geographically (often by section, city, region, or country), or developmentally (fill in the passport application, have photos taken, pay the fee, etc.)

Journalists usually call these paragraphs "the bridge" because they carry the reader from the lead into the body text. Some articles don't have bridges, most do. Study these paragraphs closely. They are pathfinders for readers. They also help keep your words from spinning off into nowhere.

Paragraph Length

If the lead seems too short, so will the paragraphs, which might also be a sentence long, usually two, sometimes three, and rarely four.

But paragraph length differs by type of publication. The lengths above apply to newspaper copy. Magazines are looser and some will have paragraphs six or even eight sentences long. As a rule of thumb, the more academic the publication, the longer (and duller) its paragraphs will be.

Books run the gamut, with novels at times having full-page sentences. With fiction, all rules are off!

Simply study the publication (or one similar) that you want to write for and fashion your paragraphs to the length it prefers. The more commercial the publication, the more it will avoid large blocks of copy because they impede reading flow and intimidate the reader.

Write like the copy in the publication in which you want to appear. Forget the old school rules that said that paragraphs ended when the subject (or the writer) expired! After a couple of sentences (or six typeset lines for newspapers) it's time for a new paragraph. Write for speed and clarity.

Seek variety too. Break up your page with quotes and anecdotes, keeping your descriptions visual, tight, and short.

Sidebars

Sidebars (also called boxes) are commonly used with travel articles, allowing you to offer additional information in a different context to add more depth and range to your copy.

Most are familiar with *Time* or *Newsweek*, both of which use sidebars extensively. A political story in *Time* might discuss, say, the Afghani travails in the main article and provide a separate, adjacent box of information (often shaded a different color) that zeros in on a smaller-focus item, like how this situation affects one family or whether life at an isolated oasis has changed.

There are three kinds of sidebars. If the article is global (or macro), the sidebar zooms in on a micro topic. Or the reverse (a micro topic with a global sidebar). The third type of sidebar is simply factual material that enhances the larger piece.

Here are two examples, both linked to whale-watching articles. The first appeared in a newspaper article in which I showed how individuals or families could board ships at the piers in southern California from December to March and venture a few miles seaward to see migrating grays. The sidebar listed the piers from San

Diego to Santa Barbara, with the names of the ships, the days and times they sailed, the cost, and specific stipulations, if any.

The second occurred in an article called "Whale Watch" in *Dynamic Years*, a publication for seniors. A few days after I sent the article to the editor I happened to sit next to a weathered fellow on an airplane. Turns out he had been the captain of the ship that had captured Gigi, the first gray in captivity, caught for scientific purposes for Sea World. I got out my notepad, interviewed Frank Mason, and called the editor the next morning, suggesting this as a good sidebar. He agreed and I sent it off, earning myself an extra $150 and providing an interesting sidelight that greatly personalized the main article.

Incidentally, this is one of the rare situations when I contact editors by phone. I sensed that the magazine was about to set the article in type and lay out the issue, so mailing the inquiry might have taken too long (those were pre-fax and pre-computer days).

Always think of possible sidebars when you send your magazine query, focusing on the main theme in the letter but suggesting that, if interested, you could also provide a sidebar about X or Y, which you explain to the editor in a closing sentence or two.

If you're writing about a winter solstice trip to a Navajo religious site, tell what else can be seen and done on the reservation. If this information doesn't blend comfortably into the text, create a separate sidebar. If you write about spending the Fourth of July on Cape Cod, let the readers know what else takes place there during the month of July. Another sidebar. If you're showing how Portugal is the best bargain in Europe, create a box comparing the buying power of the Eurodollar in Portugal for similar items in, say, France, Spain, Italy, and Germany.

Should you discover valuable sidebar information at the site, gather the information you need and, when you submit the go-ahead article, ask the magazine editor whether he or she wants the sidebar as well. Make this cover letter a short query, enclosing a self-addressed, stamped envelope (SASE) for reply.

For newspapers, submit both the article and the sidebar at the same time, noting in capital letters at the top: "SIDEBAR."

The Conclusion

All newspaper and magazine articles must come to a close, and how you write the conclusion is important.

These articles are not short stories with surprise endings. And although news articles simply stop when the news ends, travel articles (in both newspapers and magazines) must have conclusions that reinforce what their leads promise. If you're talking about saving money while touring Greece, the conclusion should return to the money-saving theme. If nostalgia is your purpose, your ending should leave a lump in the throat when the last word is read.

Let me share a well-used technique for ending articles that don't lend themselves to an obvious conclusion: Look for a word or phrase from the lead that can be comfortably returned to and repeated in the final paragraph. That gives the reader the sense of having gone full circle, of a journey fully taken. Don't force it, though, and avoid using something from the title (because often the editor rewrites or completely changes it, so that a reference to the title in the conclusion might no longer make sense).

The Title

When you write travel for the newspaper don't worry about a title unless the piece is clearly humorous. Just call it "Bodie, California" or "Railroad Bike Path, Sparta, Wisconsin."

But when you write for magazines, think of the title as the first lead. Although it's only a few words long, it should make readers want to see more. It should pull them into the actual lead (the first or first two paragraphs), which in turn pulls them into the rest of the piece. Once there, studies show, the reader will finish the article if it sustains their interest and doesn't obstruct their easy comprehension by making them wade through large blocks of copy.

A title is your article's headline. It seduces readers by telling them what the article is about. If it's humorous, write the title with the same kind and amount of humor as the article. If it's witty and full of wordplay, the title should be too. If it's so funny readers will have trouble holding on to the paper, the title should virtually laugh out loud. Editors rarely change humor titles, even in newspapers, so attention is vital here. Look for humor titles in the text itself, not in the lead. It's best to write humor titles after you've written your copy. And don't include inside jokes in the title. Since your readers haven't read the inside yet, they won't get the joke—and probably won't bother to read the article.

Stated in reverse: Don't write an article to match a title. That's like starting with a punch line, then trying to invent a joke for it! By starting with the title you set up artificial limits before you've done the research or structuring. Write the article, then a title that reflects its content.

In the sections here on style and content we've examined the characteristics that all good articles possess. Of course the best guide to how you should write is already in print, right there on the pages where you want your words to appear. Read the publication and write that way, only better.

We're now ready to look at the physical form you should give your manuscript in order to submit it (and have it looked upon favorably).

FORM

There's no absolutely "correct" form for manuscripts. As an editor I've seen them submitted in all shapes and colors, bound or looseleaf, some out of order. Once I got a manuscript with a shopping list on the back, and another time I received an article in the wrong language (I think).

In fact, between the writing and the actual form of the manuscript, editors are far more tolerant about how the words arrive than what they say or how they say it.

Still, editors do have preferences in form. And there are some editors who simply will not read copy that isn't submitted in the "conventional" style.

Some things will get your manuscript sent back about as fast as it's seen: handwritten copy, unreadable text, obvious and frequent misspellings, and English that clearly isn't. An editor's life is hard enough without working with writers who make it harder.

Still, super writing is hard for any editor to reject, however it is submitted. As the *Writer's Market* write-up for the "Sunday Journal Magazine" of the *Providence Journal* used to say, after offering the standard submission advice, "But if your stuff is really good, we'll buy it if it comes in by Pony Express." (A truly safe offer since the Pony Express never came east of St. Joseph, Missouri!)

The magic words here are *really good*. Electric, fetching prose will always overrule lousy packaging. Yet copy from new writers, and even from foot-weary professionals on lesser days, is more likely "good" than "really good."" So poor presentation is a hurdle you cannot afford.

There's another reason why sticking with the conventional style makes sense, at least early on. New writers pose as professionals while they grow into the suit, hoping the editor won't ask too many questions about their track record. It's easier to make the pose believable by doing what most professionals do: offer clean copy, proper spacing and numbering, on-time delivery, names and labels where necessary, and so on. (Yes, some professionals are slobs. Emulate them, if you must, after you've sold your five-hundredth article.)

So here are some general guidelines about a manuscript form that seem to be widely acceptable.

Manuscript Specifics

Type or print your manuscript on standard (8 1/2 x 11") white paper, one side only. On a computer, use a serif type, like Times New Roman. On a typewriter, use elite or pica, not script. The ribbon should be reasonably new and black. Clean the keys if they are clogged with ink—the *c*, *e*, and *o* should be clear (those keys are good cleaning guides).

If you're using a computer, also make sure the print is easy to read. Most editors balk at the old dot matrix printer where you practically have to connect the dots to decipher the letters and where there are no descenders (the "y", for example, doesn't descend below the line, and all letters are equal in height). Most writers now use laser, letter quality, or good near-letter quality printers, all of which can provide legible text. Some editors prefer articles on disk, so you might ask once you've received a positive reply from your query (or you might suggest its availability to newspaper editors when you submit the hard copy).

Few editors accept faxed manuscripts but you might ask about that too, once the manuscript has received the nod.

In addition to providing legible copy, remember to provide plenty of white space. Don't cover the entire page with text. Leave ample margins in every direction. Fifteen spaces for the left margin (1.5 in File/Page Setup/Margin) leaves the editor enough room to write in typesetting or layout instructions. Leave about the same amount of space, unjustified, on the right.

Start copy halfway down your first page. In the center of that empty top half write the title in CAPITAL LETTERS. Don't underline it or put "quotation marks" around it unless they are needed to indicate a nickname or other special designation.)

About three lines below the title, also centered, write "by (your name)." That is your byline. Always insert one, even if the publication doesn't use bylines—this shows the editor who should be paid!

In the upper righthand corner write the approximate word count, rounded off to the closest 25. You can write this number in by hand, since it's wisest (most accurate) to count words after the manuscript is printed or typed. (Every word counts. Even wee words.)

At the top of each subsequent page, about six lines down from the top and six lines above the copy, flush left in line with the margin, write the title (whole or abbreviated) in CAPITAL LETTERS, followed by a comma, your name (in regular type), another comma, and the page number.

Indent each paragraph five spaces. If you are using a typewriter, double-space between the lines, and you can triple-space between paragraphs if you wish. If you want the article set with white (blank) space between sections of your copy, skip about five lines and type the space symbol (#) in the center of that white space.

Don't leave "widows" (single lines, alone, on the bottom or the top of a page, "widowed" or left to fend for themselves). They bedevil editors because typesetters frequently miss them, leaving senseless holes in the middle of your article. Newspaper editors particularly loathe them—and most magazine editors started in the newspaper world.

If you wish to use *italics* or **bold face** in a manuscript, that can create difficulties for the editor. If you are typing, underline all italics. For bold, underline with a wavy line and write "BF" in large letters in the closest margin with a line leading to the copy you want in bold.

If submitted by computer, it is best sent as an e-mail attachment, if you are both using the same software (like, for example, Word of the same vintage). In that way your copy will look exactly as you intend. But if the editor wants the copy sent in an e-mail itself, the message will be converted and sent as text and will lose its distinct markings. One way to offset this is to send the text as requested but also print it out as it would appear in final form and fax or mail that second, support version to the editor as well, so your intentions can be seen in print. (This will also preserve all centering and line and space indentations, which are also lost or muddled when sent as e-mail text.)

Another way is to insert the HTML markings in the e-mail text before you send it, which will show the editor how that text is to be converted back into print form before it is used. Put <I> before and after the words to be italicized and <B> for bold. For example: "(3) <B>BIG THEME<B>: In <I>Gone With the Wind<I>, the key..." would appear as "(3) **BIG THEME**: In *Gone With the Wind*, the key..."

Use <BR> if you want a line break. Putting <P> at the end of a paragraph tells the computer to insert a break and go to the return line before the next sentence.

HTML markings are not to be confused with typesetting symbols that you may see (or may even be asked to use, particularly when reading book galleys). Most dictionaries have a typesetting section showing all of the symbols, usually near the back of the book.

Put your name and address on every page. The quickest way is to insert a one-line, full-page, centered footer like this:

Tom Goodwriter, 123 Fourth St., Alps, ID 77777, (213) 456-7890, tom@link.com

On the last page of your manuscript, a few lines below the last word, center the word *end* or write its symbol (#####). The old newspaper tradition was to put, lower right, "Page (number) of (number)" on each page, with the first number increasing from page to page. Example: "Page 2 of 4," "Page 3 of 4," and so on. You can do this on the manuscripts you submit to newspapers, if you wish.

Onionskin paper (if it still exists) made editors weep. Today it will clog your printer. Plain white 20-pound or mimeo paper is fine.

The idea is that the copy should be permanent, legible, and flat. To keep it flat you can mail the manuscript unfolded in a full-sized manila envelope or folded once in a half-sized manila, including an SASE, or SAP for postcard, for submission to U.S. publications.

Those are the usual specifics, with a few extras thrown in. Feel free to worry about content and style, but don't worry unduly about form. Simply present your copy as indicated above and improvise where the guidelines don't apply. Common sense and the editor's weak eyesight rule.

#####

Chapter Eleven

POST-TRIP QUERYING

What if you know about a potential article before you leave on a trip but can't, won't, or don't have time to query before you depart?

Or you discover a super subject you want to share in print once you are there?

Or one or several of your query go-aheads branch off into exciting directions that provide unique and clearly different article themes of their own?

In each case, if you fully researched the new article topics on-site, after your trip is the time to see which editors are eager to put your stories on their magazine pages!

When you've written your pre-trip query articles, matched them with photos, and sent them off, you can get their post-trip counterparts off, to begin the mystical life that only query letters beget.

Then, in the weeks (or months) that editors take to reply, you can write and send the newspaper articles.

Post-trip queries differ in only one way from those plotted and mailed before the trip: You've been to the site. Instead of promising a future date of departure, return, and three weeks to write gilded prose, now all you need is the three weeks, or until the editor wants the article.

Having been at the site makes the query composition much easier. You needn't rely on others' impressions and facts from which you postulate a likely article. You have a kit bag of your own true data and memories from which you can craft a tight, image-creating query to wrest an eager affirmative.

You know precisely what you can promise because you know what you have gathered and what photos you have taken. That, in turn, makes the hunt for the best markets easier.

In fact, feasibility studies for post-trip queries are fast and precise. Is it feasible to write? Of course. You know what information you have and from which angles it can be approached. Is it feasible to sell? Preparing your market list couldn't be easier: Which magazine's readers would be interested in the angles you can offer? Put them in order and start querying from the top!

What's left? Doing it! Get a query about each potential article in the mail. Follow through on each reply. If rejected, write another query to the next publication on the list. If the editor wants more, study the publication and write a top-grade article about what you promised in the query. Match the photos to the prose and get that breadwinner en route!

EXAMPLE

POST-TRIP QUERIES FOR THE BIG TRIP

I've taken the trip, written my query go-ahead articles, and posted all of the appropriate photos for the editor's downloading. Now I'm ready to write the post-trip queries to other magazine editors, getting these potential articles in motion so I can turn to the newspaper articles while awaiting a reply.

Before I left I made a note of various on-site topics to research and query editors about when I returned. I also left open the likelihood that other ideas would suggest themselves on-site.

One does—four "weekend forays" for the L.A.-bound (or residing) who want a tightly-structured do-it-yourself trip they can take by car driving just three hours into the wilderness or backlands. In fact, all I'm going to do is take the facts I gathered, repackage them, and give them 1-2-3 structure. (A few are plucked almost directly from my 13 possible query topics, but of course the magazine editor doesn't know that.)

Who might these people be? Maybe tourists. Maybe Angelenos who want more structure for their trip north. But just as likely businessfolk trapped in L.A. for a week or month and who appreciate the step-by-step planning the article suggests.

So I head to the library to see which magazines business types are most likely to read. Between the magazines on the racks and those listed in *Writer's Market* and *Business Index,* I find five (my selection is subjective, of course). I study their needs as best I can and put them in a marketing order. *B2 Magazine* is first.

Now I must write a query letter that piques the interest of Mr. Lamont Zoerner, the articles editor, as well as convinces him that what I promise must be bought for his pages (see Figure 12).

Figure 12 *Post-Trip Query Letter*

P.O. Box 6405
Santa Maria, CA 93456
June 10, 200_

Mr. Lamont Zoerner
Articles Editor, *C3 Magazine*
5543 Western Avenue
Los Angeles, CA 90047

Dear Mr. Zoerner:

Your readers have a problem: in town on business, they want to see Santa Barbara, have three days, a limited purse, and want a singularly satisfying experience. So rather than let them just go wild, end up broke, and not remember a thing they did, let me send you an article that describes four three-day excursions that are single-focused, fun, and will stretch their legs and coffers as far as they can hope! (I'm assuming they have a car or will rent one in L.A.)

These are my favorites, in summary form. (If you want other choices, just let me know.)

(1) Doing downtown, starting with the unforgettable 12-block "Red Tile Tour" that ties together the city's earliest adobe homes, plazas, flag-draped store arcades, the last Spanish *presidio* (fortress) in America, the city's first (and still active) theatre, Col. John

Fremont's headquarters, the site of the Mexican Assembly's last meeting in 1846, two superb museums (of art and history), and its most photographed hub, the County Courthouse, a Spanish-Moorish masterpiece where its 85-foot high four-direction observation tower begins or ends the 75-minute (or many-hour) free stroll through history laced with salsa and sun. Add to that the Mission, waterfront, Stearns Wharf, the harbor, and a super Sunday morning art festival. All divided into three full days that best utilize parking, driving, and less expensive motels on the outskirts of town.

(2) One day walking the beach, 18 miles from Carpinteria to Santa Barbara, or cycling nearby. A second day on the waterfront in Santa Barbara, with its open beach volleyball courts, parks, an Olympic-sized public pool, a pier with restaurants and a maritime museum, the harbor, a zoo, the bird sanctuary, surfing, the cliffs, and a large art fair held every Sunday morning at East Beach with much to see and buy. The third day? Sea fishing by ship. Much sun tan lotion recommended!

(3) The Wine Country, driving from Santa Barbara past Lake Cachuma to Los Olivos, where the many wineries begin on Foxen Canyon Road, heading north through Sisquoc, Santa Maria, and as far north as Paso Robles. The article will explain the choices, with details: (a) doing it alone, (b) joining a group, (c) going with a guide, (d) combining the wine tasting with other sightseeing in the region. Probably need a designated driver! Divided into three days with trips to the lakes, parks, restaurants, and sites north of Santa Barbara.

(4) The Missions, one day at each. The first is at Santa Barbara Mission, seeing the church, museum, and grounds. The rest of the day is spent seeing the Presidio and the other colonial sites in the city. The second day is spent driving the scenic Highway 154 past Lake Cachuma (with quick side drives to Red Rock and the dams), visiting the Santa Inez Mission, and spending the rest of the day in the Danish town of Solvang. A short drive to Lompoc on the third day will take visitors to the only secular (now state-run) mission, the excellently preserved and extensive La Purísima, where one can see the still-operating drainage and waterworks. A drive back on

Highway 101 provides a good round-the-mountain taste of the area, returning home through Santa Barbara.

I just returned from an extensive writing visit to Santa Barbara. I can have this article to you by e-mail three weeks after you give me the go-ahead. I can also provide about 60 sharp color digital photos (professional quality) to illustrate each of the three-day trips suggested, plus sidebars about any specific facet, if interested. Finally, I'll tailor-make this piece for your readers, as I've done more than 1,700 times before for other articles in print over the past 30 years.

Lots of travel fun for your readers. Are you game? Just let me know.

Gordon Burgett

Note that the trips are short, three days long, and nearby. They are also inexpensive, since the travelers will likely pay with their own money (rather than expense-account dollars). And on most they can opt to spend the night in Santa Barbara, or at least go there after dark to frolic.

I must now sell Mr. Zoerner on the four "fun" places that are the heart of the proposed article. I focus on what visitors would see at the locations, one trip per paragraph. These could be longer but I like to limit queries to one typed page. It's enough to give the editor the substance and direction of the article.

I'll wait for a reply before contacting the next of the four magazines on this market list, just as I would do with a pre-trip query list.

But let's say Zoerner does buy this article, what do I do with the four other markets thus being deprived of my intoxicating prose? I can find three or four different trips similar to those proposed and write a different query, sending it out one at a time until it too is bought (and then find new trips...) Or I can just try a completely distinct theme and send off queries (one at a time or one each on the different articles), or I can sell the article as a reprint after it appears on *B2*'s pages.

My inclination? Purely pecuniary. Since these magazines pay on acceptance—why else would I query them?—they probably won't buy reprints. And they'll pay much more for articles handcrafted for their own readers. I'd query each of them, in turn. I'll stick with modifications of the query in Figure 12 until somebody says yes, then I'll query the rest of the editors, each with a clearly different topic or combination, until I ran out of markets or ideas. Tenacity pays when you have enough stuff for good copy and sharp photos. Bless Santa Barbara!

Chapter Twelve

NEWSPAPERS:
A STRATEGIC BOMBARDMENT

The larger newspapers don't buy much copy from freelancers—except for travel, where they find it far less expensive to pay you for your words about a trip recently completed than to send a perk-paid reporter around the world for a few thousand adjectives!

The requirements are simple enough: scintillating copy that is current, accurate, more objective than fawningly biased, an appropriate length, and flat out interesting to the reader. Also, if you are describing something unimaginable to the average mortal, photos are appreciated.

First question, who buys? Almost every major newspaper buys at one time or another, though perhaps 20% are "off the market" at any one time—because of a glutted market, empty coffers, using syndicated pieces only, between editors, and less tangible reasons succinctly defined by the word *no*.

How do you find the major newspapers? You can use the *Gale Directory of Publications and Broadcast Media*, the *Working Press of the Nation*, or other reference works your library might suggest.

I created my own list, complete with addresses and ZIP codes, copying the "newspapers" section of *Literary Market Place*. I then crossed out the name and title of the book editor and replaced it with the words *Travel Editor*. This provided me with a list to work from, on the safe assumption that if a newspaper has a book editor it also has a travel editor.

Another way to get a list is to buy the "100 Best U.S. Travel Newspaper Markets" released every New Years (available from Communication Unlimited, P.O. Box 6405, Santa Maria, CA 93456 or see http://www.sops.com/100best.htm.). Following a discussion of how to sell to newspapers is a three-page list, which you could simply take to a copy shop for reproduction on Avery labels. (It's also available on disk or as an e-mail attachment.)

TWO KINDS OF NEWSPAPERS

It isn't financially wise to sell to every newspaper. To determine where to sell your writing you must realize that newspapers fall into two camps: national and regional.

A national publication wants exclusive national rights. So you can't sell to more than one of them, or to any of them and to regional newspapers (or magazines) at the same time.

Regionals, on the other hand, don't want to see the same article in their own area, in either a national newspaper or magazine or a nearby regional publication. This means that within a 100-mile radius you cannot submit an article simultaneously to another regional newspaper, national newspaper, or magazine at all. (Electronic rights sometimes interfere. See Chapter 4.)

Which further means that through regional sales you can easily send the same article to Chicago, Los Angeles, New York, Minneapolis, New Orleans, Seattle, Miami, Toronto, and Denver all at the same time—plus 100 other cities in between.

To make things simple, I exclude the nationals. The *New York Times* is a fine newspaper but it must do without my travel musings. The same for the *Christian Science Monitor*, the *Wall Street Journal*, and *USA Today*. Somehow they struggle on without my words or thoughts.

Which means that when I have a travel piece of interest nationwide, I get out my map, draw imaginary circles, and send clear copies of one master to many editors simultaneously.

SIMULTANEOUS SUBMISSIONS

A good way to create an ongoing and comprehensive market list for newspapers is to write a solid article with nationwide appeal, identify those cities that are sufficiently far apart from each other, and send your piece to as many as you can at the same time.

If there are three potential newspapers in the same area—say, from Chicago, Milwaukee, and South Bend—try one, if it says no, try another, and so on until you've made a sale or you've run out of markets!

When you receive your responses, put those that buy at the top of your new market list. Complete it with those that don't buy but that do send you a standard (or even spectacular) rejection. They are buying, although not that particular piece.

An estimated 20% will reject with a notation that they aren't currently buying freelance material. Put them on a special list to try next year. Most return to the fold eventually, buying from the public.

The nationals pay from $85 to about $220 per article, averaging about $125 each, always on publication (a few regionals and most nationals pay more). About half of the papers that buy my copy also buy my photos (99% black-and-whites [b/w's]); about half of those buy multiple photos. Black-and-whites bring $10 to $25; color (bought from freelancers almost as frequently as exposes written in Esperanto!) pay two to five times as much.

The beauty is that when you have an article of buying quality, usually three or four editors indulge. If four do buy the same article, you earn at least $500, plus another $50 or so for photos.

How many articles a year do newspapers buy from freelancers? Some pick up as few as six, if they're buying at all. Others, literally hundreds, Your competition is other freelancers, other travel editors, and staffers from that paper sent on assignment with the directive to also "get a travel piece while you're there."

Freelancers aren't very competitive for a newspaper's key articles, which often run from 2,000 to 3,200 words. Given a choice between your manuscript, however sparkling, and the editor's own humble offering, humility wins. Or the humble words of fellow travel editors.

You will generally sell at the second-article level. Fortunately, most of the larger periodicals use two to four "seconds" per travel issue. These usually include from 1,000 to 1,600 words, but I have found 1,200 to 1,350 to be just about right, with b/w's bought and used to stretch the prose where it falls short. Given the pay ranges cited, second articles pay from 40-50 cents a word (including the word "it," "the," and prepositions).

Send a Small Cover Letter with Your Article

To submit an article simultaneously to various newspapers, make a clear master and send collated copies of it to each travel editor, with a special cover note attached, and either a self-addressed, stamped envelope (SASE) or postcard enclosed.

This can also be done by e-mail in almost the same way, with the e-mail text the cover note and the article, the attachment. (Remember to refer to the attachment in the cover note!) Until you know that the travel editor wants copy sent digitally, though, I'd use snail mail. Then in subsequent contacts, like when the editor asks you to send the manuscript digitally, you can ask about querying and submitting by e-mail in the future.

The cover note contains six key elements: (1) At the top, centered, is your name, address, ZIP, phone number, and e-mail address—in an e-mail, it's at the bottom. (2) Your salutation is either to "Travel Editor" or to the editor by name. (3) Your first paragraph sells the article attached. (4) The second discusses photos. (5) The third is a closing directive. (6) Your name comes last.

Make yourself accessible to the editor. In addition to your address tell how you can be reached by phone and e-mail (or fax). Rarely will editors rush to the telephone, but I can't remember a time when a phone call from an editor didn't result in a sale.

Conversely, I never call them. They buy copy and want to see it first, so the submission process as described seems to work best. Nor do I know of any editor who wants newspaper submissions sent by fax, and some are still resistant to e-mail.

The usual process is snail mail first, then the editor e-mails back (if the piece will be used) asking you to send the digital copy as e-mail text or an e-mail attachment. Photos can be sent by snail mail, courier, or digitally: let the editor tell you which.

A salutation of "Dear Travel Editor" is fine when you're sending articles to editors you haven't submitted to before. They don't know you, you don't know them. But after you've connected or when you are sending to specific editors regularly, use their name and spell it correctly. Travel editors are just like other humans: They respond favorably to being called by name. And dislike being called by another's, particularly a travel editor who hasn't been on staff for a decade.

If you're snail mailing, attach the note to the front of the first page of your manuscript. Since travel editors are busy they'd rather read a succinct note than the whole manuscript. If it grabs their attention, they will read the submission and likely buy it. If it doesn't, they'll immediately toss it in the rejection pile.

That's why the first paragraph of your cover note is crucial. It must tell what your article is about, convey the flavor of the text, and make the editor want to read more—all in a few sentences. Ideally in two concise sentences since almost all newspaper paragraphs are two sentences or less. But you can stretch it a bit here because so much must be done in so little space. The editor can quickly confirm that the article itself adheres to that two-sentence paragraph length by glancing at the first page of the manuscript.

In the second paragraph you indicate whether you have b/w photos (or, less desired, color) to illustrate the article, how you can submit them, and that you'd be happy to do so, if the editor is interested.

If a photo is the most important part of the submission, elaborate on it in detail. You might even consider switching the second and first paragraphs! For instance, if I'm submitting an article about whale watching from canoes in Scammon's Lagoon and I have a shot of a watcher actually petting a docile cetacean, that would be the highlight of my cover note! (But I'd still not send the actual photo until requested.)

In the third paragraph you simply ask the editor not to return the manuscript but rather send the verdict in the enclosed SASE, on the postcard, or by e-mail. What good is a crumpled manuscript, often decorated with doodles? And why pay additional postage to get it back when a single stamp for a small envelope or a postcard will do? (If the editor regularly e-mails, you can stop sending the SASE or postcard.)

Note that at least in the beginning you must send something stamped with your manuscript submission to get a reply—unless you specifically ask to be e-mailed. If you send an SASE, you often get your note torn off and returned in it, with comments on the back. Postcards work just as well (see Figure 13), with boxes to check and space for comments on the back, your name and address on the front, and (for best results) an actual stamp in the upper right-hand corner. Again, some will simply e-mail even though you sent the envelope or postcard.

Figure 13 *Sample Postcard for Reply to Newspaper Simultaneous Submission*

Regarding the article titled _____

submitted on _____ by Gordon Burgett

[ ] I am holding it for future use and will either let you know soon or will pay upon publication.

[ ] Not for us now, but thanks for sending it.

[ ] Let's see your photos: _____

[ ] Comments:

Name _____ Newspaper _____

You must fill in the article title and the submission date. (You can do this by hand as long as it's readable.)

All you must do now is sign your name to the cover letter (it's okay is this is illegible since your name appears in print elsewhere: on the byline, on the SASE or postcard, and at the top of the cover note itself, above the address). Just so the editor knows how it should be spelled on the check.

What length should the cover note be? Short enough to let the editor read it quickly and long enough to do its job. But another factor enters in. Even though the best place to put this note is on top of the first page of the manuscript, stapled in the upper lefthand corner (if you are snail mailing it), I want to avoid covering any copy. I make my note short enough so that my lead paragraph is visible.

The first page of my manuscript has the title and byline on the top half, plus the word count in the upper righthand corner, with the rest of the space left open so the editor can write in layout instructions. I cover only the top half with my note, leaving the lead and the rest of the first-page copy readable on the bottom half. And I usually include the title, plus my name, in the note itself.

I want editors to become so intrigued by the cover note that their eyes will involuntarily drop to the actual article lead; there they become enraptured, continue to the second paragraph, remain enchanted, slide to the third paragraph and turn the page....

Ideally, after reading the entire article the editor will return to the note, finish it, and let me know immediately that the manuscript is being kept and the photos are wanted *now*!

The beauty of the cover note? It simplifies everybody's job and increases your selling ratio and response time considerably. Newspaper travel editors are too busy for the kinds of queries that magazines accept. Although they must see the actual copy, the note gives them a thumbnail sketch to read first. Done right, that note piques their curiosity, gets them to read the text quickly, and closes—or loses—the sale. But a loss is better than no-reply limbo. Widespread, multiple submissions deftly done are the key to success when writing newspaper travel.

Don't Dally!

When you return, after sending out the pre-trip query go-ahead articles and the post-trip query letters, get your newspaper articles written and sent. Prepare the manuscripts and either e-mail them (with a cover note for each) or print out a clean manuscript, attach a cover note, insert a return SASE or postcard, and send the package either flat in a full-sized manila envelope or with a single fold in a half-sized manila envelope.

Don't wait too long. Situations change. Even the Holy Lands change daily. The oldest buildings eventually crumble, seas pollute, resorts close their doors, and restaurants change chefs. Get your copy in print quickly, before the topics become inaccurate, obsolete, dangerous, or uninteresting.

What if you have a hot item, say, Octoberfest in October? Change the order of your work, and possibly the medium. Here is where e-mail works best. You can even send the cover note, copy, and a thumbnail sheet of digital photos from Munich! At least, when you return, write and send your hot item first, while the photos or slides are being quickly developed.

Would I call an editor first? I might if I'd sold regularly to his publication. Ninety nine percent of the time, though, what is urgent to you isn't to him or her, and the editor isn't that receptive.

Two more points. What shouldn't newspaper travel articles say? And how do you avoid glutting the market?

Obviously some things should not to be found in your manuscript: vulgarity, sexual innuendo, racial or religious slurs, and anything else you normally don't find in public print, or wince at when you do.

I'd also avoid much negativity, as I mentioned earlier. Travel sections contain travel ads. And even though newspaper editors champion the division between the freedom of the press and the business of selling advertising, you'll notice a dearth of articles that talk down what the adjacent advertisements talk up. The mere existence of a travel section promotes travel. If you blatantly discourage it, you will quickly find yourself without a printed platform.

And finally, if you've just returned from Moravia or Easter Island overflowing with material for at least seven different, super newspaper articles, how do you best get those into print? By not flooding the market all at once.

The public's reading appetite for Moravia or Easter Island is quickly sated. If you simultaneously send all seven articles to one editor, you will get six or seven rejections. It's a simple supply and demand problem. The demand is low, you're bursting with supply.

So write the seven articles while they're fresh. Pick the most newsworthy—changes, new facts, unknown circumstances—and send it out first. Then send one article at a time at measured intervals thereafter. For England, Germany, Japan, and perhaps Mexico, a new piece every two weeks. For most larger countries, maybe once a month. For places like Moravia and Easter Island, every six months.

EXAMPLE

SUBMITTING YOUR ARTICLES AND PHOTOS TO NEWSPAPERS

Submitting Newspaper Travel Articles

Time to hit the newspapers nationwide! My pre-trip go-aheads are long gone, the post-trip queries are in the mail, and now it's the newspapers' chance to taste my verbal delicacies. Alas, a meal this good ain't free.

So I check my list of potential newspaper article topics, written before I left and added to during the trip, to see which articles have the best chance of being bought. From those I pick the most urgent or the most newsworthy to write first.

If they just found alien remains near Las Positas Road, I move that item up. If the road has been buried by a landslide near Ventura and Highway 101 (Santa Barbara's coastal link to the rest of California) will be closed for months, I write about that first. Then I write the less urgent items.

Santa Barbara is always fetching and ever-green, so I draw from my query go-ahead research on the Red Tile Tour, add the observations and quotes I gathered while taking it, look through the printed matter I picked up locally, and write a 1,300-word manuscript clearly different from any similar magazine article I am writing about it. Then I write an appealing cover letter, a half-page long, to send to each of the ten (or one hundred) newspaper editors that I think might buy this topic (see Figure 14). I staple each cover letter to the front of a complete manuscript.

Figure 14 *Cover Letter for Newspaper*
   Simultaneous Submission atop the First Page
   of the Newspaper Manuscript

GORDON BURGETT
P.O. Box 6405
Santa Maria, CA 93456
(800) 563-1454 / Gordon@sops.com

1300
words

Dear Mr. Billy Jim:

It's hard to imagine a more attractive setting almost 365 days a year: sun, sea breeze, the Santa Ynez Mountains in the backdrop, and a gentle, friendly city dotted with Spanish colonial architecture, a fort, adobe houses, two museums, an 85-foot free overview from the County Courthouse building, and a self-guided 12-block tour that will let you wend your way through the heart of Santa Barbara, California, map in hand, music and flags and food within sight...

Let me take your readers there in the attached 1,300-words article, a detailed rewalking of the Red Tile Tour. I also offer 24 sharp digital photos and captions (plus 60 more, if interested). Those can be seen and downloaded at http://www.sops.com/_____.

Please don't return the ms, just your verdict in the SASE or e-mail or call me at the addresses above. Thanks.

Gordon Burgett

SANTA BARBARA's RED TILE TOUR

by Gordon Burgett

America's Pacific Coast has one Riviera, it has the best Spanish Colonial Revival architecture in the world, and it's all there to be seen free 365 snow-free days a year on a bustling 12-block Red Tile Tour plunk through the middle of Santa Barbara's spotless, vibrant downtown.

King Carlos III didn't plan to put his last colonial *presidio* in the heart of a sunny city of 85,000 in 1782. He had the fortress built to prevent invasion, pacify the Chumash Indians, and house his administrators, plus 55 soldiers and their families. What stands today is the whitewashed adobe museum, church, and archeological trenches of an ambitious project that will become a living museum several blocks square.

The Presidio is but one of several dozen, scattered adobe homes on the self-guided foot tour, buildings that housed Fremont's conquering troops in 1846, the last Mexican Assembly the same year, and the author of *Two Years Before the Mast.* The casual walk includes two museums, colonial plazas, festive arcades, an 85-foot overview of the city, restaurants, and street performers. Even a full statue of Carlos III himself!

Comments About the Cover Letter

Newspaper travel editors aren't going to spend hours laboring over what I want them to buy. They'll read a manuscript, if they have to. But a cover letter—really, a cover note—is much better, since it gets right to the point, offers a tasty writing sample, and talks about black-and-whites all at once.

A mixed blessing because if I write a lousy note, the gem of a manuscript attached probably gets thrown out with the note.

This note is directed to Mr. Billy Jim at *The Newspaper.* The first paragraph says it all: Santa Barbara is one great place to visit, I can bring it alive, and your readers will run 50 miles at double-time to read it! Well, not exactly, nor would I boast about my writing in this note. But if my note doesn't have vigor my article probably isn't going to be bought.

Mr. Billy Jim may have been to Santa Barbara so I must remember not to overdue the adjectives and make unfounded claims. Just keep it honest, upbeat, and descriptive in the same tone as the manuscript attached.

The first paragraph of this cover letter is inevitably different from that of the manuscript. I must say more and I must say it faster in the cover letter. The purposes differ.

The second paragraph does more of the same: why that editor needs these words on his or her travel page. In the second part of the third paragraph I tell what digital photos I have for them to see, assuming they can convert the color to black-and-white if that's what they need. I give them what's available here (24 shots, with captions plus 60 more if they want to see the full acceptable assortment) and the download page from my website.

I provide three response addresses in the last paragraph: by snail mail in the SASE, by e-mail, or if the editor is frothing with excitement, my phone number. And my third paragraph specifies that I don't want to pay the postage to get back this full manuscript. (I include a small [#9 envelope] SASE if that's the preferred method.)

How does this submission actually look? See Figure 14 for the first page of the manuscript (of course I send *all* of the pages!) with the cover letter stapled in the upper lefthand corner.

Then I wait. Since I sent basically the same cover letter and manuscript to many travel editors, some will reject it—but others will want it, some with photos, and some will just use the words without illustrations. All pay upon publication, and 90% will send me a copy of the piece in print.

What do I hear from Mr. Billy Jim? Good news! He'll use the article and will download one or two photos at that time.

Submitting Newspaper Travel Photos

While photographing Santa Barbara I took almost 100 sharp digital shots, so I have no trouble finding a good assortment of shots for Billy Jim, which I post on a special page on my website. Here, I post the 24 that I think will work best for a newspaper format. I send all travel editors to the same page. This is a different photo page than the one I'm sending to magazine editors, with different photos and, of course, different captions. I don't have much control here over their use since many editors may select the same shots. And I don't want to have to reject a plea of exclusivity by a magazine editor for a photo that may appear in print, in a newspaper or many, without my prior knowledge.

Figure 15 *Reply to Newspaper Manuscript Submission*

> The Newspaper
> 1234 Main Street
> Buggle, Nebraska
>
> Gordon,
>
> I'm holding your article about Santa Barbara's "Red Tile Tour." A bit more picturesque than Buggle! Hoping to use it next month. I will download a photo or two and will pay for the package when it sees print. A copy of the article will accompany the check. Thanks.
>
> Chester Billy Jim
> Travel Editor

I take far more verticals than horizontals at the site since newspapers prefer them. Of the 24 on this website page, 18 are verticals.

With each photo is a short one-line caption; the last includes a longer caption for each shot. The editor can simply download what they want to use.

Mr. Billy Jim now has the manuscript and the cover letter that accompanied it. In that letter it explains how he can access the available photos at my website address.

If he requests the other 60, I will send those to him on a CD-ROM by snail mail. He can download anything else he needs from that. All I ask is that he send me a copy of the printed manuscript so I have an idea of the photos he did use.

Chapter Thirteen

SELLING YOUR COPY AND PHOTOS AGAIN AND AGAIN

Since you've lathered yourself into a froth writing a super article and illustrating it with unforgettable photos, why sell them only once?

With your newspaper pieces you've already followed the multiple sale route, offering both the copy and a choice of photos to as many regional newspapers as you wished or that didn't overlap each others' circulation area. Now you can do the same with your magazine pieces and their corresponding photos.

RESELLING MAGAZINE ARTICLES

You can resell your magazine articles and photos, unless you sold all rights to the manuscript or sold the photos on an exclusive basis. Both are unlikely, but if either is the case then that element has come to the end of its short but lucrative life. The buyer bought those words in that order, forever. Or that image captured, forever.

But all is not lost. You can sell a similar photo. Or a rewritten manuscript. You didn't sell the subject to the buyers, just a particular, singular treatment of it. Anything else you sell must be clearly different. To rewrite an article, change the title, lead, conclusion, and order. Better yet, approach the topic from a new angle or slant, so everything else naturally changes. You can even use some of the original quotes, if they are in a sufficiently different setting. But for a photo sold on an all rights basis? Use a different shot, period.

Almost all magazine travel editors buy first rights to the copy and buy the photography on a one-time rights basis. Therefore, once an article or photo has actually appeared in print in a magazine, you may sell those words and that photo again and again.

What if an editor buys and pays for your journalistic gem but it never reaches print? Limbo. This has happened to me three times. In each instance I waited a year, then wrote the editors asking them if they planned on using the article they had bought a year ago. If not would they please release the rights back to me? All three said yes, did so in response to my letter, and apologized (as much as editors apologize) for not using it, saying roughly the same thing: They had to restructure a certain issue at the last minute, planned to use my article later but it had become dated, and now after a year they wouldn't be using it at all. The payment was mine. So were the copy and photos, to rework if possible into another first rights sale for some other publication. (I sold two but the third, about the bicentennial, I'll just have to keep until 2076, to modify and resubmit again.)

REWRITING THE ORIGINAL

The moment you convert an original pre-trip query letter into an article and sell it, all you need do is rewrite it, albeit substantially, to sell it again. And again, rewritten. And again, rewritten.

You've collected a pool of usable information, quotes, anecdotes, and photos. Why use them only once?

Most article themes can be approached from many different angles. The house where Lincoln lived in Salem, the store where he worked, Lincoln's life in the town (with Salem as the backdrop), what happened to the town since Lincoln's time, and so on. All using Salem as the primary focus or as a secondary one.

If you queried about one angle, you can query about any other angle, before or after visiting Salem. Just so each article is clearly distinct, each has its own life. Each is sold, probably, on a first rights basis. (And each can be sold again, as often as possible, as a reprint! More about this below.)

Rewrites exist only in my mind and on my desk. The editors receiving the queries don't know of the original query, nor should they. My rewrite query is of a different topic. It doesn't mention the other query, or if the original is in print, the article.

The process has already been described: Write a query, send it—include a self-addressed, stamped envelope (SASE)—and if the response is positive, write what you promised and put it in the editor's hands in three weeks. For that reason you do most rewrites after your trip is completed, when you have a pool full of usable material at your disposal.

SELLING REPRINT (SECOND) RIGHTS

Let's assume that a magazine does buy the first rights to your article and photos and that these appear in print. The publication has used what it bought. But you can still sell the copy on a reprint (also called second rights) basis. You needn't contact the editor to whom you sold the article. The rights are automatically yours. There are no third or subsequent rights.

You sold the photos on a one-time rights basis, unless otherwise stated, and you can continue to sell them on that basis, forever.

How do you sell your article and photos to other magazines? The process is simple.

Editors at every buying level normally send you a copy or two of the issue that includes your material. Take one of the copies of that first rights sale, cut out your material, reassemble it in a consecutive fashion, and adhere it to standard 8 ½ X 11" paper. If it's not obvious, also write the name of that publication in which your article appeared, the date it appeared, and the words *first rights sale* on the master. Then make as many clear copies as you need.

Which publications do you query for second rights? Those that pay on publication are by far the most likely purchasers since few professionals do original work for them. Those magazines buy the bulk of their copy this way. But don't forget magazines that pay on acceptance whose readership doesn't overlap much with the original buyer's. Sometimes these magazines are interested. Make a list of all the publications you think might buy the second rights and then query them. All it costs to find out is a copy of the original article now in print, a cover letter, and some postage.

There is one situation, though, in which you may not wish to simultaneously submit even though it is perfectly legal and ethical. That's when both publications are direct competitors. Many years ago I sold the PSA and Air California in-flight magazines when both airlines served the West Coast. They were tooth-and-nail competitors. I would send my article first to one, and if it said no, then to the other. Even though there was no exclusivity, had I sold the same article to both and both used it, each editor would have been hopping mad at me and probably wouldn't have bought in the future. In a similar situation, prudence and patience are better than a closed market.

Sometimes an article doesn't quite fit your new market. It uses examples of welders whereas the new publication sells to flower arrangers. In those cases I suggest modest changes to the editor. In the first two paragraphs of the cover letter I describe the article in print and how I could modify it for the editor's readers.

What kind of modification? Different quotes, or interviews with people of interest to the magazine's readers. If the original talks about the school system in Ceylon for the general reader and the second publication is for school teachers, I might suggest inserting special interview material from several Ceylonese teachers. Or I might simply restructure the facts of a piece to more closely match the reader's interests.

The only problem with offering extensive modifications is that you must have access to the information needed for the substitution. That can be difficult if the site is half way around the world!

The Cover Letter for Reprints

Once you've produced the clear copies of your article and photos as described above, compose a sharp cover letter, one for each potential buyer, to accompany those copies. These can be sent simultaneously, each with an SASE enclosed, to as many editors as you wish since second or reprint rights do not carry any exclusivity. The one-time rights for photos also convey no such guarantee or implication.

What do you say in the cover letter? Describe what you have to sell in the first two paragraphs. You can then state the publication history and rights information in the third paragraph, and perhaps explain what photos or slides you have available for sale in the fourth. You may wish to offer the manuscript as digital text in an e-mail attachment in the fifth paragraph. Then a closing, if any, followed by your name.

Those first paragraphs sell the manuscript so they should carry the same excitement or punch that made the piece sell originally, written in the same style as the article itself. If humorous, they should contain humor to the same degree. If serious, a sober mien but lots of information so the piece has the proper feel of substance.

The third paragraph contains the legal necessities. In it you tell who bought the first rights, when the article first appeared in print, and what rights you are now selling. (This refers to the copy only. The editor will assume that the photos were and are currently being sold on a one-time rights basis.) I usually say something like "First rights to this article were sold to X publication and it appeared in print on Y date as you can see on the copy enclosed. I am offering you reprint rights."

The first editor may have bought three slides and an inside b/w photo from a choice of 120 slides and 72 b/w's (in proof sheet form). But you will want to offer the editors of the second rights publications access to all the illustrations, those bought in the first sale and those not chosen then. The fourth paragraph is a good place to do this, describing what you have and how you can submit it, and encouraging the editor to request the photos (rather than having hundreds of slides and proof sheets cruising profitlessly through Uncle Sam's tentacular snailmail world).

Incidentally, if you have some truly spectacular photos or slides, here is where you laud their value and availability. But don't send them until requested.

The last paragraph serves two functions. One, it tells the editor that, if interested, you will gladly send the original digital manuscript by e-mail, rather than their having to type or scan it again. Two, it lets you know which editors are seriously considering using that article, since those who request the original usually end up publishing it.

Why is the latter important? Because some publications that pay when the item is used are very slow to send you a check, meaning you must prod them. So if you know which of the pay-on-publication magazines are sincerely interested (those that requested the original manuscript), you can keep an eye on subsequent issues. If your piece appears, wait a few weeks or a month for payment. If you don't receive it, write the publication. Though editors have failed to pay me only twice in more than 1,700 sales, I suspect that

I picked up 25 or so reprint foot-draggers by just letting them know that I was pleased with the appearance and use of the article but had still not received the payment. They knew that I knew, and payment followed.

How much do editors pay for second rights or reprints? The current *Writer's Market* will give the range, but rest assured that reprints will be near the bottom. Often only one-half to one-third of the top pay rate.

On the other hand, all it takes to get double or triple yardage out of one set of words and illustrations is some digging, some copying, writing a few letters, the price of envelopes and stamps, and the energy to get all this in motion. Plus, of course, an original sale!

EXAMPLE

QUERYING FOR REWRITES AND REPRINTS

There are two main paths suggested above to turn your words over often and profitably. I plan to follow both with the copy I wrote about my trip to Santa Barbara, because I think that site offers enough new material for creating some marketable rewrites and generates enough interest to sell the original as a reprint. I'll divide the example into two parts, focus on each, and share the critical selling letter in both cases.

Rewrite of the Original

I will focus here on my pre-trip query and the resulting article focus about the Red Tile Tour. It is easy to branch out from that base, gather more information about related sites in the city, plus and other nearby attractions, and then match it to the needs of various magazines.

For example, we already spoke of a piece for a hiking magazine that responded favorably about a trek up the mountain wall between Foothill Road and Gibraltar Road at the top. But why stop there for another publication? Why not backpack it up, then keep going over the top and west to the campgrounds near Red Rock? An easy addition to the gathered facts and a new challenge to those wanting to explore. That's how a special interest magazine could be queried in a similar way. Others might be magazines devoted to water skiing, Buddhist temples, hang gliding, or Hollywood hiding in the hills. All could be easily tied into Santa Barbara.

The system of finding markets for rewrites is no different than it is for the original query, consisting of a two-part feasibility study: It is feasible to write and is it feasible to sell? If it is both, find markets in the *Writer's Market* or the academic discipline indexes, prioritize them, and get the queries moving.

Let's continue the example of the second hiking magazine. See Figure 16 for my rewrite query.

This query is no different in form from the original pre-trip query, except that I've written it after I return and have the new hiking information and a destination in hand.

The lead talks about a warm-up hike on the "Red Tile Tour," but then moves on to a much more challenging hike heavenward from America's Riviera, promising more details in the article itself.

Figure 16 *Query Letter for a Magazine Rewrite*

P. O. Box 6045
Santa Maria, CA 93456
July 18, 200_

Mr. Kim Pierce
Editor, *C3 Magazine*
448 Elm Avenue
Birmingham, AL 35214

Dear Mr. Pierce:

How can we combine backlands hiking with the greatest urban scenery in mid California?

Why not a warm-up town hike on Santa Barbara's unforgettable 12-block "Red Tile Tour" that ties together the city's earliest adobe homes, plazas, flag-draped store arcades, the Guard's House, its first (and still active) theatre, gardens, Col. John

---

Fremont's headquarters, the site of the Mexican Assembly's last meeting in 1846, two superb museums (of art and history), and its most photographed hub, the County Courthouse, a Spanish-Moorish masterpiece where its 85-foot high four-direction observation tower begins or ends the 75-minute (or many-hour) free historical stroll.

Then a no-nonsense backpacking challenge from the center of town past Foothill Road up the Santa Ynez Mountain range to Gibraltar Road on the top, and along it west to Highway 154, then down the old stagecoach route to the Los Padres National Forest campgrounds near Red Rock, on the other side of the range? Once there, a decision: farther back into the wilderness (the forest covers 2/3 of Santa Barbara County!) or return to the evils of the not-so-big (85,000) city? A true win-win conundrum.

I propose plenty of photos of both sides of the Santa Ynez Mountains, plus lots of needed logistical information that would make either or both choices fun and rewarding. Or, if your readers would prefer a quick stay in the city the first and last day but a true trek of about 100 backpacking miles in between, that will be the slant.

If any of this rings a positive bell, Mr. Pierce, let's design precisely what would work best for your pages. I've been in print 1,700+ times just that way: tailor-making text that link travel to specialty needs. Hiking is my own peculiar bent so those needs I know particularly well.

Should we share hiking in and near Santa Barbara with the readers of *C3 Magazine*? Just let me know.

Gordon Burgett

The letter ends with why I am qualified to write the article (I'm a hiker) and how I can tailor this for the editor's readers "as I've done 1,700+ times before..." I close with a question to elicit a response from the editor.

I may discover four hiking magazines that would be interested. Using the same criteria that I used for my pre-trip research, I'll determine the desirability of each magazine (from my standpoint) and then I'll prioritize them. I'll either send the same query to each magazine on my list, one at a time, or I'll send different queries (different hikes and settings) to each publication simultaneously.

The logic is straightforward: Keep a chunk of the original article (though rewritten to meet the new readers' needs), since the original has already proven successful and you have solid research on it. Then patch on other information to create an altogether different article. As much profit again for half the work. By the fifth rewrite it's almost a sin.

Reprint of the Original

In Chapters 9 and 10 we noted the progress of the original Red Tile Tour article for the *A1 Magazine*. The article finally appeared in print in November.

Actually I received my copy in mid-October, before it reached the stands. A few days later I went back to the file and reviewed the earlier markets I had planned to query, to see if there were any I hadn't queried or any that would be likely to buy a reprint of the original.

Since all the publications on my original market list paid on acceptance, which ones, if any, would even consider buying second or reprint rights? Only those that regularly use this kind of material, whose circulation is small, and where readers wouldn't likely have seen the original in print (usually because the two publications are in different fields).

As it is, the only magazines left on my list I had either queried or they simply weren't good candidates for a reprint. So I returned to *Writer's Market* to compose a new list of travel-interested magazines that paid on publication. They are my target market for reprints!

First I prepare a paste-up of the article so that it reproduces clearly, and then I make as many copies (plus one for myself) as I will send out to potential buyers. In case my article gets separated from my cover letter, I put my name, addresses, and phone on it. And, if it's not obvious, the name and date of the magazine it comes from.

Then I write an enticing cover letter that does what it must do: Sell the subject, state the conditions, offer the original text, and ask a question. See Figure 17 for that letter.

Figure 17 *Cover Letter for a Magazine Reprint*

P.O. Box 6405
Santa Maria, CA 93456
gordon@sops.com
December 2, 200_

Ms. Michela Conor
Editor, *D4 Magazine*
358 Lookout Hill Road
Dalton, MA 01226

Dear Ms. Conor:

It's hard to look from the base of his statue on the parade grounds of Santa Barbara's oldest building and not wonder if Carlos III isn't kicking himself in his grave for being so stupid. It was 1782 and the last Spanish *presidio* (fortress and administrative seat) he built in the New World was a zero-hour effort to hold on to his distant, empty territory. Too late. How could he have let this gilded gem, the Riviera of the Pacific, slip away?

Today the state historic park sits plunk in the center of the narrow city of 85,000, stretched between the Santa Ynez Mountains and the sea. Its shimmering walls, festive chapel, and trenches of archeological digs are the strongest tourist magnet in one of California's favorite resort cities.

Let me take your readers on an unforgettable 12-block "Red Tile Tour" that ties together the city's earliest adobe homes, plazas, flag-draped store arcades, the Guard's House, its first (and still active) theatre, gardens, Col. John Fremont's headquarters, the site of the Mexican Assembly's last meeting in 1846, two superb museums (of art and history), and its most photographed hub, the County Court-

---

house, a Spanish-Moorish masterpiece where its 85-foot high four-direction observation tower begins or ends the 75-minute (or many-hour) free stroll through history laced with salsa and sun.

The article attached appeared in the November issue of *A1 Magazine*, which bought first rights. I am offering you reprint rights and access to any photos you see in print, plus some 95 more that will bring this verdant, flower-decked city even more alive for your readers.

I know it's hard to typeset against a magazine article, so I'll gladly send you the piece in its original manuscript form as an e-mail download. Should we share Santa Barbara with your readers now, before another King Carlos comes and takes it back?

Gordon Burgett

This reprint cover letter looks suspiciously like the original query! And why shouldn't it? The first query worked, the article contents are the same, and these editors have never seen it before. All I will do is change the address and salutation and this becomes a one-fits-all letter. Therefore it had better be good!

I've only trimmed the first paragraphs a bit since I want it all on one page.

The fourth paragraph includes the three obligatory items: who bought first rights, when the article appeared, and what am I offering the editor (second, or reprint, rights). That done, I can simultaneously submit and am legally in the clear!

In this particular cover letter I included information about photos in the fourth paragraph as well. The form for this type of letter isn't rigid, though I don't think I'd lead with the legal business until I had softened the editor up with some alluring opening paragraphs. (A copy of the article accompanies the letter so the editor already knows you're hawking a reprint!)

Once I've addressed the legalities, the last paragraph is standard, though lately I just offer to e-mail the original text. If the editor requests that original manuscript I know he is likely to use it—and I know to watch for payment! In this paragraph I also like to include a "should-we-share?" to prompt the editor's response.

If the editor says no? All it cost you was a bit of time to run off the letter and address the envelope and the SASE, plus some postage—or an e-mail. If an editor says yes? Bring on the gravy train! Well, maybe the gravy bowl.

Chapter Fourteen

OTHER WAYS TO SELL YOUR TRAVEL WRITING INFORMATION AND SKILLS

Many exciting things happen when you travel. You have fun, you explore new sites or revisit favorite places, you create new friendships or strengthen old ones, and you learn new things.

It's that knowledge that you share with others in magazine and newspaper articles. Yet there's a funny thing about knowledge. It has the miraculous powers of Silly Putty. It can be recast, reshaped, and combined into myriad new forms, each of which can be sold under its new identity.

There's more. In developing skills to find and then share your travel information in print, you also develop skills that serve you well in related fields. So the question becomes: How can you sell that information and those skills other ways?

SELLING YOUR TRAVEL WRITING INFORMATION IN OTHER WAYS

You've already seen how magazine articles can be sold once, then resold as reprints without a whit of change. Or how the same information in an article can be approached from a different angle or slant and rewritten into an entirely different piece, which in turn can be resold as a reprint of a rewrite!

And how newspaper articles can be sold widely in their original form by offering them to readers sufficiently distant from each other.

But why couldn't your trip form the crux of a book? Or be the setting for a novel? Is there a need for one or a set of brochures about the region? Could you develop and sell a travelogue based on your adventures and photography? Could you sell your photos alone or through a stock agency? How else might you sell your core of information again and again?

Let's take a brief look at each of these possibilities, less to provide definitive how-to information than to suggest additional avenues worth your consideration and perhaps later your in-depth investigation.

Writing a Travel Book

On the one hand, there is always a need for new travel books. Current books go out of date quickly, local economies and skylines change, "in" activities fly out as fast as autumn leaves fall, and buyers look closely at travel book copyright dates.

On the other hand, the demand for such books is intimately related to the volume of Americans headed to a particular place. A guide to London always outsells a guide to Fernando de Noronha. And sales are the name of the game. Bookstores want books from publishers that will sell in volume and quickly, so publishers seek precisely the same from writers: books that people want to buy.

If you're interested in trying your hand at a travel book, consider two kinds. One, the all-you-need-to-know book, a compendium of encyclopedic knowledge, with illustrations. Two, a more tightly focused approach that serves a more specific need.

Examples of the latter might be titled "Backroad Cycling Trips Through ...", "Pub Crawling in Downtown...", "Summer Fairs in ...", or "The Complete Guide to Medieval Castles in ..."

These books are easier to write than the encyclopedic books because their scope is more limited and better fit your field(s) of interest or expertise. But often the markets are likewise smaller. Rather than approaching a major publishing house that sells full-spectrum books, you might best approach niche publishers whose clientele eagerly buy books about a specific field. Cycling book publishers, for example, for "Backroad Cycling Trips Through ..."

How necessary your photos are to the book's production will be decided by the publisher, but you're ahead of the game if you have a possible topic in mind before you take the trip. You can either begin the querying process well before leaving so you'll know whether you need to take photos and what kind. Or, at least, while there you can take plenty of photos similar to or better than those in other books of the same kind.

Travel books often require two trips. During the first you survey the topic, take the basic photos, and gather as much working information as possible. From this compilation you write the query and prepare the supporting data. During your second trip you go to the heart of the research and take more and better photos.

Will publishers pay you to take those trips? Almost never. Ultimately you'll be paid from royalties—and (the more creative publishers might suggest) by God, later, for having made others' lives fuller on earth! (Try that one on your banker if your trip requires a loan!)

Can you use the same material for articles now and for a book later? You bet. Sell the information in article form to magazines and newspapers first, using the income to justify tax deductions and to pay for the initial trip. Then send an article or two with your book query and other attachments, both to show the interest that already exists in the topic and how you write about it. The article copy is yours. Others buy the rights to use it first in magazines and/or newspapers. If you don't sell all rights, the book rights are still eagerly waiting to be sold!

Querying for Book Sales

I can't go into details here regarding the querying process for selling an idea for a book. Basically, however, it is this: Send a two-page query letter accompanied by an outline or annotated table of contents, a synopsis (if needed)), and a reference/resource sheet. You can vary this format somewhat depending upon what you have ready or what you think the particular publisher would like to see. If interested, the editor will request sample chapters. If you receive approval, you'll then send the complete manuscript. I discuss this process more fully in my book *How to Sell 75% of Your Freelance Writing*.

Incidentally, for a local regional book, seriously consider self-publishing. For how-to details, see the current editions of Dan Poynter's *Self-Publishing Manual* and John Kremer's *1001 Ways to Market Your Book*. If it's a niche travel book, first read my book *Publishing to Niche Markets*.

Using Your Trip in Another Book

Sometimes the knowledge you gather on a trip will find its way into print indirectly. You might be writing a tome on tapestry, and while in Egypt you obtain valuable insights that add depth to your book.

Or you might be writing a thriller that requires your hero, thought by the authorities to be a machete-wielding lunatic, to hide away for a few weeks while he proves his innocence and catches the true villain. Where better than in Manaus, Brazil? So while there to write articles you compile notes about the setting, a *pensão* where the hero might hide, the weather, the difficulties, the dialogue. Later, your visit and those notes will imbue your work with pungent reality.

And you can convert that specific information into articles for magazines or newspapers. Or later you could devote an entire book to Egyptian tapestries or to life in Manaus, using the information obtained on your trip to form the core of a query letter with attachments.

Can you deduct part or all of your travel expenses for the initial trip if this information finds its way into print? Probably only part of the expenses, and only after the book is in print and earns you as much as the percentage allowable. In the first case the problem is that you didn't lay a foundation to prove you took the trip to write articles or a nonfiction book. In the second case you can't deduct expenses for fiction until the book materializes, when the income equals the necessary expenses. But in both cases, keep records of the costs. And if they aren't already deductible through article sales, check the IRS for guidance.

Preparing Travel Brochures

Travel brochures are hard to sell generally but might be worth serious consideration if you are already well positioned in a niche market.

Let's say that your specialty is backpacking. You already have written a book about the subject, are a member of several related associations or groups, and perceive a need for specific booklets about trails, rules, and date ranges for particular countries, one small enough to fit in the pack yet durable and waterproof.

You design the product, prepare the maps and data, and produce the booklets—you become your own publisher. How do you sell them? By mail specifically to the backpackers belonging to backpacker associations, to subscribers to magazines read by backpackers, and to any others you have included on your own in-house mailing list. Plus to secondary markets through display ads in the appropriate publications, at selected sports stores (probably through a sales representative), even at a booth at a convention for backpackers. Again, my *Publishing to Niche Markets* should provide specific guidance here.

You might also be able to interest a larger publisher if you think your series of brochures or booklets could be anthologized into one volume.

Creating a Travelogue

When I was young, when *National Geographic* was as close as most ever got to jungles or the Orient, travelogues were the rage. People filled auditoriums straining to see movies and slides of the Belgian Congo and gaze upon bushy-haired explorers who had survived the wilds of northern Alberta.

Then television came along and made tapirs and Tangiers as everyday as soap and water. Out went the greatest hope held by travelers who weren't given to writing to convert thousands of dollars spent on travel into many thousands back, for years and years.

Nowadays if you have a travelogue in mind, you must explore television as the most receptive purchaser. For starters, that means identifying every program that features travel both primarily or secondarily, contacting the producers, and doing what they suggest, often on speculation.

Minitravelogues, the best of your video, photos, or slides plus exciting narration, are still in demand by church groups, schools, and senior centers. But your pay, if any, will most likely come as food and fame. Hard to convince the IRS on deduction day that those are the things upon which a profitable business can be built.

Selling Your Photos Again

Rohn Engh, in his fourth edition of *Sell & Re-Sell Your Photos*, says that 20,000 photos are sold every day in little-known, wide-open markets at fees of $20-100 for black-and-white (b/w) and often twice as much for color!

Give the editors who buy your magazine and newspaper articles first crack, of course. But why retire a fetching slide or a telling photo without trying to turn it over, and over, and over?

The question is how much you wish to involve yourself in the photography. You can do it all: your own stock agency, full effort, maximum profit. Or you can dabble, using other agencies and personally zeroing in when a market seems obvious.

One thing is certain. The need for good photos is huge, the income can easily equal what you earn from writing, and the details can drive you nuts.

Read Engh's book: it's excellent, thorough, and very clear on the process one follows. Then do as much as you want to make travel photography a solid source of dependable income, to help offset the costs of the trip and bring in a fat profit.

SELLING YOUR TRAVEL
WRITING SKILLS

Freelance travel writing is hard and economically insecure work. Planning tightly, pursuing diligently, and writing deftly, you might eke out a decent income and see much of the world. But as a steady diet most writers have other jobs around which they can write travel articles part-time. I did it for years while deaning and teaching Portuguese and history at the college level. Almost any vocation works. The four that seem the most compatible with travel writing might be:

As a Travel Editor

As the popularity of travel continues to grow, the travel market continues to seek more outlets for advertising. And advertisers want their ads placed in the midst of travel copy that will attract readers, who will read the ads. The tail wags the dog. The desire for travel copy requires travel editors to solicit and manage it.

What's the chance that over time your stellar prose and scintillating insights will prompt the editor-in-chief of a newspaper to beg you to run the travel department?

About as likely as a live interview with Honest Abe. That's a plum spot often rewarded to a faithful in-house workhorse easing toward retirement, a journeyperson long on writing who can learn about travel on the job as editor. Your best hope would be to join a newspaper staff and work up to an assistant editorship, then cross your fingers.

Magazines, on the other hand, are more likely to hunt for a specialist with both journalistic and travel experience. Here your writing credits, travel mileage, and grasp of page composition and content requirements might put you in the running.

You can draw attention to your qualifications three ways. One, keep producing top-quality travel pieces over a sustained period of time. Two, join one or several associations of travel writers. And three, learn the other skills that editors need by becoming one at a small, nearby publication, even for minimal pay. After you have established a solid reputation as a travel writer and have proven you can perform as an editor, let magazine editors and association colleagues know that you are available for an associate or assistant editorship.

As a Photographer

By dividing your talents evenly between writing and travel photography you can quickly increase your overall income.

Most travel writers at best dabble with a camera, and some refuse flat out to look through the lens. But the two skills, each paying modestly, can be combined to sweeten the end product, raise its perceived value, distinguish its producer as uniquely twice talented, and open a future in both areas.

How do you do it? Read every book about writing and photography, take every needed course or workshop, then go into the field and work single-mindedly to create a rare, unforgettable blend of words and art.

Travel Agent or Tour Director

The life of a travel agent has radically changed since airlines dropped commissions and the agents added service fees.

One used to think that if they worked in the travel industry they would get to travel at a greatly reduced rate, they could afford to venture farther and more often, would be in a position to write more, and between their employment and their freelance writing would live happily ever after.

But reality now waves a red flag. The pay range was already low, the work is too often seasonal, free flights are all but gone, and the higher up you progress in the industry, the less time you have to travel at all.

Tour directors might be better positioned to turn their activities into copy, though often on-site responsibilities preclude much free time to pursue facts, quotes, and anecdotes.

If interested, TTT (transportation, travel, and tourism) courses are widely available nationwide, usually at the junior or community college level. Or contact one of the related associations—ASTA, ARTA, ICTA, or CLIA—for information about travel agency careers or courses.

Through Public Relations

Public relations may well be the field most compatible with commercial travel writing. In many cases it is the same bird with different feathers.

Most outsiders presume that the sole purpose of "p.r." is to put their client before the public eye (or ear) as often as possible in as favorable a light as can be cast, truth be damned.

Favorable, almost always, but disregard for the truth is done at peril. Access to most media is closely guarded by editors seeking facts objectively framed. The common ground where public relations and media meet best is through information clearly and honestly shared, with the degree of objectivity a major determinant to whether the information is reproduced.

Since print is the communications medium most used for public relations, somebody must prepare the press releases, brochures, reports, newsletters, and magazines. And when the client is travel based, who better than an experienced writer with an objective travel writing background?

In addition to writing and editing, photography and graphics skills are sought. Developing special events is a natural for a travel writer where the site or subject is travel related or involves different cultures and locations. And public speaking, another aspect of public relations, often requires the same degree of articulation that writing does.

The key most important qualification sought by public relations departments? Experience in print journalism! A college degree is highly desirable, a master's degree in public relations is widely available (although rarely mandatory in this job market), and the field continues to grow as business and government expand. Best yet, the pay range is comfortable.

There is more to travel writing than just writing travel. Sell your information and your skills again and again. Knowledge and craft are the very best investment. They always pay compounded dividends.

Chapter Fifteen

IT GETS BETTER
THE MORE YOU SELL

The writing and selling process described in this book is primarily directed at newer writers eager to learn the steps to follow so they can travel, write about it, and sell that writing often and profitably. A related question often comes up in my "Writing Travel Articles That Sell" seminar: "Later on, doesn't it get easier—or at least different?"

Well, yes, it does. Not easier, necessarily, but the process gets faster and the results, more certain. The trade-off is that you are expected to produce ever higher quality material each time you submit. That means more pressure—and almost always more money.

For example, the more you write and sell, the easier it gets to see things to write about. As you grow in your profession, you read more. There you see what your colleagues proposed and the slant they took to bring it to print. You also learn what doesn't sell, either from getting your concepts rejected or from never seeing unsought topics or angles on the pages where you want to appear.

The more you sell to an editor and the more familiar they become with your competence and reliability, the more favorably they read your queries. Some encourage you to pitch ideas by phone; others aren't opposed to your doing so as long as you don't spread the word! And almost always they will give you more instructive responses to those queries. They will explain the rejections more fully, give you more tips on what they expect in the "go-aheads," and occasionally even suggest a modification in your proposal that will move it to the acceptance pile.

After two or three sales, they are more likely to talk with you in detail about specific concerns you have with your "go-aheads," and they may indeed be more lenient (once) if something extraordinary delays your copy or even your trip.

Money becomes easier to discuss. The first time through you are likely to receive the lowest end of the pay scale suggested for that publication in the appropriate *Writer's Market* write-up. If they pay $200-500, unless there is something exceptional about your piece (like its length, depth, unusual interviews, time involved, verbal eloquence, or hardships undertaken), you can expect $200 flat. That may soar to $300 for your second sale. After that, you can suggest (and have reason to expect) some extra perks like an assignment and/or some expenses or travel paid, in addition to even more money for the article.

After sufficient time and sales can you expect editors to pester you with pleas to write this or that, all fees paid, at your leisure? Not that I or my friends have ever heard of. But sometimes they do call with an idea similar to something you queried or wrote earlier, and a go-ahead results. They are more likely to give you a second chance to rewrite a lead, insert an obviously missing section, and recheck a dubious fact, thus saving a piece that would be certain death to a rookie.

They are also more likely to treat you like a valued business colleague from whom they expect to benefit during a long(er)-term relationship.

It's obvious why all of this is happening. You have become a dependable contributor to that editor. Your ideas are in sync, your writing meets or exceeds their needs, your facts are reliable; you bring home a usable product on time. That value can be significantly amplified if your photography is of the same high, reliable quality each time. Is it any wonder that any editor would want you to continue to help them produce a quality publication? And why, if funds are available, that editor would be eager to pay you progressively more for such quality output?

Does that mean you will become the editor's buddy or sidekick and attend the fabled (but mostly non-existent) roundtable luncheons where great literature and cutting-edge ideas are swished about with fine wine? Hardly. I've yet to meet most of the editors I've written for, and when I did it was usually by accident or because we were thrown together to speak on a writing panel. A perfect example was the editor of a European car magazine to whom I hold sold six articles who joined a Marine colonel and me talking, huffing, and running a 20-kilometer race in Ventura, California some years back. Two miles from the finish, before we unleashed our respective death sprints, we exchanged names, professions, and rank. Only after we had crossed the finish line and had been revived did the editor and I seek each other out, each asking "Are you the guy who..."

You also learn how to find and when to take the perk trips. You learn how to plan better, collect more needed information and photos, and yet have more "fun time" on excursions. You learn how to spend your money better, and what is worth spending the extra, unplanned dollar on for even greater after-trip selling rewards. You learn to balance your time better between first sales to magazines, reprints, and newspaper simultaneous submissions. And you learn to pinch out more good copy from the same site, even the same topics, all unique and each worth the price paid. None of which can be properly taught in a book like this since most of it becomes as peculiar in form as the writer. Those insights are some of the rewards of having survived the first years of freelancing.

And you become more professional in how you handle the business of writing. You join associations, keep files, balance your books, kibbutz with other writers, take (and later lead) workshops, conquer paranoia, move into nonfiction books, and learn that editors and writers desperately need each other. Like love, there is nothing like the first sale and the first check from some editor who doesn't even know your Dad. In the beginning every aspect of it is exciting, fearful, and mystifying. But after a while that unknown becomes less frightful, the thrill of each sale diminishes, and beating the odds becomes expected. Writing, especially with a travel kicker, becomes much more enjoyable and fun for all its predictability.

Done right, your travel is better than free—you can live from it! But it all starts with a first idea, then a query or a newspaper submission. The rest is doable.

PART FIVE

Related Information

Chapter Sixteen

THOSE MARVELOUS FREEBIES!

FANTASY

Newcomers to the travel profession envision a wide world of free-bies—open tickets to anywhere any time from globe-girding air-lines, complimentary passes to showcase hotels, and nonstop ban-quets and booze from four-star chuck wagons. All the writer has to do on the way to the beach is fax copy and photos to enraptured editors, who of course will pay tomorrow!

Nice Fantasy, but not quite accurate.

REALITY

Freebies exist—but not quite as you may imagine. Some foreign countries do transport planeloads of travel writers, wine them and dine them, and ply them with press releases and photo kits. All for free, or just about.

Occasionally resorts will pop for a few nights or a weekend, in-cluding drinks and food. Amusement parks give free all-ride passes. Restaurants feed those with a tap to publicity. In fact, almost any person or business that stands to win big by cultivating your good favor might cut you in on the freebie game.

The hardest touch, oddly, is the airlines, who used to let travel agents see the world on standby but invoke 300 regulations when it comes to travel writers—except when the airlines are touting a new route!

Free?

Alas, nothing is free. And freebie givers aren't fools. They aren't interested in a would-be writer long on hope but short on clips (copies of earlier articles or items in print) or credits. In exchange for footing part or all of the bill, they expect, or at least are betting on, a favorable comment (or a raving, three-page review) in print for plenty of potential customers to read. The better your credentials and the broader the circulation of your magazine or newspaper, the more likely you are to get the nod.

But freebie takers can find themselves in a bit of a pickle. Beholden to the gift giver, how do they try to slip in a plug or positive comment without writing obvious public relations blather, all the while attempting to maintain a wider, professional perspective?

Putting Freebies in Perspective

There's a way out of the freebie dilemma. Make it known up front that, should some of your tab be paid or special favors extended, you are nonetheless an objective journalist and there can be no strings attached. You will give whatever it is that the business or organization sells an honest and straightforward look, nothing more, nothing less.

However, it's rare that a travel writing novice even gets tempted. The killing question is "Where have you been in print?" Later it becomes "Let me see your assignment letter." So you usually have to pay dues for months or years—getting your feet firmly planted, your writing skills honed, wooing editors with sharp copy tailored to their readers and delivered on time. Once you've established your reputation as a travel writer, you will be approached for freebies, or you will know how and when to solicit them.

Joining one of the several travel writer's associations is usually a rite of passage to freebieville. (See "Sources for Travel Writers" at the end of this book for names and addresses). Yet acceptance by these associations often requires a certain number of travel articles in print. A second set of dues to be paid. Once a member, your best benefit is your contact with true vets who can tell you precisely how freebies can reward you, the giver, and most important, the reader.

Be aware, though, that some of the major newspapers will not use your copy if any part of your travel was sponsored or subsidized (paid for). Some even go further: Sponsored once, you are a pariah forever. It's a quandary that every writer must resolve.

Some Advice for Beginners

My advice to beginners about freebies is simple: Pay your own way, 100%, in the beginning. Focus on the place and topic rather than the "extras." Keep queries in circulation, organize well and research deep, pluck out winning prose from well-structured trips, and accumulate clips and credits. All kinds of rewards will result, including no-strings freebies that accrue to the successful.

Do I take the freebies? Almost never. The best freebie I ever accepted was one I engineered myself: a trip to Canada in the winter, to show through vivid and fact-filled writing what there was to do up North rather than bask in the Bahamas sun. The Canadian government was as mystified as I was but nonetheless footed the bill for two of the coldest weeks I've ever spent, shunting me from Chicago to Edmonton, Winnipeg, Calgary, Banff-Jasper, Vancouver, and Victoria.

The result? Six articles, about snow castles, having to plug your car heater cable into the parking meter, skiing, the art center in Banff where Shakespeare was performed while starving wolves patrolled the edge of town, shirt-sleeve golfing on Saltspring Island in January, and Victoria, that wee bit of England, snow-free.

I got the credits and cash and Canada got honest press exposure at a time when, to most people's way of thinking, it was best left to freeze. Probably never did get a convert from the Caribbean but it was the best kind of mutual aid, without a string to be seen.

Of course, I had been in print probably 400 times before, mostly in travel, so the Canadians knew what I could do. This reinforces my point: Forget freebies until you've got a competitive edge, then you can decide for yourself whether to accept them.

It must be said again: Write for the reader and the gold will follow. Do it right—be honest, dig deep, make your words jump off the page—and the rewards will come your way.

Chapter Seventeen

COMPUTERS AND
COPY SUBMISSION

Computers have become so commonplace in the writing world that for simple manuscript preparation and printing they have all but replaced the typewriter. But other means of information submission or exchange are still in flux, such as the use of e-mail versus snail mail (sent through the Post Office), faxes, and the phone for query and copy submission.

Nine years ago, when the second edition of this book was released, submitting anything by e-mail was either *verboten* or limited to insiders who were quietly provided a specific e-mail address. Faxing was heavily discouraged and editors did not want phone queries, particularly from newcomers.

Today, not only are most or all of the e-mail, fax, and phone addresses or numbers readily available in the current *Writer's Market*, you are usually encouraged to use them—except the phone.

For example, the editors of the 46 publications in the "Travel, Camping, and Trailer" section of the *2002 Writer's Market* would accept query letters submitted these ways: all 46 accepted snail mail; 41 of 46, e-mail (two by e-mail only, one in Greece, the other from Michigan), 19 would look at faxes, and three of 46 wanted phone queries (while another three emphatically stated "don't call!")

Many would accept queries by more than one medium: 14 would accept snail mail, e-mail, or fax and 13 wanted snail mail or e-mail, while 12 editors didn't specify (presumably indicating a preference for snail mail) or pointedly requested snail mail only.

What are we to conclude? For queries, don't guess. Simply check each submission write-up to see the respective editor's current preference. And forget phoning. Why? Because even if you do somehow reach the editor and manage to explain your article idea with sufficient persuasion and clarity, the editor is still most likely to respond, "Hmm, that might work. Send me a written query." In other words, they must see it in print to see if you can write as well as you speak. Most will also resent the lost time spent talking to a rookie who should know better.

The editor's question isn't whether you have an IBM or a Macintosh, not even whether your printer is a dot matrix or the newest five-function ink jet, but is the copy easy to read? In that sense, nothing has changed. Editors hated typed vowels filled with black by crummy typewriters; today they hate unreadable copy just as much. And the result is the same: manuscripts rejected, mostly unread.

So computers, faxes, modems, or even whether information should be sent as part of the e-mail text or as an e-mail attachment aren't the issue. You are expected to provide the item in the proper form and by an acceptable means. You must figure out how to get the query and manuscript there, then do it. Technological troglodytes won't survive in today's freelance writing world.

The greatest problem with queries, whether typed or computer-prepared, is not their legibility but that they are simply poorly written, or have no point to them, or even that they are good queries sent to the wrong editorial eyes, like "how to find Bolivia's wildest exotic dancers" rushed off to the editor of a missive for new ministers.

The speed of e-mail exacerbates the problem of quality. It's so easy to peck out a quick query during a coffee break and send it off with the touch of a key that it takes extraordinary, though much needed, control to first print a draft copy of that query, set it aside, and rework it repeatedly until it is as good as the article promised, before submitting it. If there was any selling advantage to typing a query letter, it was that the process was slow and final clean copy almost always required retyping the text once or several times. To minimize the retyping, the first draft was revised and restructured repeatedly, by pencil, with careful scrutiny given to every word before the "final" typing began.

Typing, and retyping, also involved a more disciplined use of a dictionary and thesaurus. Your computer's "spell check" and thesaurus programs are far less complete, sacrificing word choice for speed. The electronic dictionaries are a blessing only if you know when you have used a wrong word spelled correctly or the right word spelled incorrectly. The editors' old adage still holds: if a query letter writer is so lazy that he won't spell correctly, you can imagine the accuracy of the facts in his article to follow!

THE CASE FOR SNAIL MAIL

Sometimes old-fashioned first-class snail mail is the way to go.

A dozen editors in the *2002 Writer's Market* tally just mentioned give you no choice. Three reasons why many editors prefer snail mail queries? The slower pace may fit their decision-making process better. They may be so overcome by the hundreds of unsolicited e-mails they receive daily that they delete queries, inadvertently or with joy, along with other porno come-ons and stress-reduction cures. Or they simply think there is more élan in a 20-pound bond letter specifically addressed to them. A snail mail letter surely looks and retains form better than a curling fax or an 8-point e-mail query printed on the same page with several others.

COPY SUBMISSION

In the old days (several decades past) you typed out a query, received a reply or the letter itself with a hand-written comment, typed out the copy (often two or three times), and mailed it in.

Now you probably e-mail your query, hear back soon, and send the copy as an e-mail attachment. But woe to you if yours is the piece that crashes the editor's computer or snags it for 40 minutes while it tries to get protocols in sync.

How do you get your own protocols in sync so the editor gets precisely what they want with a minimum of hassle? Once the query has been accepted, you ask:

"Do you want me to send this piece as an e-mail download? If so, is the address the same as the one I used for the query?"

"Should I send it as a Word (or WordPerfect) file? Or do you want me to send it in the e-mail itself, in text, and fax you my printed version so you can see the specifics that the format removes (like centering, bold face, italics, etc.)?"

If digital illustrations or photos are involved, these questions become even more important. "Do I send them as a jpeg or a gif file? Any specific instructions? Do you want me to send them later at night so that it doesn't slow down your computer during the day?"

Sometimes you will get incomprehensible instructions from well-meaning editors who simply don't understand computers. When that happens, take the humble road and explain that you don't understand computers all that well. Would they please explain their instructions again, using other words, so that you know exactly what to do? Then be patient until you get it right.

How often will you be asked to send (or resend) the final copy by computer if it was originally snail mailed? For me it's been 100% of the time for the past eight years.

The editor approves the copy in hand—or, rarely, suggests a few more, specific paragraphs or a slight rewrite to include other information he provides (or sends you to find)—and directs me to e-mail the same or revised article as an attachment.

It's been the same with magazine articles. All I needed to know was to whom the final copy was to be sent, by what means, the correct address, and any particulars. If that isn't provided, I'd ask.

One of the critical questions in the past was whether the recipient computer was a Macintosh or an IBM since neither, then, could read the other's files. Now there is software that permits files in either to be accepted and read by the other. But if you are uncertain, that is also a proper question to ask the editor. If they don't have the right software, both computer formats will accept your material as e-mail text.

YOU HAVE NO FAX OR COMPUTER?

Okay, I won't scold you, though you must excuse me while I scratch my head.

You can rent computers, print, fax, and e-mail at copy shops. Libraries and college computer labs will sometimes let you use their computers; a few will also let you send e-mails. In each case you must provide your own disc. (Get a small box of them at a stationary store.)

To send and receive e-mails from your computer, you need a modem and an account with a server, like AOL. Check your computer's directory to see if your software doesn't include a modem, even though you may have never used it. If it doesn't, go to a computer store, tell the salesperson the kind of computer you use and request the needed linking software for an external modem, which is often available on discount for as little as $50.

Chapter Eighteen

AIR COURIERS

Want to travel abroad at a 50-85% discount, be assured a seat both ways on the best airlines, and be met at both ends to help expedite your passage through customs? Become an air courier!

Contrary to popular assumption, you won't be smuggling drugs, gems, or radioactive isotopes. Mostly you will be a body accompanying baggage, since the courier firms can't send personal baggage unaccompanied, yet they must transport containers overnight. The baggage—mostly paper contracts, X-rays, computer disks, medical records, small repair parts, and backup systems—becomes yours while you are in-flight, though it's stored safely below in the luggage hold and you are assured a seat, though it may be the last one in steerage. Dress conventionally, stay sober, and you had better guard your manifest envelope with your life or you will swim home!

What about *your* baggage? Well, there are some sacrifices or conditions you must make or meet to save $500-1,000 or more in flight costs.

First, you should live near the major courier airports. A vast majority of the flights leave from major hubs: New York, Los Angeles, San Francisco, or Miami.

Next, you must match the U.S. hub with a city you want to visit. Most New York flights go to Europe (primarily London, Frankfurt, Paris, Rome, Brussels, and Zurich) or South America. Miami flights head south, particularly Caracas, Mexico City, Buenos Aires, and Montevideo. And most California flights head west to the East: Hong Kong, Singapore, Sydney, Seoul, Tokyo, and others.

So you must find the courier firms that serve your airport and desired destination, then usually book well in advance. (Most flights are in and out of the same airport and are round-trip only.)

Forget the *Yellow Pages*. Check Hogsett's new edition of *Bargain Travel Handbook* (Travel Easy, 2002) with an excellent explanation of the process and lists of both courier companies and consolidators (airfare discounters). There are also chapters or sections about air courier travel, some getting dated, in Kelly Monaghan's *Air Courier Bargains* (Intrepid Traveler, 1998), Robert William Kirk's *You Can Travel Free* (Pelican, 2002), and Bruce T. Northam's *The Frugal Globetrotter* (Fulcrum Press, 1996).

You must figure out how to carry the bare essentials for a visit of seven to sixty days (the length of stay you arrange with the courier firm in advance) in a 9" x 14" x 22" bag (plus another small personal item, like a purse or camera bag). Check Hogsett's Travel Easy Bag, just this size and a courier's favorite.

Finally, both coming and going, you must be at the airport well in advance of the departure hour, which means when you are overseas you will probably return to the airport city at least a day in advance and be in the airport hours before. If you are a no-show, you lose any deposit the courier firm has demanded plus your return ticket.

The biggest sacrifice for most is that couriers travel alone, unless your mate or friend can arrange a trip with another courier company at the same time or you both travel as couriers but on different days! Or you can buy a ticket on the same flights directly from the airline or a consolidator, whichever is cheaper.

The best part of being an air courier? You can afford to go, you are on your own, and you have plenty of time to explore, interview, experience, and photo. Just stay out of jail—or at least get free in time to return on the flight. There can be extra bonuses. Often you can get frequent flyer miles. And you will know at the time you sign the contract exactly when you will fly, how, and where, so it's easy to work up a travel writing schedule around the trip.

The worst part, in addition to the shortcomings mentioned above? It's not for the aged, infirm, or anybody in whom change provokes the vapors. Sometimes couriers are bumped to the next flight. Rarely, the trips are canceled altogether. And if that writing haven so electric on paper turns out to be a festering hellhole that no sane person would encourage others to visit in print, you are there to fester until your ship comes home!

Chapter Nineteen

365 IDEAS FOR
TRAVEL ARTICLES

Some travel writers have more ideas than a lifetime of article writing could match. If their ideas were falling leaves, life for them would be a perpetual autumn in the woods.

But for other writers life is Antarctica. No leaves for a thousand miles! Such writers need help until their eyes and minds learn to see that travel ideas abound at every turn.

So here are 365 ideas that should work almost anywhere (except maybe for Antarctica). In some cases one idea will be sufficient to create a full article. In others several ideas might be combined to produce one piece.

The easiest way to structure a selling article is to ask a question first, then make the article answer it, through facts, quotes, anecdotes, and perhaps photos. An article brimming with excitement, information, gusto, and accuracy.

Therefore, the ideas in this list are posed as questions. This requires you to determine who would most benefit from knowing the answer, and why. This, in turn, suggests which publications would be most likely to buy your article since once you've determined who would be most interested you can determine which publications they read.

Future Travel Ideas

Books like this are frozen in print once they've left the press. But new travel ideas are dynamic. There are new places to visit, new conditions to confront, new circumstances to describe and report.

Bless the Internet because we can now provide occasional updates that will expand this basic 365-item list and keep it relatively current. To check those updates, please visit the following site: http://www.sops.com/travelideas.htm. The information is free, of course. There is even a way that you can help us share your ideas with other travel writers.

Enough preamble, there's writing to do. Best wishes for happy traveling, good writing, and bountiful selling!

1. What are the ten "hottest" travel destinations this year or season, and why?
2. Of those top ten, which of those at or near the top of the list are new? Why would travelers want to go there?
3. If one wanted to visit all ten, what is the best route, season, and means?

For each or any of the next ten:

4. What are the five most interesting things to do there? Why? How can each be done? When is the best time?
5. What are the five best hotels or accommodations? Why? Describe each: cost, location, attractions, restaurants, etc.
6. What are the five best restaurants? Why? Describe each in detail.
7. What five places must one visit at night? Why? Should visitors plan to spend a whole evening at each or can they go to several? Describe the best itinerary and give details for each location.
8. What should visitors do during the daytime? Why? What itinerary allows them to do the most and reap the greatest benefits?
9. What are the best athletic facilities open to the public? Describe each: cost, accessibility, availability of equipment, friendliness, condition of the facility, etc.
10. What is the shopping like? What are the best stores? Bargains? Things to avoid? "Must buys"?
11. What would children most enjoy doing there? Describe each activity fully.
12. What would seniors most enjoy doing there? Are there conditions like terrain or altitude that might limit older people? Describe each activity fully.

13. What is there to do in the way of cultural activities? To what age group are these directed? Describe and evaluate the quality of the activities.

14. Using each site as the center, what of interest can the traveler see within a day's range? Describe each major attraction and how it can be reached. Rank the attractions.

15. Again using each site as the center, how can an exciting weekend be spent in that area? Suggest an itinerary, explaining each item in detail and why it is included.

16. How could an exciting weekend itinerary best be expanded to a full week? Two weeks? A month?

17. How would you rank the top ten, or any combination of the top ten sites, by any of the mentioned criteria: hotels, restaurants, activities, etc.? Why?

18. As you rank the top ten by a chosen criterion, what other sites not mentioned must be included? Why?

19. What were the top ten sites last year or season? Which ones are not included this year? Why?

20. Historically, which sites have remained at or near the top for many years? Five years? A decade? What makes them perennial favorites?

21. What other sites have many or most of the same qualities or characteristics but are not presently among the top sites? What are their prospects for the future?

22. What are "travel spots to watch" in the short or long range? Why?

23. Since many travelers are interested in investments in prime travel locations, what places look promising for present or future investments? Why?

24. How might travelers' money best be invested? Hotels? Restaurants? Services? Other?

25. What is the local climate like for foreign or outside investment? Should or must the investor live on-site?

26. How can travelers get more information about investing in a particular place?

27. How can travelers get details on the local currency? Current exchange rates? Where it is best exchanged? Long-term prospects? What to do with extra pocket money after returning?

28. Where can travelers learn the customary tipping practices of various countries? Of cruises? In dining and social situations?

29. Why should—or shouldn't—a traveler get tickets from a travel agent? How can an agent minimize a traveler's risk while increasing the service supplied to the traveler?

30. How can travelers find the best (and the best type of) agent for their various travel needs?

31. What recourse does a traveler have when a travel agent acts dishonestly, unfairly, suspiciously, or in any other way seemingly improper?

32. Along that line, how can one select the best carrier—air, sea, whatever—for the trip planned? Select the criteria one could use: safety, comfort, adherence to schedule, price, food, service, appearance, prestige, etc.

33. How can travelers secure guarantees that the criterion or criteria will be met?

34. If the guarantees are secured but not fulfilled, what recourse do travelers have? How do they exercise that recourse?

35. Lost or damaged baggage is a common problem while traveling. How can one find out the incidence of this for the various carriers?

36. Should one's baggage be lost or damaged, what recourse is there? How does one initiate that action?

37. What should travelers do if their tickets are lost? When? If that brings no results, is there any recourse?

38. One reads of extraordinarily low-priced tickets in the newspaper classifieds. Are those generally legitimate? How can one check before buying? Any recourse later?

39. One also hears of "bucket shops" where low-priced tickets are found. What is the story here? Legitimate? How do they do it? What risk does the traveler run?

40. Some carriers are completely unknown. How can one check on their legitimacy, reliability, safety record, adherence to schedule, etc.?

41. Which U.S. carriers have foreign branches or affiliations? What are the names of their other lines? Will tickets from them be honored, or accepted for credit, by the U.S. firms? Will the U.S. firms accept full responsibility for their actions?

42. What should the traveler know about purchasing airfare before leaving? How much in advance? Round trip?

43. Some airlines charge considerably less than others. Is there any danger implied in the lower costs? What questions should the buyer ask?

44. Often a ticket has additional air mileage included beyond the stated destination. When is this the case? How can the flyer know this and plan for it?

45. Do all airlines serving food make special dietary arrangements? Which do not? Why?

46. How can travelers arrange for special diet meals? How can they be assured that this request is met?

47. Are there items that one should not use while flying? Do portable computers, cell phones, or digital hand-held games, for example, interfere with the plane's radio transmission?

48. How does one travel with prohibited items when these are needed at the destination? For example, hunting rifles and camping knives.

49. How does one carry delicate but odd-sized baggage, such as cumbersome carvings or large, mounted display boards?

50. Are there ways to streamline the registration, exiting, and baggage retrieval process?

51. What does "standby" booking actually mean? Is it less expensive? Are there levels of priority for standby customers?

52. What are the services customarily performed by flight attendants? What additional services can the customer expect but not know about? Is tipping ever expected or accepted?

53. Does the flyer have recourse if seatmate(s) are abusive, drunk, excessively noisy or troublesome, or otherwise unpleasant?

54. If a movie or other service is advertised but not provided on a flight, does the flyer have any recourse, financial or otherwise?

55. What is the air industry's policy regarding flying with children? How does this vary by airline?

56. What regulations prevail concerning minors flying unaccompanied? How does this vary by airline?

57. When a plane arrives behind schedule and connections are missed, what must the airline do in the way of accommodations, meals, transportation, and rescheduling?

58. How has the air industry changed over the past 50, 25, 10, 5 years? Since 9-11? What does that mean to the traveler?

59. How do the various airlines compare in fares, time spent traveling, comfort, and other ways between the U.S. and a particular destination?

60. If you miss a flight and did not cancel the ticket, can you receive a full refund? How do the airlines differ on this? What questions should the buyer ask in advance?

61. How can one travel and earn U.S. tax benefits at the same time? By conducting business? Writing? Attending conventions? What are the current tax laws in these areas?

62. To receive U.S. tax benefits, what kind of paperwork and/or proof of activity or intent is required before or after the trip?

63. Is the U.S. traveler ever taxed by the country or countries visited abroad? How? Where? How much? Can it be avoided?

64. If the U.S. traveler pays taxes abroad, direct or indirect, can this be deducted on the 1040 tax form later? What kind of validation or paperwork is required?

65. Which countries charge an exit fee at the airport? Prepare a list of these countries by continent and indicate the cost. Payable in U.S. or local currency? Is it also payable if you are in transit?

66. Is there a way to avoid paying exit fees? Where? How?

67. Are there any other official "hidden" fees at airports or in overseas countries that the traveler would likely be unaware of? Where? How much? For what?

68. Which countries require tourist visas? Prepare a list by continent, stating where such visas can be obtained, how much they cost, and what is required to receive them.

69. How can one obtain a tourist visa when they are abroad and wish to travel from one country to another?

70. What other kinds of visas, besides tourist, are available? Are any preferable, if the traveler qualifies? What is their cost, how are they obtained, and what is required to receive them?

71. With a tourist visa, does any foreign country require additional paperwork before exiting? Do any require tax or police clearances?

72. What happens to tourists who remain in a foreign country beyond the expiration period of their tourist visa?

73. In planning an extended stay abroad, what potential visa-related problems should be considered? Are there actions that can be taken in advance to alleviate or reduce these potential problems?

74. What should every traveler know about U.S. customs before traveling?

75. How can the traveler find out the most recent information about customs before each trip?

76. How can travelers speed up their customs inspection? What should they do beforehand? What papers and receipts are necessary? Must these be in English? What if these are lost?

77. What are the penalties for exceeding the customs limits? Are all enforced? What do travelers do if they can't pay the penalties?
78. In general, what kinds of items are most likely to give travelers difficulties with foreign customs?
79. What are the most common restrictions enforced against U.S. travelers by different nations? Prepare a list of countries by continent.
80. What are the most common requirements for driving a car or truck from country to country? Flying a plane? Docking a watercraft?
81. Can one use a U.S. driver's license in a foreign country? Prepare a list or chart explaining the regulations in each country by continent. Where local licenses are required, what must a traveler do to obtain one?
82. Is U.S. car insurance applicable in foreign countries? If not, can an extension be secured? Or can one buy insurance there?
83. Is U.S. health insurance applicable in foreign countries? How can travelers best secure similar protection abroad?
84. Who is responsible for injury and health care payments, the person or the country? If the country, does that apply to U.S. tourists? Who does one contact? Prepare a list or chart of countries by continent.
85. How does one find English-speaking doctors or dentists when traveling outside the U.S.?
86. In what countries would it be advisable to seek medical attention from doctors or dentists trained in the U.S. or another nation of similar training standards?
87. In some countries injections are customarily given in pharmacies. What are the dangers to be avoided in this situation? How can they be avoided?
88. In which countries should travelers return home for particular operations or treatments of a non-emergency nature?
89. How can a traveler bring medications and neither be detained nor have the medication confiscated by customs?
90. What medical conditions might make the traveler unacceptable by carriers or for admission into other countries? Are there ways in which that unacceptability can be modified?
91. How can travelers learn of unsafe health conditions in areas they wish to visit?
92. What are the most serious health threats in the world today? Where are these primarily found? Can travelers take precautions against them, other than staying out of the area altogether?
93. What is jet lag and how will it affect the traveler?

94. What can be done to lessen the effects of jet lag or to alleviate or avoid them completely?

95. What consequences can many travelers expect in high altitude sites? What can they do to lessen or alleviate these consequences?

96. What care should a traveler take when drinking local water? Why? Where is this not a concern? What precautions are possible?

97. Are there areas where fresh water swimming or bathing can be health threatening? Where? Why? Any precautions possible?

98. What should the traveler be concerned about when swimming in unknown seas? What precautions are advisable?

99. Often the sun is more direct and intense in sites closer to the equator. What concerns should the travelers have, and what precautions should they take?

100. How can travelers learn of local health threats (such as the Chagas disease in Salvador, Brazil) so they are neither unduly frightened nor inadequately prepared?

101. Are there local foods that should be avoided as potential health threats? Which ones, and where are they found?

102. For those with breathing difficulties, which cities or areas in the world are the most polluted?

103. Which cities are held to have the cleanest air in the world?

104. Which parts of the world house the oldest living people? Describe the evidence, life style, food, explanation(s). Can the areas and people be visited?

105. Where are the most healthful spas in the world? Says who, and on what evidence? Give details, costs.

106. Where are the most popular spas found? Give details, costs. How do these compare with the most healthful spas?

107. How are the world's time zones determined? How do the various countries alter this (with daylight savings, etc.)?

108. What consequences can the time zones have on scheduling, telephoning, transacting business, etc.?

109. What parts of the earth have the longest and shortest nights? How are these celebrated? Can visitors participate in these activities? How?

110. How can travelers synchronize their biological clock with the local time of day to diminish the negative effects of disharmony between the two?

111. Is time, in the sense of a 24-hour day, told the same worldwide?

112. In what areas of the world are different calendars used? How does this affect the traveler?

113. Winter and summer are reversed in the two hemispheres. What should the traveler know about this, and how might it affect their planning?

114. Holidays vary from country to country. Are there any holidays that are honored worldwide? Which? When do they occur?

115. What are the major holidays celebrated in each nation, the date(s), the occasion? What everyday activities are altered at those times? Make a list of countries by continent.

116. In much of the world, pharmacies take turns staying open 24hours a day. How can the traveler find out which pharmacies and which other vital services are open around the clock?

117. Are there areas of the world offering the kind of relief that the desert Southwest does for people allergic to the more common pollens in the U.S.?

118. What are the most humid areas of the world? How does this affect traveling in the area?

119. Where are the highest tides in the world? Can these be seen by travelers? When? From what viewing point?

120. For traveling golfers, which are the ten most enjoyable courses in the world? Why? Give details, including the best season to play.

121. What equipment should the average golfer bring on a trip? Is there any country that won't allow golf equipment through customs or charges extra for it? Why, and how much? What equipment is available locally? How can golfers find out about the best local courses?

122. Does the golf etiquette differ in other countries? How? Any other peculiarities the traveler should know?

123. Is golf played and scored the same in every country?

124. For the traveling businessperson, is business conducted on the golf course in foreign countries as it is in the U.S.? Where? How does it differ?

125. What are ten wildest courses in the world? Why? What should the traveler know to play on each or all?

126. Golfers on vacation might enjoy watching tournaments elsewhere. When and where are the major golf tournaments held outside the U.S. each year? How can one obtain tickets to watch?

127. When playing outside the United States, do golfers have access to the clubhouse? How does this differ from country to country?

128. How much can a golfer expect to pay elsewhere? Are there greens fees? Are caddies required? Golf carts? Special shoes or attire? Other costs?

129. Which major golf courses outside the U.S. are connected to hotels? Is access guaranteed to hotel guests? Supply costs and details.
130. How does playing tennis in a foreign country differ from playing tennis in the U.S.?
131. Do travelers have access to the major tennis tournament courses outside the U.S., such as Wimbledon? How do they make advance arrangements?
132. How do travelers arrange temporary use of tennis clubs and courts in foreign lands? How do they find out about them?
133. Is there any country where tennis equipment cannot be brought through customs, or where they will be charged extra? Why, and how much?
134. Where in the world can the traveler expect to see baseball played professionally as it is in the U.S.?
135. How does a professional baseball game played in a particular country differ from one played in the U.S.? What presumably American traits are practiced there?
136. How can U.S. tourists find out the playing schedule in a particular country so they can watch a game while there? Can they reserve seats in advance?
137. Which former American major leaguers could a traveler watch play in the professional leagues outside the U.S.? Where do they play?
138. How and where can a visiting American practice or play baseball abroad? Softball?
139. Does the American community in the larger cities abroad have regular outings the tourists could join to play ball? Where and when?
140. Are there any cities that prohibit or discourage jogging and running in the parks? On the streets? Which, why, where, and when?
141. Must one wear attire different from than worn in the U.S. when jogging or running abroad? How does it differ? Where? Why?
142. Athletes regularly spit while exercising in the U.S. Is this prohibited or heavily discouraged elsewhere? Where? How is the offender penalized?
143. Is the etiquette of running different outside of the U.S.? How and where?
144. How does one gain access to showers and locker facilities at major stadia or parks outside the U.S.? Must this be arranged in advance? How is that done?

145. How can runners find out the schedule of competition in other countries so they can coordinate their visit with these activities?

146. Are requirements for running competitions abroad different from those in the U.S.? Doctor's form? Evidence of previous times?

147. Are there running events that last for days and/or cross the country or cover long distances that the traveler could enter and thereby see much of the land? Where? When?

148. How could each of the running questions above be applied to triathloning, biathloning, marathoning, and ultramarathoning?

149. How does the visiting trackperson gain access to tracks abroad, for practicing, informal racing, and competition?

150. Are there track clubs and groups abroad that allow visiting American trackpeople to participate in their workouts? How can this be arranged in advance?

151. What are the ten prettiest running trails or roads outside the U.S.? Why? Any problems simply running on them?

152. Of those ten, which is the most exciting? Most difficult? Most daring?

153. How might one cross a country by running and walking a reasonable distance daily, stopping at super locations each night and seeing the best that land has to offer? Lay out such a trip, with details.

154. Are there any "Runs For Peace," or other runs for similar purposes, being planned inside or outside the U.S. during the coming year that might attract travelers? Where and when? Whom should they contact?

155. How and where can one find good bicycles to use for seeing the countryside abroad? What might they cost? What kind of security would be required?

156. How do the cycling regulations differ outside the U.S.? Are licenses required? Can one use all regular roads?

157. How can travelers bring their bicycle with them? Do the carriers require special packing? Is there an additional charge? Will customs allow them to enter?

158. Is special cycling attire required? Helmets? Are these available for rent abroad?

159. How can travelers join cycling clubs and tours outside the U.S.? How can they find out about them? What is the customary charge to participate?

160. Where can traveling U.S. football fans find football played outside the U.S.?

161. How does football played abroad differ from football played in the U.S.?
162. How can travelers find out schedules, ticket information, and whatever else they need to know for football games outside the U.S.?
163. Where is rugby normally played and how can one find necessary information about the schedule and tickets?
164. How can spectators unfamiliar with rugby learn the rules and intricacies of rugby before seeing a match?
165. The same for cricket: Where is it normally played and how can travelers secure information about the schedule and tickets?
166. Again, how can one learn more about it before observing it?
167. Do rugby or cricket have a special etiquette that the visiting spectator should know? What is it?
168. Soccer is widely popular. When are the major world matches scheduled and how might this affect the traveler's plans?
169. How does one learn the exact schedules of soccer matches and the ticket information?
170. What might the traveler read to fully understand soccer before observing a match in person?
171. Is there a special etiquette for the spectators? Must one be careful about the color of their clothes to avoid perhaps unpleasant or dangerous results of implied partisanship?
172. What other sports can be observed in the country in question? What should travelers know about these in advance? How can travelers view or participate in the event?
173. How can travelers arrange to visit a business similar to their own while outside the U.S.? What would be the proper way to do that in a particular country?
174. Once the business has been visited, is a gratuity expected? Would it be well received even if unexpected? How might that be done?
175. How can one get information on the kinds of the business, trade, or professional associations of a particular country? Contacts (names and addresses)?
176. Is there a U.S. governmental agency that can help arrange a business visitation schedule for travelers with their counterparts abroad?
177. How can travelers visit the stock or commodities exchanges outside the U.S.? Where can one find information to read in advance to understand what they will see?

178. How can one learn about trade shows, or their equivalents, in the countries they wish to visit?
179. Is there a way to learn of fairs held outside the U.S., with the related ticket and schedule information?
180. Every nation has beauty contests. How can one find out when they are held, where, and what the visitor must do to attend?
181. What natural wonders or phenomena are there to see in a particular country? Why would the traveler want to see these?
182. Does the public have access to the phenomena? Are there fees? What arrangements must be made in advance? How can that be done?
183. What dangers, if any, can the traveler expect to encounter when viewing the natural phenomenon? How can these dangers be protected against in advance?
184. Who would find viewing the phenomena difficult or inadvisable? Is it rigorous? Must one be at a particular state of training to participate fully or wisely?
185. How does a particular phenomenon fit into its natural setting? Is it singular or one of many such phenomena?
186. What is the geological history of the area or site? Is this typical or atypical of the surrounding area? If unique, what makes it so?
187. What is the history of human habitation in the area or site? To what degree is it a result of the geology?
188. What can the visitor see that shows the geological history of the area? Are there guided tours? Where? When? How does one participate?
189. What evidences can be seen of the early human habitation? Are there archaeological digs there or nearby? Where? How and when can they be visited?
190. Are there guided tours of the digs? Can one participate in the dig? How can more information be obtained?
191. Is there a good museum display in the vicinity that shows the geological formation and/or the early human habitation? Where? When is it open to the public? What does it cost?
192. When did the historical period of the site or area begin? How were the first writings made? Are copies still available to be seen by travelers?
193. What of significance has occurred in the site or area during the time of recorded history?

194. Which of those significant sites can be visited by the traveler? What physical evidence can be seen today? Where is it? Give details.

195. Can one read historical accounts of the events? Can one read actual historical documents while present at the site? How?

196. Are there symbolic reenactments of these events today? When? Are they worth viewing? How can that be done?

197. Do ancestors of those involved in the historic events still live in the area? Who are they? Can they be visited? How?

198. Is the area currently undergoing a change of historical significance? What is it? How can it be viewed? Can one participate in it?

199. Who are the most famous personalities of the area or site? Where did or do they live?

200. If they have died, can the place(s) where they lived locally be visited? When? Cost? Is a guided tour possible? Are they buried there? Where?

201. If they are still living, can one meet with them? When? How does one make the arrangements?

202. Is it possible to visit the home where they are presently living? Where they used to live? When? How does one make the arrangements?

203. What would children enjoy doing at the site or area?

204. Are there programs solely for children, where they can be left and retrieved later, that will enlarge their understanding of the site or area?

205. If so, can the traveler's child(ren) participate? What does it cost? How can arrangements be made in advance?

206. If one visits the area during the school year, is it mandatory to enroll children in school during the visit? What are the regulations? Are they enforced?

207. How can the traveler's children get to know local children? What is the best means and setting for that interchange?

208. What dangers exist for visitor's children in the area? Is kidnapping common? What precautions should the parents take?

209. Are there cultural activities specifically directed to children that are open to youngsters traveling in the area? What are they? Can newcomers participate? Can arrangements be made in advance?

210. What sports activities or facilities are open to traveler's children? Are they supervised and safe? What are the details?

211. For the traveling parents with youngsters, are babysitters available? How trustworthy are they? How can one tell? How can they be hired? What is the going rate?

212. Are there any health precautions parents should know about before bringing children to the site or area? Anything they should do while the children are there? After they have returned home?

213. Are there any health care limitations such as inadequate hospital facilities or the absence of medical care that one should know about the area or site before visiting or bringing children?

214. Conversely, are there particularly healthful activities or locations that children (and probably adults) should avail themselves of while in the area?

215. Is there anything in the local diet that should be avoided by children? What? Why?

216. If the children are very young, is it possible to buy the necessary food and diapers locally?

217. If needed for infants, are reputable doctors available? How can they be contacted?

218. Are there summer camps in the area that will accept visitor's English-speaking children? How can a camp's reputation be checked? Provide details.

219. Are there similar camps or programs where the English-speaking children of travelers can learn the local language and customs and associate with peers?

220. What are the local customs concerning children accompanying parents to social or cultural activities?

221. Can the visitor's children safely sightsee alone or with other children during the day? Play at the beach or at parks? What areas or activities are unsafe?

222. How safe is it for children to carry pocket money, cameras, radios, watches, or other items of value?

223. What phone numbers should every child visiting the area carry on a card in his or her pocket, on the remote chance they would get lost, ill, etc.?

224. What clothes should the parents bring for the child to wear? What can be bought locally, if needed?

225. What kinds of shoes do children most need in this area? If needed, are the local shoes worth buying?

226. What would teenagers find particularly interesting to do in this area?

227. What can teenage girls see and do that is worthwhile yet different?
228. What advice should teenage girls receive before exploring alone or in pairs in this area? Where or at what hours is it always advisable to be accompanied or chaperoned?
229. How can they meet other girls roughly their own age and with similar interests?
230. How should the teenage girls dress both to feel comfortable and to avoid sending the wrong message?
231. What would teenage boys find different yet worthwhile to do here?
232. Any advice they should heed to avoid trouble or problems? Any attire that should be avoided for the same reasons?
233. How can visiting teenage boys or girls participate in sports in this area? Can they make any arrangements in advance?
234. What are the dating standards for teenage girls here? How much should a visiting girl adhere to those standards? Any outright taboos?
235. How do the dating standards for boys differ here from the U.S., and what is proper behavior?
236. How prevalent is drug use among teens in this area? What are the penalties if caught, and how regularly are they enforced? Would they be stiffer for a tourist caught abusing the laws?
237. What are the regulations concerning alcohol or tobacco use as they apply to teens both local and visiting? Anything else prohibited that the visiting teen should know?
238. How does the local social dancing done by teens differ from that in the U.S.? Anything visiting teens should know or behavior they should avoid?
239. Where can the visiting teens dance? Should they attend in pairs? Is chaperoning ever advised or required?
240. Should U.S. teens bring radios with them? Could they hear familiar music? Programs in English? Any advice on radio use there?
241. How much money should teens carry with them? In what form?
242. How much anti-Americanism is present in this area? How might it affect teens? What should they respond?
243. What are teen home parties like in this area? If invited, what would be expected, or desired, of U.S. visitors?
244. Can teens rent cars in this area? If so, what advice do they need to avoid injury, stay safe, and not run afoul of the law?

245. Given one full day in this area, what would be the best combination of things to see and do for teenaged girls? Boys? A mixed group?
246. Given two days? A weekend? A week? Two weeks? Give details.
247. Are there many extra-academic activities at the universities in this area that would interest visiting teens? How might they participate?
248. Are there academic activities, in or out of the university, that visiting teens might enjoy? Can they participate? How?
249. Are there secular or religious institutions in the area that encourage teen visitation and interaction? If so, give details.
250. In this area or society, what is the proper role of teens as they relate to the elderly, parents, teachers, and peers? Are visiting teens expected to act in the same way?
251. What would honeymooners enjoy doing in this area or at this site?
252. Do they make special provisions locally for honeymooners? What kinds of provisions? Should couples identify themselves as honeymooners at hotels, restaurants, other locations?
253. How do local newlyweds celebrate honeymoons? Could visiting honeymooners do the same? Explain.
254. What would be an ideal one-day schedule for visiting American honeymooners? Two-day? Weekend? Week-long? Two-week?
255. Is there anything commonly done in the U.S. that would be improper or embarrassing for visiting newlyweds? For any married couple?
256. What would be particularly interesting to do in the area for seniors, alone, in groups, or as couples?
257. Are there local accommodations for seniors—lower rates, elevators, special stairs in buses, etc.?
258. Is there an age at which one can first use these accommodations? Is there a local card or pass needed? How does one secure it?
259. Are there special tours for seniors to places that might otherwise be physically inaccessible or inconvenient? How can one learn of them? Can one participate?
260. Are there health facilities in the area of particular interest to the older traveler? Explain.
261. How can seniors meet their counterparts in this area? Is that to be encouraged?
262. For seniors dependent upon continued medical care or medication provision while traveling, how can arrangements be made in this area? How can this connection be established in advance?

263. What would constitute an ideal day for a visiting senior to this area? Two days? Weekend? Week? Two weeks? Describe.

264. What are the best months or seasons for visitors to come to this area? What can be done best during that period?

265. What is the next best season? What can be done best during that period? Which activities differ from those of the best months?

266. When shouldn't one visit this area? Why?

267. Are there special accommodations for the handicapped in this area? Explain.

268. Would visiting American tourists who are handicapped be looked down upon here? How would their treatment differ? Why?

269. Are there special telephone and TV accommodations for the hearing-impaired?

270. How do the deaf sign in this area? Anything the visiting deaf should know?

271. Are there any difficulties bringing Seeing Eye dogs to this area? Explain.

272. What major sites in the area can be fully visited by those in wheelchairs? Which cannot? Explain.

273. What local religious centers or attractions would most interest the American visitor?

274. Must the visitor wear any special attire to see the local religious attractions? Is the attire available there? Any cost?

275. Are guided tours offered at the religious attractions? When? Open to anybody? Cost?

276. If a visitor wishes to preach or explain his or her religion to local residents, would this create any difficulties? Explain.

277. Are there activities or places that are inaccessible to those who are not believers of the national or official church or faith? Explain.

278. How can one find private guides in this area? Are they licensed? How can they be evaluated before hiring them?

279. Are there official taxi rates in this area? Where are those rates listed? How does one learn of the exceptions?

280. Is there a Traveler's Aid, or equivalent, in this area? Where is it located? How can one contact it?

281. Where can one find maps in English of the region, city, or site? Are there various maps? Which is best? What do they cost?

282. What services does the closest U.S. consulate or embassy provide for visiting Americans? Who should be contacted there? What days/hours?

283. How can one receive mail in this area? What kind of identification is required to retrieve it?
284. Which credit cards are commonly accepted in this area? What does one do if the cards are lost here?
285. Can the visitor bring pets? What shots or papers are required? What are the local rules regarding those animals?
286. If one buys a pet locally, what must be done to bring it back to the United States?
287. What are the most common local scams tried on visitors? What should the newcomer be particularly aware of?
288. Are there local bookstores or libraries with books in English?
289. Are there video stores with English-speaking films? Can one rent VCRs for use with hotel TV's? Do the hotels have TV's?
290. For the single visitor, what are the possibilities of meeting congenial peers of the opposite sex? Of the same sex?
291. What must the single visitor beware of in this area when socializing? Any absolute taboos?
292. How is a visiting single considered by the local residents? Any way to reduce the discomfort that might create?
293. Are there precious works of art or legitimate artifacts available for purchase? Where might one find them? How can they be authenticated?
294. Must any purchase have a special antiquities release before it can be taken out of the country? If so, explain.
295. Can visitors pan, mine, or otherwise remove ores or metals from the ground, then sell them or take them home? What are the rules?
296. What can horticulturists take home of the plants or seeds they find in the area? How can they get permission to do so?
297. What local food should be tried by visitors? Where is it best prepared and available? Where might one find authentic recipes for preparation back home?
298. What sites or attractions are overblown and not worth the time or expense?
299. What deserves close attention but few outsiders know about? How can the visitor see it? What information should they have in advance?
300. If travelers want to write about this area, or any area, and later use their earnings to help offset the trip costs, plus deduct some or all of them for their taxes, what seminar should they attend or

tape series, with workbook, should they consult before taking the trip?

301. How has the fall of European communism changed European countries? Socially, economically, personally, educationally?

302. What happened to the more visual symbols, like the Berlin Wall and the mined fields along the boundaries? Have those totally disappeared? What can the visitor still see?

303. How have the former communist countries changed regarding border crossings, prohibited items one can carry, visa requirements? What should a potential visitor know?

304. Is there a commerce in memorabilia of those earlier regimes? Stores selling old communist posters, for example? How can one visit these? Any problems dealing in such matters?

305. Are there any tours built around the remnants or physical manifestations of the old communist rule? Describe them.

306. Along the same line, with the recent worldwide focus on the holocaust and World War II, what can be seen today of the earlier Nazi concentration camps? Which ones are open to visit? Describe them and details visitors should know.

307. Are there tours built around the old Nazi buildings, monuments, or remnants, particularly in Berlin? Give details.

308. Where does communism still rule? What are the current regulations about visiting or touring? Changes since the collapse of the U.S.S.R.?

309. Where in the world can gays visit without hassle? Where is it encouraged? Any stipulations? Anything outsiders should know to fit within the accepted range of freedoms?

310. Does this differ for gays versus lesbians? Where? How?

311. Where is the climate particularly negative to their visit and gathering? Why? What might happen to them?

312. How might gays find out about the local activities of places they wish to visit, either before the trip or once they are there?

313. Are there travel agencies that particularly cater to gays? Which?

314. Are there travel agencies that particularly cater to blacks? Other ethnic groups? Which? Will they also help others interested in the sites and activities of their focus group?

315. In the past few years ecotravel has become important. Describe that, how it has changed the travel scene, and what it means to the reader, with examples.

316. Where, for example, can the travelers most quickly and fully integrate themselves into the environment to sense and experience

life and nature to its fullest? List the top ten foreign ecotravel sites.

317. How does ecotravel affect the countries catering to it? What limitations does that have on the number and kind of visitors it can accommodate? How does that affect the cost?

318. How can the average traveler keenly sensitive to the ecology change their own activities to leave all sites they visit less ecologically damaged?

319. How are U.S. parks accommodating themselves to this new sensitivity? What can the traveler do to assist or provoke them into making more changes?

320. Which of the parks—national, state, or local—are the best ecotravel sites? What makes them so exceptional?

321. Which are the worst? What can Americans do to alter that?

322. Americans are becoming more conscious of the perils of city visitation. Which cities in the world are currently the worst to visit in terms of an individual's safety?

323. Which are the safest? Why? Is each likely to be as safe in the next five years? Ten?

324. The same questions for American cities: safest and least safe. Any predictions for the future?

325. What can tourists do in any large city to enhance their safety? What are the tips that seem to work anywhere in the world?

326. Are there specific things travelers can do in particular cities that will increase their safety? Cultural taboos that incite unsuspected response? Americanisms that put that person in exceptional, unknown danger?

327. What is the best way to carry money, passports, and other needed papers and documents so that it is unlikely to be stolen? Does this vary by sections of the world?

328. More people yearly rent cars abroad. What is the best way to find out the regulations, restrictions, and rates? How can you be certain the cost will be the same when you arrive as it was when quoted at home?

329. Do you need anything beyond a U.S. driving license? Insurance? An international license? If so, give details.

330. How does driving differ in various parts of the world? For example, which countries drive on the left hand of the street, as in England? Do hand signals differ? Do all use red-yellow-green lights?

331. Explain how gas stations function in different countries? Self-service? Open at night? Does each handle repairs? What do you do if you are stranded in the middle of the night?

332. In what countries does it makes sense to bring your own car for an extended visit? Or purchase your own car there? Explain the stipulations that entails.

333. In the U.S. it's possible to drive somebody's car for them from one site to another. Explain how this is done: where you find out about it, make the arrangements, and so on.

334. Travelers are intrigued by the prospect of becoming air couriers: flying at huge discounts in exchange for giving up their baggage space. Explain how this operates.

335. Where can they find more information about this activity; those air courier firms currently hiring; their routes, needs, rates?

336. How can they also find out about foreign air courier firms that will employ Americans?

337. How can one learn about working on steamers or cruise ships? What skills or talents are required? Who do they contact? Does it pay more than just getting to the destination? Must you work both ways?

338. Frequent flyer miles are a boon to many travelers who, by traveling, get to travel more at less charge. Explain how this whole phenomenon works, and how it has changed over the years.

339. Which airlines offer this program? Do frequent flyer miles differ from line to line? How can miles be increased through hotel and car rentals plus taking advantage of bonus opportunities?

340. Explain the pitfalls of the system: what not to do, when it doesn't work, and how it can be used poorly.

341. Any tips you know that aren't common knowledge about how to use the system legally yet to its absolute maximum?

342. How does one "cash in" on unused frequent flyer miles? Can they be given to charity or be used for charitable means? Can you give, sell, or trade them to others?

343. Where can credit cards be used abroad? Which cards? Any cards that simply have no use overseas?

344. What danger does the traveler have carrying credit cards? How can travelers safely store and use them? What do they do to get replacements if they are lost or stolen?

345. Generally, overseas purchases are made in a foreign currency. How can the traveler be certain of the currency rate when the

card is converted into dollars and that additional fees aren't added to the card?

346. Often cards in the U.S. act as warranties of product quality. Is that the same abroad? Should the item being mailed home prove to be a different one than purchased, for example, what recourse does the traveler have? Anything they can do there?

347. How difficult is it to use bank checks abroad? How does one set up the proper conditions for their use before leaving? What do travelers do once they arrive?

348. Letters of credit can be created for use abroad. Explain how they work, where they are useful, and what the traveler must do both at home and overseas to put the letter in effect.

349. Banks are not used for money exchange or overseas transfer in some countries. Such commerce is rather done by private parties. If that is true in a particular country, what should travelers know about it before participating? How can they verify the reliability of the process and the involved parties?

350. Where outsiders are welcome to participate in archeological digs, explain precisely what one does at a dig. The amount of work involved: digging, lifting, sifting, sitting, etc. Also, the living conditions and the time expectations.

351. When digging abroad, what additional requirements exist: registration in the sponsor's institution or program, shots, waivers, etc.

352. For archeological digs, who pays for what: airfare, food, local travel? Are the workers actually paid anything? When?

353. Often universities have overseas learning programs that travelers might include in their itinerary. Explain how one finds out about these and participates.

354. Sometimes university facilities go unused during part of the year, both in the U.S. and abroad. Since these can often be rented at a nominal rate, how can you find out where these vacancies exist and how a traveler can fill them?

355. Many travel readers are interested in utilizing various travel means on the same trip. Explain, for example, how one might box a cycle, fly it to another city, unbox it, and ride to a campsite.

356. Expand that to any of the many combinations possible: trucking to the shore and canoeing into the wilderness; flying to a remote strip, then backpacking away; etc.

357. Explain how the traveler can pack for an overseas trip of several week's duration in one suitcase: what's needed, what isn't.

358. Do the same for travelers of varying ages: what must be brought for the youngster, teen, adult, senior.
359. Create a chart showing various things one might do in different countries, then the minimum attire one must bring to match each activity.
360. Another kind of chart could be created by season: what one does in specific countries, say, in spring. One for each season.
361. Travelers can compensate for underpacking by buying clothes abroad. Indicate what clothes are best bought where, with a possible price range.
362. Describe travel in the future: how will trips differ in 10, 25, 50 years based on what we know of the industry and the world?
363. Explain what effect the sub-Channel tunnel is having on travel from England to France. Future impact on travelers?
364. How much negative reaction already exists in specific countries to intrusion by foreign travelers? Where? How does it manifest itself?
365. As the world shrinks, how will that change in the future? Give specifics of current trends and future projections.

BIBLIOGRAPHY AND CITED SOURCES

BOOKS AND REPORTS

Travel Writing

Anderson, Brian and Eileen. *Writing About Travel.* How To Books (U.K.), 2000.

Burgett, Gordon. *Travel Writer's Guide*, 3rd ed. Communication Unlimited, 2002.

Cropp, Richard, et.al. *Writing Travel Books and Articles.* Self-Counsel Press, 1997.

Dial, Cynthia. *Teach Yourself Travel Writing.* NTC Publishing Group, 2001.

Farewell, Susan. *How to Make a Living as a Travel Writer*, 2nd ed. Marlowe & Co., 1997.

O'Neil, L. Peat. *Travel Writing: A Guide to Research, Writing, and Selling.* Writer's Digest Books, 2000.

Sedge, Michael. *The Writer's and Photographer's Guide to Global Markets.* Allworth Press, 1998.

Zobel, Louise. *Travel Writer's Handbook*, 4th ed. Surrey Books, 1997.

Travel Photography

Engh, Rohn. *Sell and Re-Sell Your Photos.* Writer's Digest Books, 4th ed., 1997.

Engh, Rohn. *Sell Photos.Com.* Writer's Digest Books, 2000.

Hicks, Roger and Frances Schultz, *Travel Photography: How to Research, Produce and Sell Great Travel Pictures.* Focal Press, 1998.

I'Anson, Peter. *Travel Photography: A Guide to Taking Better Pictures.* Lonely Planet, 2000.

Photographer's Market, current edition. Annual. Writer's Digest Books.

Air Couriers and Bargain Travel

Hogsett, Suzanne. *Bargain Travel Handbook.* Travel Easy, 2002.

Kirk, Robert William. *You Can Travel Free*. Pelican, 2002.
Monighan, Kelly. *Air Courier Bargains*. Intrepid Traveler, 1998.
Northam, Bruce T. *The Frugal Globetrotter*. Fulcrum Press, 1996.

General Writing

Bowerman, Peter. *The Well-Fed Writer: Financial Self-Sufficiency as a Freelance Writer in Six Months or Less*. Fanove, 2000.

Bly, Robert W. *Secrets of a Freelance Writer: How to Make $85,000 a Year*. Henry Holt, 1997.

Bly, Robert W. *The Online Copywriter's Handbook*. McGraw Hill-NTC, 2002.

Burgett, Gordon. *How To Sell More Than 75% of Your Freelance Writing*, 4th ed. Communication Unlimited, pub. date 1/2003.

Metter, Ellen. *Facts in a Flash*. Writer's Digest Books, 1999.

Metzler, Ken. *Creative Interviewing: The Writer's Guide to Gathering Information by Asking Questions*. Allyn and Bacon, 3rd ed., 1996.

Writer's Digest Magazine (Amanda Boyd and Thomas Clark, eds.). *Writer's Digest Handbook of Making Money Freelance Writing*. Writer's Digest Books, 1997.

Yudkin, Marcia. *Freelance Writing for Magazines and Newspapers: Breaking In Without Selling Out*. HarperCollins, 1993.

Finding Markets

Burgett, Gordon, "100 Best Travel Newspaper Markets," report by print, disc, or e-mail; revised every January 1. Communication Unlimited.

Writer's Market, current edition. Annual. Writer's Digest Books.

Legal Matters

Bunnin, Brad and Peter Beren. *The Writer's Legal Companion: The Complete Handbook for the Working Writer*. Perseus, 1998.

Kirsch, Jonathan. *Kirsch's Guide to the Book Contract: For Authors, Editors, Publishers, and Agents*. Acrobat Books, 1998.

Query Letters

Cool, Lisa Collier. *How to Write Irresistible Query Letters.* Writer's Digest Books, 1990.

Wood, John. *How to Write Attention Grabbing Query and Cover Letters.* Writer's Digest Books, 2000.

AUDIO CASSETTES

Burgett, Gordon. *"How to Sell 75% of Your Travel Writing!"* Two-hour seminar on audio cassette, with workbook. Communication Unlimited, 1999.

Burgett, Gordon. *"Finding Ideas for General and Travel Articles."* 60-minute audio cassette. Communication Unlimited, 2002. (Also available in print or by e-mail.)

DIGITAL SOURCES

Photography

http://www.nationalgeographic.com/photography. A wide variety of travel-related photo information.

http://www.fodors.com/focus. Nearly 100 easy-to-follow tips, with accompanying photos, covering every aspect of travel photography.

http://phototravel.com. Publishes a bimonthly newsletter containing detailed guides to great photo destinations, plus 26 additional guides.

http://www.naturephotogallery.com. Look here for wildlife landscape and macro photos. How to's, and equipment reviews.

ASSOCIATIONS

FIJET (World Federation of Travel Writers and Journalists), One Ballinswood Rd., Atlantic Highlands, NJ 07716. (732) 291-2840, email fijetusa@aol.com, http://fijet.org.

IFWTWA (International Food, Wine, and Travel Writers Association), P. O. Box 8249, Calabasas, CA 91372. (818) 999-9959, email ifwtwa@aol.com, www.ifwtwa.org.

ITWEA (International Travel Writers and Editors Association), 1224 N. Nolcomis NE, Alexandria, MN 56308. (320) 763-7626, www.iama.org.

SATW (Society of American Travel Writers), 4101 Lake Boone Tr. #201, Raleigh, NC 27607. (919) 787-5181, email shaw@satw.org, www.satw.org.

TJG (Travel Journalists Guild), P.O. Box 10643, Chicago, IL 60610. (312) 664-9279.

SOURCES CITED IN *Travel Writer's Guide*

Acrobat Books, P.O. Box 870, Venice, CA 90294. (310) 578-1055, email acrobooks@cs.com.

Allworth Press, 10 E. 23rd St. #510, New York, NY 10010. (800) 491-2808, email pub@allworth.com.

Allyn and Bacon, 75 Arlington St. #300, Boston, MA 02116. (617) 848-6000, email AandBpub@aol.com.

Communication Unlimited, P.O. Box 6405, S. Maria, CA 93456. (800) 563-1454, email sops@sops.com.

Focal Press, 225 Wildwood Ave., Woburn, MA 01801. (781) 904-2550, www.focalpress.com.

Fulcrum Press, 16100 Table Mtn. Pkwy. #300, Golden, CO 80403. (800) 992-2908, email fulcrum@fulcrum-books.com.

HarperCollins, 10 E. 53rd St. 20th Fl., New York, NY 10022 (800) 742-7831, www.harpercollins.com.

Henry Holt & Co., 115 W. 18th. St., New York, NY 10011. (888) 330-8477, www.henryholt.com.

How To Books Ltd., 3 Newtee Place, Magdalen Road, Oxford OX4 1RE, U.K. (01865) 793806.

Intrepid Traveler, 371 Walden Green Rd., Branfort, CT 06405. (203) 488-5341, email info@intrepidtraveler.com.

Lonely Planet, 150 Linden St., Oakland, CA 94607. (800) 275-8555, email info@lonelyplanet.com.

Marlowe & Company, 632 Broadway, Seventh Floor, New York, NY 10012.

McGraw Hill, 1221 Avenue of the Americas, New York, NY 10020. (212) 512-2000, www.mcgraw-hill.com.

NTC/Contemporary Publishing, 4255 West Touhy Ave., Lincolnwood, IL 60712. www.mhcontemporary.com, (877) 226-4997.

Pelican, 1000 Burmaster, Gretna, LA 70053. (800) 843-1724, email office@pelicanpub.com.

Perseus Books Group, 10 E. 53rd St., New York, NY 10022. (800) 386-5656, email perseus.books.group@perseusbooks.com.

Self-Counsel Press, 1704 N. State St., Bellingham, WA 98225. (877) 877-6490, www.self-counsel.com.

Surrey Books, 230 E. Ohio St. #120, Chicago, IL 60611. (800) 326-4430, email surreybk@aol.com.

Travel Easy, 1259 El Camino Real, Box 111, Menlo Park, CA 94025. (650) 529-0421, email TravelEasy@aol.com.

Writer's Digest Books, 1507 Dana Avenue, Cincinnati, OH 45207. (800) 289-0963, www.writersdigest.com.

INDEX

T

tape recorders, 24
taxes, 53-9
tax plan diagram, 58
thesaurus, 28, 222
third person, writing in, 74, 156
title, article's, 75, 162-3
topic(s), 47-9
tour agent, job as a, 207-8
tour director, job as a, 207-8
transitional paragraph, 5, 159
travel associations, 255-6
travel book, 202-4
travel editor, job as a, 206-7
"Travel Newspaper Markets, 100 Best U.S.," 175
travel photography, 253
travelogues, 202, 205
travel writing, books, 253
trip cost, total estimated, 42

U

U.S.A. Today, 176

V

variable costs, 42
vertical file, library, 33
voice, writing, 74, 156

W

Wall Street Journal, The, 176
Who's Who, 128
working hours, 110-1, 121-2, 138

Working Press of the Nation, 175
Writer's Digest Magazine, 29, 72
Writer's Market, 29, 35, 66-8, 71-4, 79-80, 86, 89, 91, 144, 163, 197, 212, 221, 223
writing books, general, 254
writing plan, 37-8

OTHER PRODUCTS
by Gordon Burgett

Gordon's books, reports, and audiocassette programs have helped tens of thousands of writers grow and prosper. All written in the same no-nonsense, step-by-step way (with fun occasionally permitted), here are the items that travel writers might most enjoy. Specific details, sample chapters, and an order form can be found at http://www.sops.com, under writing. (An asterisk [*] below indicates that the product is available in both print and digital form. Check the website for digital costs and formats.)

BOOKS

Sell and Resell Your Magazine Articles (2nd ed.)	$17.95
How to Sell 75% of Your Freelance Writing * (4th ed.)	$17.95
Publishing to Niche Markets	$14.95
Empire-Building by Writing and Speaking	$12.95
Treasure and Scavenger Hunts * (2nd ed.)	$17.95
How to Create Your Own Super Second Life * (2nd ed.)	$19.95
The Travel Writer's Guide * (3rd ed.)	$17.95

REPORTS

100 Best U.S. Travel Newspaper Markets * (annual)	$12
Travel-Writing Trip to Germany (e-mail only) *	$10
Professional Query and Cover Letters *	$12
Finding Topics for General and Travel Articles *	$12

AUDIOCASSETTE PROGRAMS (with workbooks)

How to Sell 7% of Your Travel Writing (2 hrs.)	$29.95
How to Publish Your Own Book and Earn $50,000 Profit (2)	$29.95
How to Set Up and Market Your Own Seminar (3)	$49.95

HOW TO ORDER

By **telephone**: With VISA or Mastercard, call (800) 563-1454, M-F 8-4 PST (or leave message 24 hours a day).

By **mail, fax, or e-mail** (to the addresses below): Provide us with the following information and your remittance, with shipping and (in CA) 7.75% sales tax—the product(s) you wish to order, plus your name, address, city, state, ZIP, and phone number. *Checks to Communication Unlimited.* If using a credit card, we need the 16-digit card number, expiration date, and your authorizing signature.

Shipping: $3.50 for first item, $1 for each successive item in U.S. for media mail. Please call for PRIORITY or other mail as well as shipping to Canada and other nations.

E-mail downloads: no shipping or tax is charged.

COMMUNICATION UNLIMITED

P.O. Box 6405, Santa Maria, CA 93456
Phone (800) 563-1454
Fax (805) 937-3035
Website http://www.sops.com
E-mail order@sops.com